IBSEN AND THE GREAT WORLD

IBSEN AND THE GREAT WORLD

Naomi Lebowitz

LOUISIANA STATE UNIVERSITY PRESS
BATON ROUGE AND LONDON

Copyright © 1990 by Louisiana State University Press
Manufactured in the United States of America

First printing

99 98 97 96 95 94 93 92 91 90   5 4 3 2 1

Designer: Amanda McDonald Key
Typeface: Goudy Old Style
Typesetter: G & S Typesetters, Inc.
Printer and binder: Thomson-Shore, Inc.

Library of Congress Cataloging-in-Publication Data
Lebowitz, Naomi.
      Ibsen and the great world / Naomi Lebowitz.
          p.   cm.
      Includes bibliographical references.
      ISBN 0-8071-1543-6 (alk. paper)
          1. Ibsen, Henrik, 1828–1906—Criticism and interpretation.
      I. Title.
      PT8895.L37   1989
      839.8'226—dc20   89-12988
                                                                CIP

For Al: *vi to*

Oh, dear Brandes, it is not without its consequences that a man lives for 27 years in the wider, emancipated and emancipating spiritual conditions of the great world. Up here, by the fjords, is my native land. But—but—but where am I to find my home-land.

Henrik Ibsen

A beautiful thing is something great—and far away.

Pillars of Society

As long as you were living out there in the great, free world that gave you the courage to think great, free thoughts yourself.

Pillars of Society

I felt as if a new, great, wide world was opening up for me.

Rosmersholm

The mountains oppress and weigh down your spirit. There's not enough light for you here. Not enough space. Not enough strength and sweep to the wind.

Lady from the Sea

Imagine—to be free—and to come out—into the unknown.

Lady from the Sea

But my mind—my thoughts—all my longing dreams and desires—those you can never constrain! They'll go raging and hunting out—into the unknown that I was made for—and that you've shut out for me!

Lady from the Sea

That she'd like some glimpse of a world that—
That—?
That she's forbidden to know anything about.

Hedda Gabler

Oh, you beautiful, big world—!

The Master Builder

For now she has her chance to go out in the great, wide world that I once dreamed so hopefully of seeing.

John Gabriel Borkman

Far, far up on the reeling heights of a mountain top. You inveigled me up there and promised to show me all the glories of the world.

When We Dead Awaken

CONTENTS

ACKNOWLEDGMENTS

My deepest gratitude goes to Joseph R. Roach, whose work and inventive insights continually inspired my interest and effort; to the participants of an Ibsen–Strindberg class in the Masters of Liberal Arts Program at Washington University, whose intelligent and eager readings of the plays exercised my thoughts and feelings; to the cast and crew of a Washington University production of *A Doll's House,* who helped me to experience Ibsen's depth and power; to Milica Banjanin, Janice M. Carlisle, Tony Earls, Molly Elkin, Alaina Genakos, Gerald N. Izenberg, Emma Kafalenos, Herbert E. Metz, Ruth Newton, Lynne Tatlock, and Jarvis A. Thurston, for information, perceptions, and shared enthusiasms; to Al Lebowitz for constant support, intellectual stimulation, and editorial suggestions; and to Kaye Norton and Teresa Rittenhouse for help in preparing the manuscript.

ABBREVIATIONS OF IBSEN'S
WORKS CITED IN THE TEXT

I   *Ibsen: The Complete Major Prose Plays.* Translated and edited
by Rolf Fjelde. New York, 1978.
Pillars of Society (PS)
A Doll House (DH)
Ghosts (G)
An Enemy of the People (EP)
The Wild Duck (WD)
Rosmersholm (R)
The Lady from the Sea (LS)
Hedda Gabler (HG)
The Master Builder (MB)
Little Eyolf (LE)
John Gabriel Borkman (JGB)
When We Dead Awaken (WWDA)

M   Henrik Ibsen. *Brand* (B). Translated by Michael Meyer. London, 1981.

W   Henrik Ibsen. *Peer Gynt* (PG). Translated by Peter Watts.
Harmondsworth, Middlesex, 1966.

O   *The Oxford Ibsen.* Translated and edited by James W. McFarlane et al. London, 1969–77. 8 vols. Volumes used in this
book are:

O.1   Vol. I: *The Early Plays: The Burial Mound* (BM) and *Olaf Liljekrans* (OL). Translated by James McFarlane. *Catiline* (C)

and *Lady Inger* (LI). Translated by Graham Orton. *St. John's Night* (SJN). Translated by James and Kathleen MacFarlane.

O.2 Vol. II: *The Vikings at Helegeland, Love's Comedy, The Pretenders. Love's Comedy* (LC). Translated by Jens Arup.

W.1 *The League of Youth* (LY). In Henrik Ibsen, *The League of Youth, A Doll's House, The Lady from the Sea.* Translated by Peter Watts. Harmondsworth, Middlesex, 1965.

N Quotations from Norwegian taken from *Ibsens Samlede Verker i billigutgave.* 3 vols. Oslo, 1977–78.

IBSEN AND THE GREAT WORLD

INTRODUCTION

For being one of the most under-
read of great writers, Ibsen must take part of the responsibility. If
Kierkegaard and Nietzsche were right to insist that all genius must
hide behind a mask of misunderstanding, Ibsen was almost too successful a craftsman. His crude surfaces mask his subtlety; his hopeless endings obscure his will. His concern with social freedoms disguises his passion for Freedom; his virulent parodic depiction of the
small world of bourgeois duty camouflages the rich and relentless
presence of the Great World of liberated spirit, desire, and art. This
most profound of writers has been taken for a political activist; the
finest manipulator of the mysteries of motive has been reduced to a
lover of ideas and fact. The Great World which beckons us to an
innocent coming into fullness of being, love, and power has been
dismissed as a sadistic siren of delusion.

The passage from the constricted society of "moral invalids"
(*I*, DH, I, 140) to the large and generous world we remember in our
dreams is terrifying and perilous, a painful exile sure to fall short of
the Promised Land. Yet the parody that punishes every ascent,
every going forth, is the means by which Ibsen keeps the Great
World open and alive, indifferent to the premature postures of deforming idealism, immune to absorption by the moral imperatives
of petty prophets and priests. His own creative will must undergo,
as well, the purgatory of maiming and mocking in order to get on
with its task of holding the Great World waiting beyond the pathos
of resignation. The power it liberates through parody stays in the air
and is felt as a thrilling value: *depth*. That dimension is a permanent

and not altogether cruel reminder that we, rendered dependent and fearful by a despotic religion of morality, have both tragically and comically abbreviated our natural scope and renounced our realm. It is perhaps because Ibsen's demands for spiritual expansion are so difficult and merciless that his readers have taken vengeance by reducing the scope and subtlety of his plays. Theodor Adorno insists that the epithets of "old fashioned" and "outdated" are covers for a "shame that overcomes the descendant in face of an earlier possibility that he has neglected to bring to fruition."[1] That possibility was the journey towards a remythologized universe, the beckoning medium of our deepest being. In this book, I describe the means and motives Ibsen exploited to recover for us our homeland.

In Chapter One, while demonstrating how the political morality of bourgeois Christian humanism indicted, in the name of self-preservation and the preservation of the species, the creative will driving towards self-realization, I have raised around Ibsen a Great Society of thinkers and writers also dreaming of the utopian Third Empire.[2] In Chapter Two, Ibsen's private history enters his plays. By moving his body and art into an exile from which the relentless parody of his early dream of innocent creative power and complete understanding helps his will to responsible energy, the playwright counterattacks the small world's divorce of house from home and homeland. Chapter Three reviews the public history taken into the plays and describes the strategic scene-crashing of the small world's theater by liberating mythological and biological metaphor, materializing in bursts of passionate language and figures. And, finally, Chapter Four treats the problem of the artist's crippled and crippling ambition in marriages, communions, and communities that cannot serve it and do not know how desperately they need it as the punished agent of the Great World, patiently waiting for the re-education of its future citizens.

Since Ibsen's meanings are so layered and subtle, and no character embodies his full values, a progressive analysis will not be able to do justice to his scenes and strategies, and that is, of course, what

1. Theodor Adorno, Minima Moralia: Reflections from a Damaged Life, trans. E. F. Jephcott (London, 1974), 93.

2. Ibsen used this phrase in Emperor and Galilean to describe a place in which pagan sensuality and Christian ethics could marry each other in the rich climate of our full nature. See discussion in Michael Meyer, Ibsen (Harmondsworth, Middlesex, 1971), 399.

makes directing his plays so difficult. Each chapter approaches the Great World from a different beginning, often through the same scenes and critical designs, continually modulated by changing contexts. I hope that gradually the fullness in his plays of the Great World's presence and the endless permutations of our self-deceptions will become apparent, to suggest how Ibsen's vision stirs in his audience, in the face of our fears, a longing for the depth we have abandoned. For we cannot *think* our way to its recovery; we must *feel* our way there.

January, 1989

ONE

The Great World

The climate, topography, and architecture of Scandinavia, in the works of its greatest writers, are symbolic almost before they are literal. If the moralizing of geography was already a tendency in Goethe and the émigrés about whom Georg Brandes wrote, the liberation from the provincial constriction of cozy northern homes to the generous South of Europe, traced in the Danish critic's essays in European literature, is a central and obsessive trope of spirit as quickly as it is a fact.[1] Strindberg might complain: "The home here in the North is much praised in song. The homes in the South are less stifling. It is a question of climate. The Scandinavian home with its double windows that ruin the air, with its porcelain stoves (the domestic hearth!), with the long winters and autumns and springs that torment people by forcing them together, make these homes unlovely in my eyes." When his character Bertha in *The Father* appropriates the contrast, she shifts it into a moral, psychological, and spiritual distinction by a passage more intimate and vulgar than that of the symbolists: "How I'd like to get to town, away from here, anywhere at all! Just so I'll get to see you occasionally, often. It's always so heavy, so terrible in there as if it were a winter night but when you come, Dad, it's as if we

1. See Georg Brandes, *Main Currents in Nineteenth Century Literature*, trans. Diane White and Mary Morison (6 vols; London, 1901), I, 141–42.

4

were taking out the double windows on a spring morning."[2] Ibsen's preference is for children to *leave* the father. As Erhart walks out on his role as family redeemer, he complains: "My God, Mother—I'm young! The air in this room—I feel it's going to smother me completely" (*I, JGB*, III, 1002). And the power to make spirit of landscape is so evident in Ibsen's plays that admirers as disparate as Maurice Maeterlinck, Henry James, and Rainer Maria Rilke were spellbound by his characteristic "atmosphere of the soul." Noting the frugal charm of his stark scene, Henry James—himself a persistent converter of architecture into state of mind—is captivated by the quickness of the translation from outer to inner sign: "There is no small-talk, there are scarcely any manners. On the other hand there is so little vulgarity that this of itself has almost the effect of a deeper, a more lonely provincialism. The background at any rate is the sunset over the ice. Well in the very front of the scene lunges with extraordinary length of arm the Ego against the Ego, and rocks in a rigour of passion the soul against the soul—a spectacle, a movement, as definite as the relief of silhouettes in black paper or of a train of Eskimo dogs on the snow."[3]

One of the reasons *Pillars of Society* is thought of as the first play of Ibsen's major period is that its external pointers "out there" and "in here" immediately work on two levels—"the whole canvas," as James observes, "charged with moral color"[4]—so that we are made aware of both a challenge and a threat to the bourgeois stage, character, and audience, terrified of losing generic and moral security. We feel this, of course, when Mrs. Bernick asks if the curtains should be drawn agains the unsettling pageant of character trooping off the docked Indian Girl, about to bring the new world crashing into the "good home," into the "little closeknit circle where no disturbing elements can cast a shadow" (*I, PS*, I, 33). But a more in-

2. August Strindberg, *Getting Married*, trans. Mary Sandbach (London, 1972), 43; Strindberg, *The Father*, trans. Walter Johnson, in August Strindberg, *Pre-Inferno Plays* (New York, 1976), 31.

3. See Maurice Maeterlinck, "The Tragic in Daily Life," trans. Alfred Sutro, in Toby Cole (ed.), *Playwrights on Playwriting: The Meaning and Making of Modern Drama from Ibsen to Ionesco* (New York, 1960), 34; Henry James, *The Scenic Art: Notes on Acting and the Drama, 1872–1901*, ed. Allan Wade (New Brunswick, N.J., 1948), 293.

4. James, *The Scenic Art*, 252. In "The Dimensions of Ibsen's Dramatic World," in Daniel Haakonsen (ed.), *Contemporary Approaches to Ibsen: Proceedings of the Second International Ibsen Seminar* (Oslo, 1971), 179–80, Rolf Fjelde speaks of a tenuous hope inherent in the natural extension of scene for those bourgeois doomed to terrible fates.

teresting transposition is that of the schoolmaster Rørlund who worries that when Martha dreams of distance, of the wild sea, she finds more than aesthetic value: "The sirens of temptation, my dear Miss Bernick. You have to bar the door to such unruly guests. The wild sea—of course you don't mean that literally" (*I*, PS, I, 18–19). The stage directions of *Ghosts* are indistinguishable from spiritual and psychological signs marked by eruptions in dialogue. Jung opens the metaphorical door to the bourgeois parlor to "unprecedented uncertainty, with apparently no inside and no outside, no above and no below, no here and no there, no mine and no thine, no good and no bad." And, literally, on this stultifying side of the door, Mrs. Alving, at last listening from the inside, scorns Manders's shallow and dangerous judgments from the outside, and Osvald is compelled to distinguish here from there because the minister prosecutes the below by the above. The dovetailing of physical and psychic maps makes Ibsen's stage the scene of what Heidegger calls the drama of "the darkening of the world," the hysterical closing out of those unruly guests of instinct, imagination, spirit, and desire by a monolithic morality that conflates categories of value and discourse, freezes the relationship between ideals and customs, and represses the deepest needs of our being.[5] Layered representational dimension calls attention not to an aesthetic revolution but to the loss of poetic, ethical, psychological, and spiritual depth that is our only value.

The dwindling of our natural habitat to dollhouses constricts divine and elemental powers and passions, and we are cut off from the heights and depths of a universe we once experienced as home. Barred from provincial parlors are the scenes and cast of a larger world—great halls and rivers of death, the gods and goddesses of Olympus or of the sea, ambivalent mythical monsters of desire, our pack of hounds untamed by priestly castes,[6] heroes and lovers of leg-

5. C. G. Jung, *Psychological Reflections: A New Anthology of His Writings, 1905–1961*, trans. R. F. C. Hull, ed. Jolande Jacobi and R. F. C. Hull (Princeton, N.J., 1978), 243; Martin Heidegger, *An Introduction to Metaphysics*, trans. Ralph Manheim (New Haven, Conn., 1959), 45. Among others, Rolf Fjelde calls attention to the psychic scenery in his admirable foreword to Vol. I of the two-volume Signet series of his translations of major Ibsen plays (New York, 1965); see also his prefaces in *Ibsen: The Complete Major Prose Plays* (New York, 1978). And see Aage Henriksen, "Henrik Ibsen som moralist," *Kritik*, II (1969), 72–73. Henriksen notes the persistent identification in Ibsen's major plays between the elements and gradations of consciousness as a moral reminder that we must live on all planes at once.

6. See Friedrich Nietzsche, *The Genealogy of Morals*, trans. Francis Golffing, in Friedrich Nietzsche, *The Birth of Tragedy and The Genealogy of Morals* (Garden City, N.Y., 1956), 276.

end, oracles of the future. And trapped in them are the aborted adventures of stinted epic leaders whose books on the future, memorial orphanages, and houses are burned. Our souls were not made to live in one dimension, one time, or one grammar, and Ibsen—with the remythologizing subterranean prophets of the last half of the nineteenth century and first decades of the twentieth—tunneled up under the nice and cozy ("lunt og hyggelig") Helmer houses to open their foolish and treacherous secrets and formulas of moral romance and justification into a greater world, unburdened by moral history and deaf to its commandments.[7] The community they all lamented as lost was recovered in a communion across the years and across mutually derogatory epithets.[8] When they answered Nietzsche's call to arms for "bold and industrious comrades" willing to overcome morality in the name of a higher one, they became the future citizens of that Great World to which they led us. Anticipating and joining the philosopher who, in the preface to *Daybreak*, calls himself, with Dostoyevsky's antihero, an underground man— "one who tunnels and mines and undermines" not only the public world of moral universals but the "blocked subterranean passages of our own psyche"—Ibsen already, as a young man, imagined himself a miner compelled and fascinated by darkness, by the treasures hidden in the mountain, by what John Gabriel Borkman will later call

7. This is an obsessive measure of cultural pleasure in Scandinavian society and of cultural disgust in its corrective writers. The characteristic doublet was used, for instance, to describe an ideal domestic atmosphere, in a Christmas letter to Ibsen from his wife: "It was all so snug and cozy." Bergliot Ibsen, *The Three Ibsens: Memoirs of Henrik, Suzannah, and Sigurd Ibsen*, trans. Geri K. Schjelderup (London, 1951), 115. In *Continuities* (New York, 1968), 149, Frank Kermode rightly names D. H. Lawrence a qualified remythologizer after the great "literary and academic and clinical revival of mythology with which we associate such names as Frazer and Harrison, Freud and Jung." Of course, many writers and thinkers—Nietzsche, Rilke, Joyce, Yeats—join the group that continues the Romantic German poets and philosophers of art, whose Greece was adequate to spirit, a golden mean between northern introversion and the passionate southern senses, a place intolerant of barriers between gods and men. See M. S. Silk and J. P. Stern, *Nietzsche on Tragedy* (Cambridge, England, 1981), 7. Particularly parallel to Ibsen's emphasis on homelessness is the utopian vision of the epic world and its loss in the young Hegelian Georg Lukács's *The Theory of The Novel*, trans. Anna Bostock (Cambridge, Mass., 1971).

8. In a letter to Nietzsche, Georg Brandes wrote of Ibsen in 1888: "With him too you have some kinship, even if it is a very distant kinship"; Georg Brandes, *Friedrich Nietzsche*, trans. A. G. Chater (New York, 1909), 96. Nietzsche became one of those who underread Ibsen, calling him "an old maid" for fighting for women and for idealizing moral freedom; *Ecce Homo*, trans. R. J. Hollingdale (Harmondsworth, Middlesex, 1979), 76. See the note of Walter Kaufmann in his edition of Nietzsche's *The Will to Power*, trans. Walter Kaufmann and R. J. Hollingdale (New York, 1968), 53n; Harald Beyer, *Nietzsche og Norden* (2 vols.; Bergen, Norway, 1959), II, 29.

"my deep, my endless, inexhaustible kingdom" (*I, JGB, IV,*
1021).[9] But, trapped in metaphor, the romance of depth and
darkness yields its treasures most often, in the modern world, only
to the pick-axe of irony. Perhaps Kierkegaard was the first to realize
that, in an age possessed by the conceit of self-preservation, the
prophets of transvaluation, in order to be heard, must step down to
the rank of dialectical poets pressed into indirect communication,
forced to pit darkness against darkness—to be, in fact, deliberately
"incomprehensible, concealed, enigmatic."[10]

Not the least of Brand's misfortunes is his impulse to confront
the age directly and aboveboard, as if he had the privilege and presence of Christ. This stubborn position, like that of Don Quixote,
has its portion of absurd nobility. But Ibsen, with Kierkegaard a
master of projected self-parody, prefers to refuse prophetic authority,
especially when faced with those who would claim him as an advo-
cate of political liberties. To the Norwegian Society for Women's
Rights, he insisted in 1898: "I have been more of a poet and less of
a social philosopher than people generally tend to suppose. . . . My
task has been the portrayal of human beings."[11] He was a poet to
keep from being a moralist, but he was careful to chasten the aesthetic power and authority of that term. When his Svanhild plays a
Regina engaged in Kierkegaard's incessant act of renouncing into
freedom, she casts an aura of irony around Faulk's assertion that
"everyman's a poet / Who in his work expresses his ideal" (*O.2,
LC,* II, 196). Ibsen endorses this, but it is in his last play that the
full implication of the demotion to the category "poet" and the
qualification of "dialectical" are most fiercely felt. When Rubek
asks Irene, "Why do you keep calling me poet?" he receives this
scorching answer: "Because, my friend, there's something extenuat-
ing in that word. Something self-justifying—that throws a cloak

9. Nietzsche, *Genealogy of Morals,* 155; Nietzsche, *Daybreak: Thoughts on the Prejudices of
Morality,* trans. R. J. Hollingdale (Cambridge, England, 1985), 1–2; C. G. Jung, "Symbols
of Transformation," in Violet S. de Laszlo (ed.), *The Basic Writings of C. G. Jung,* trans.
R. F. C. Hull (New York, 1959), 9. See Ibsen's poem "The Miner" ("Bergmannen"), trans.
Michael Meyer, in Michael Meyer, *Ibsen* (Harmondsworth, Middlesex, 1971), 89–90. In an
interview in *Ibsen News and Comment,* II (1981), 7, Austin Pendleton uses Borkman's mining metaphors as a paradigm for the experience of an Ibsen director who finds that "as deep as
you go in an Ibsen play, you always feel you can go deeper."

10. Nietzsche, preface to *Daybreak;* D. H. Lawrence, *Phoenix: The Posthumous Papers,
1936,* ed. Edward D. McDonald (Harmondsworth, Middlesex, 1978), 400.

11. Michael Meyer, *Ibsen,* 817.

over every sin and every human frailty" (*I*, WWDA, I, 1074). Refusing the consoling cover of the "fig-leaf of the word," Ibsen is the greatest dialectical poet of his age, hounding us by indirection beyond the political shallows into a passionate and psychological depth. It is no accident that both Rilke and E. M. Forster refuse to separate his critical scrutiny from his spiritual profundity. While the one imagines him crouched in the deepest rooms of our soul simultaneously analyzing the capillary twitches of our sick conscience and projecting them into perilous and alluring symbols of height and distance, the other calls him subterranean, a lover of "narrow passages and darkness," and pictures him carrying his criticism to the bottom of the sea, underground.[12]

Even in his last play, Ibsen has Maja's critical realism ironically lay the groundwork for a poetry of heights and depths. Stranded between the grammars of anatomy and spirit, the language of this dreamer of demolition[13] is hung up between house and home:

> *Maja.* We could have it so nice and cozy down there in our lovely new house.
> *Rubek.* Or, to put it more exactly: our lovely new *home.*
> *Maja.* I prefer house.
> (*I*, WWDA, I, 1032)

Ibsen's houses, gnawed and nibbled by lies and laws, are the very sign of our spiritual homelessness and the parodied preserve of the idea of home. In his exile, Ibsen may have drawn "a breath of relief when coming out of the Christian sick-house and dungeon atmosphere into [the] healthier, higher, *wider* world," and it is when he *returns* to Norway that he wonders "where [he] is to find his homeland." In his coming as in his going forth he laments: "That is the accursed thing about small surroundings—they make the soul small." But his liberating exile is tenaciously attached to his critical complaint. His yearning for the northern sea is what reminds him that no modern man has any country in which he is at home.

12. Søren Kierkegaard, *Fear and Trembling* and *The Sickness unto Death*, trans. and ed. Walter Lowrie, rev. Howard A. Johnson (Garden City, N.Y., 1954), 72; Rainer Maria Rilke, *The Notebooks of Malte Laurids Brigge*, trans. M. D. Herter Norton (New York, 1949), 76; E. M. Forster, *Abinger Harvest* (London, 1946), 85.

13. This is a metaphor from D. H. Lawrence's review of an anthology of Georgian poetry, 1911–12, *Phoenix*, 304. Lawrence names Ibsen, Flaubert, and Hardy as the nihilist dreamers who cleared the ground for the future literature of creation.

Having raised the geographical place to a spiritual one, he still cannot embrace the unqualified transvaluating romance of Nietzsche the conqueror who rejoices in converting the longing into a homeland for the higher type. It becomes "a world still rich and undiscovered" to which we journey, driven by our strength to the sea, preferring "even to perish" there than to "become half-hearted and poisonous."[14] Clearly, Ibsen records this thrill in his scene of value, but never without irony or parodic distortion. Even Brand manages a Schopenhauerian smile of pathos when he relates this anecdote from his author's own childhood:

> When I was a boy, I remember,
> Two thoughts kept occurring to me, and made me laugh.
> An owl frightened by darkness, and a fish
> Afraid of water. Why did I think of them?
> Because I felt, dimly, the difference
> Between what is and what should be; between
> Having to endure, and finding one's burden
> Unendurable.
>   Every man
> Is such an owl and such a fish, created
> To work in darkness, to live in the deep;
> And yet he is afraid.
> (M, B, I, 24)

The ferocity of Ibsen's attacks on his times might well have been stimulated by his recognition that he himself harbored the double fear of the necessity and the impossibility of healing the ontological, psychological, and historical split between house and home.

As Kierkegaard assaulted the eudaemonists and Dostoyevsky the Grand Inquisitors of Christianity for protecting us against the kind of fear and trembling that could expand our medium, so Ibsen, with Nietzsche, exposed the direct relationship between education against fear (the opposite of Wordsworthian education by fear) and our "overpowering homesickness for the sea" (I, LS, II, 623). His Wangel comes to know there is not enough space in his house for

14. Friedrich Nietzsche, *Twilight of the Idols*, in *Twilight of the Idols and The Anti-Christ*, trans. R. J. Hollingdale (Harmondsworth, Middlesex, 1968), 57; Henrik Ibsen to Georg Brandes, June 3, 1897, in *The Correspondence of Henrik Ibsen*, trans. J. N. Laurvik and Mary Morison (London, 1905), 447; Ibsen to Magdalene Thoresen, October 15, 1867, *Correspondence*, 139; Nietzsche, *Will to Power*, 219.

the soul to spread out when it is haunted by "pictures of the teeming life of the sea," the scene of our old home, almost beyond the memory of evolution.[15] To unpreserve ourselves and spend our souls in the larger medium for which we were intended is our task. Because none of us is quite up to it, Ibsen shames us by leaving a space around our formulas insulating the lazy poetry of our projections and transferences, which is never fully lived in by any character, and never fully appropriated by its author.

This is a place of spiritual value, resistant to idealization, because it is nurtured by irony. To those readers and watchers of Ibsen's drama who deny this dimension any positive value, we can only appeal to the absence of feelings of despair, cynicism, or entrapment in our reception of his endings, despite the failure of any character to embody, dominate, or live in the medium.[16] The space Ibsen opens is, in fact, by our failure to travel beyond our projections, freed from them. That space is fully inhabited by consciousness in the novels of Henry James and virtually refused us in Flaubert's bourgeois fiction. Through self-parody, Ibsen shares as possibility the space that beckons his characters, so that it stays open for all of us as a recessive reminder of what we have wilfully closed off.[17] His critical determination to make an expansive poetry of value out of a lost dimension aligns him with those phenomenologists of psychology, philosophy, and anthropology who, by recalling the totem and taboo of our cultural and personal origins, disturbed refuges from

15. William Archer (ed.), *From Ibsen's Workshop*, trans. A. G. Chater (New York, 1978), 331.

16. See John Northam's comments on *Brand* in *Ibsen: A Critical Inquiry* (Cambridge, England, 1973), 71: "And yet the ending does not feel like a simple rejection." Critics like Errol Durbach, in *Ibsen the Romantic: Analogues of Paradise in the Later Plays* (Athens, Ga., 1982) and John S. Chamberlain, in *Ibsen: The Open Vision* (London, 1982), who most convincingly chart the double direction of Ibsen's critical and spiritual tendencies, speak of his open form, of the dialectic between the Romantic and counter-Romantic voices that "instructs by negative example, by irony," on the one hand and "celebrates joy in the jaws of death . . . sees in the law of change not decay but the continuous transformation of the self" on the other (Durbach, *Ibsen the Romantic*, 30). Although this double direction secures us, to a certain extent, from the metaphysical projections that Nietzsche thought drained the world of value, it is important not to overvalue the compensation of immanence. Ibsen's "negative Romanticism" stimulates a third world, beyond the void, free of our torment and contradiction.

17. It is this space that keeps Brand's impasse from being merely the blockage of morality in the face of spirit that Janko Lavrin claims it to be: "Ibsen himself undermined, perhaps contrary to his own intention, the loveless puritan Brand, whose striving will was moral, but not religious"; *Ibsen and His Creation* (New York, 1972), 59.

conflict and ambivalence—projections propelled by a fearful morality towards places of peace. The legacy of Ludwig Feuerbach who demythologized our longing is still alive in Ibsen's work of recovery. *That* part of him would always agree with Bertolt Brecht's retort to Walter Benjamin: "Depth doesn't get you anywhere at all." The response was meant to detach consciousness from consoling bourgeois promises of the noble progress of the race and to prevent escape through the feelings from reason's responsibility. He would similarly agree with Alain Robbe-Grillet's claim that the myths of depth have romanced us out of reality into sentimental readings of the universe.[18] This is the hard-bitten negative side of the perspective carried into the twentieth century by Henri Bergson and William James, through which the buzz and bloom of life reclaimed rich depth and complexity from transcendental abstraction. From our contemporary perch, however, we see how far Ibsen is from the undialectical minimalists of literature and philosophy who, in a post-psychoanalytic age, politically suspicious of depth, cling to surfaces, terrified of the old romance of metaphysical and psychological seduction into the sky and sea. The poet keeps open what the critic closes, and for all his ferocious parody and satire, Ibsen still sees man in the image of his mythological and spiritual possibility, fissured, unfinished, but available to the call of being.[19] Like Kierkegaard, Ibsen used depth as a scandal and a stumbling block to the bourgeois and provincial expectations of progress.

In his spiritual solitude, Kierkegaard enjoyed imagining himself as a merman whose "real life is not in the external and visible world but deep down in the secret chambers" of his soul and who "faintly" hears "the din of the world, not anxiously clamoring but quietly dying away and really irrelevant." Yet in his literature he continually tortured himself back into the apparent world, imagining in his various guises all the complex ethical issues he could suppose.

18. Hannah Arendt (ed.), *Understanding Brecht*, trans. Anna Bostock (London, 1973), 110; also, Terry Eagleton, *Walter Benjamin: Or Towards a Revolutionary Criticism* (London, 1981), 55; Alain Robbe-Grillet, "Nature, Humanism, Tragedy," in *For a New Novel*, trans. Richard Howard (New York, 1965), 123. Brecht's distrust became a common one in Holocaust analysts like Hannah Arendt.

19. This image of man is maintained by Martin Heidegger, *An Introduction to Metaphysics*, trans. Ralph Manheim (New Haven, Conn., 1959), and Thomas Merton, *New Seeds of Contemplation* (New York, 1961), religious and philosophical advocates of the need to court the unknown.

As good a self-torturer in his representations as Kierkegaard, Ibsen could not even fantasize a transvaluation so complete that the world we live in becomes a baffle to a metaphysical reality. Ibsen looks into the sea and views the same life that moves on the earth, only in a different form. As he climbs up and down the Nietzschian ladder of free spirits who persecute morality into problems, his double nature insists on opening the used and banished worlds to each other. His runged irony is not content to pit artificial mythologies of poetry against artificial mythologies of bourgeois conduct, a compensation of great consolation to Flaubert, nor is it set, like Conrad's stoic conduct, against a will-less universe stranding projections and aspirations frantically netted by storytellers. If, with D. H. Lawrence, Ibsen would find Conrad too sad and resigned, he could not be a prophetic Lawrentian hero of conversion and creation.[20]

The space that awaits the transformation of moral solutions into moral problems lures and frightens spiritual men and women, terrified to surrender the self-preserving hope that bourgeois imperatives may be able to save the race from anxiety and contradiction.[21] Although it constantly recedes from the rationalizations and displacements of characters, though we never see it lived in, it waits patiently for the time in which individuals and cultures can work free of the ghosts of repressed desires and spirit. This is the true protagonist of Ibsen's drama. This home that beckons us—this thrilling, terrifying home—is called, in every play, the *Great World*, a term subjected to ruthless parody and irony as long as it is attached to our deceptions, but elsewhere free of qualification and worship, of the idealization that screens inevitable ambivalence and guilt. Joyce felt this space to be almost "wholly independent of . . . characters" and James felt it as the catalyst of a drama that is so powerfully alive and moving that it repels analysis and interpretation.

20. Søren Kierkegaard, *Letters and Documents*, trans. and ed. Henrik Rosenmeier (Princeton, N.J., 1978), 72; Ibsen, quoted in Meyer, *Ibsen*, 605; Friedrich Nietzsche, *Human, All Too Human: A Book for Free Spirits*, trans. R. J. Hollingdale (Cambridge, England, 1986), 7. Nietzsche gives his free spirits the right to say: "Here—a new problem! Here a long ladder upon whose rungs we ourselves have sat and climbed—which we ourselves have at some time *been!*" (p. 10). For a discussion of Flaubert and artificial mythologies, see Roland Barthes, *Mythologies*, trans. and ed. Annette Lavers (New York, 1972), 109–59.

21. See Friedrich Nietzsche, *The Gay Science*, trans. Walter Kaufmann (New York, 1974), 36, 283–84.

This atmosphere, like that of Kafka, depends upon the subsumption of personality by state of mind, and it alone demands the empathy Brecht associates with traditional characters. For Rilke, as for so many other Ibsen admirers, there rises around the tragicomedy of a play like *The Wild Duck* an aura invulnerable to the grotesque, something "very great, deep, essential. Doomsday and judgment, something ultimate." Howells, sensitive to the anti-apocalyptic nature of the dramatist, preferred to think of Ibsen's vision as one giving out the sensation of Judgment Day, but without the judgment.[22]

A dot or line drawn on a plane surface has difficulty entering its medium. So stubbornly does the eye maintain the integrity of the plane that it bars the intruder from penetrating it, forcing it to race back and forth on top of the paper. Rudolf Arnheim humanizes the line's struggle by imagining only one available avenue of freedom: the third dimension, depth. When the world into which we have been educated is too poor for our spiritual aspirations, its formulas deforming the language of the heart into empty rhetoric, it is im-

22. James Joyce, review of *When We Dead Awaken*, in James Walter McFarlane (ed.), *Discussions of Henrik Ibsen* (Boston, 1962), 63–64; James, *The Scenic Art*, 318; Rainer Maria Rilke, *Letters: 1892–1910*, trans. Jane Bannard Greene and M. D. Herter Norton (2 vols.; New York, 1945), II, 217; W. D. Howells, "Henrik Ibsen," *North American Review*, CLXXXIII (July, 1906), 4.

I support the sense of John Northam, "The Substance of Ibsen's Idealism," in Daniel Haakonsen (ed.), *Contemporary Approaches to Ibsen: Proceedings of the First International Ibsen Seminar* (Oslo, 1966), 9–20, that there is a separation between the idealism embodied by characters in the plays and that directed beyond them by Ibsen's will. The atmosphere of Doomsday without the security of judgment prevents, as well, the appropriation of life and reality by morality that Nietzsche ceaselessly complained of. See Nietzsche, *Will to Power*, 364, 189; and for a parallel emphasis, Charles R. Lyons, *The Divided Consciousness* (Carbondale, Ill., 1972), xxiii, 85: "Ibsen's scene is not primarily the projection of the consciousness of the protagonist. Rather, the scene which contains this spatial image is the environment in which the hero's consciousness exists." Yet Lyons does not, it seems to me, seize upon the transformation of dimension into value that this separation implies. This larger scene is featured by Brian Johnston, *The Ibsen Cycle: The Design of the Plays from Pillars of Society to When We Dead Awaken* (Boston, 1975), 3, and is one of the advantages of opening Ibsen to Hegel's cosmology. Aside from the obvious deformations that occur with the application of system to art, however cogent the disclaimers, there is still too much universal optimism in the Hegelian climb of consciousness through history's tragedy, and Ibsen is almost as wary as Kierkegaard of immanent systems, though wary as well of transcendental ones. Concentration on medium over character allows for less distortion in the ascription of cause to fate. On this point, see Daniel Haakonsen, "The Play-within-the-play in Ibsen's Realistic Drama," in Haakonsen (ed.), *Second International Ibsen Seminar* (1971), 117; Joan Templeton, "Of This Time, of This Place: Mrs. Alving's Ghosts and the Shape of the Tragedy," *PLMA*, CI (January, 1986), 57–68. Ibsen's refusal to appropriate atmosphere might be seen, too, as an example of the antihumanism favored by Robbe-Grillet, *For a New Novel*.

possible to go forth without first finding a way to freedom in the confined space.[23] Nothing so resembles the dot racing back and forth as the pacing of the most celebrated, frustrated heroines of the nineteenth century—Emma Bovary, Hardy's Sue and Tess, Anna Karenina, and Nora and Hedda. Lawrence could not forgive Tolstoy and Hardy for allowing their heroines to die in the wilderness, impotent to create a world past convention and worthy of their wishes. The nomadic circling of Hardy's characters is forced by an antithetical world that does not even want to find a way to the third dimension. And what are we to do with the comic pathos of Kafka's Abraham, his going forth blocked by fussy doubt? Distance is ethically and aesthetically useless without the privileged and sanctioned perspective of exile. The perplexity of setting out from a community so spiritually shallow, smug, and stupid that it does not know morality is a problem but feels it to be "the hallowed place of peace" is to all the major writers of the modern world, from Flaubert to Joyce, an aesthetic as well as an ethical dilemma. Madame Bovary, sealed in a provincial world of formulas that trap her longing in sentimental rhetoric, is offered no homeland for her desire freed from her pathetic projections. We see the intimate connection between her sense that "certain parts of the world must produce happiness, as they produce peculiar plants which will flourish nowhere else" and "lacking the words, she had neither the opportunity nor the courage." The novel's surface stubbornly resists penetration, and her soaring thoughts are absurdly leveled: "She wanted to die, and she wanted to live in Paris." Even complaint is caught at the door by cliche and refused the key of self-irony that might find the "mot juste": "They spoke of the dullness of the country, the lives that were smothered by it, the illusions that perished there."[24]

Henry James lamented this confinement and wished Flaubert could have "listened at the chamber of the soul," which would have "floated him on a deeper tide." As a master of depth, who wondered at the magical and vibrant remainders in Ibsen's plays that could

23. Rudolf Arnheim, *Art and Visual Perception: A Psychology of the Creative Eye* (Berkeley, 1966), 212; see Gustave Flaubert to George Sand, December 20, 1875, in *The Selected Letters of Gustave Flaubert*, trans. and ed. Francis Steegmuller (New York, 1953), 251.

24. Lawrence, *Phoenix*, 411, 420; Nietzsche, *The Gay Science*, 284; Flaubert, *Madame Bovary*, trans. Alan Russell (Harmondsworth, Middlesex, 1970), 53, 73, 151.

not be appropriated by character, he guides Isabel Archer towards a great world high enough to meet the requirements of her imagination, amply compensating her for defeats of expectation by growth of consciousness that knows how to make the small world of delusion a large one to live in. Excluded from the romance of history and depth she senses in Osmond and Madame Merle, Isabel is thrilled and terrified by a future beyond her control: "Her imagination . . . now hung back: there was a last vague space it couldn't cross—a dusky, uncertain tract which looked ambiguous and even slightly treacherous, like a moorland seen in the winter twilight." When she is inside the deception, she calls the treachery "deep." Since Mme. Merle had been "deeply false . . . deeply, deeply, deeply," the history of Rome is taken in as depth. Returning to Gardencourt, to "those muffled chambers," she envies Ralph his death, which slides into a depth "as sweet as the vision of a cool bath in a marble tank, in a darkened chamber, in a hot land." Ralph's is a stalking death, like Dr. Rank's, that opens up its fellow consciousness past both its terror and attraction. Earlier, Isabel had noted in Goodwood a "want of easy consonance with the deeper rhythms of life"; in a final interview, she says to him, "The world's very small," but *thinks:* "The world, in truth, had never seemed so large."[25] The marriage of Isabel's consciousness and the fully scoped reality available to us is as nearly complete a universe as it could be. The journey to depth had been full of delusion, but it has deposited her, in the midst of her constrained circumstances, in the great world. The cramped houses Ibsen likes to stage—a reflection, perhaps, of the social, economic, and physical demotion of the Ibsen family after bankruptcy—are jealous surfaces; the community, run by pillars of society, is a "whited sepulchre" of any thought or word that would live.[26] Ibsen will not, himself, escape by aesthetic exorcism, but neither will he let his characters absorb the great atmosphere raised by the impure longings of frustrated wills. As a sub-

25. Henry James, *The Portrait of a Lady,* ed. Leon Edel (Boston, 1963), 158; James, "Gustave Flaubert," in *Literary Criticism: French Writers; Other European Writers; The Prefaces to the New York Edition,* ed. Leon Edel, assisted by Mark Wilson (New York, 1984), 314; James, *Portrait of a Lady,* 207, 260, 423, 424, 457, 105, 481.

26. See Else Høst, *Vilanden av Henrik Ibsen* (Oslo, 1967), 235. Ibsen uses the biblical metaphor of the whited sepulcher several times in the plays; see, for example, *I,* PS, I, 17 and *I,* EP, I, 298.

terranean poet, the playwright must find a way to depth, not just for himself, but to keep charged that atmosphere of possibility that will be neither canceled nor mastered.

Where is he to find and recover the numinous value of a world drained by longing for a better one behind and beyond it—a longing that has succeeded in ghosting this apparent world, as Nietzsche tirelessly claims, of anything but moral philistinism? Not only have years of projection of ethical and spiritual value into the *true* world beyond left this world a prey to dead and dangerous ideals and the language that rehearses and receives them, but they have also, in pursuit of innocence, closed off the only kind we could host—the innocence of becoming, rich with the joys of change and oppositions. Ibsen's Great World has obviously been foreshadowed by a long history of prelapsarian golden ages buried beneath the heavy years of civilization and available to repossession by moral and spiritual revolution.[27] Romantic manipulation and appropriation of theological and cosmological designs, still in the hope of marrying the mountains and valleys of nature to those of the mind, justified the public use and power of poetry. The extreme symbolist mentality is represented by Des Esseintes who disdains the literal for the mental journey to England, shutting out the public and private connections to moral history and reality. Ibsen comes between the two and cruelly prevents either kind of victory for the aesthetic consciousness. For a while, Solness might satisfy his sense of guilt by imagining the cracked flue as the cause of fire, and his sense of innocence by sharing castles in the air, but he is, finally, forced—by the logic of a universe devoid of metaphysical and historical authority, mature muses, and a public vulnerable to poetry, and ruled by a morality of puppet-masters—*literally* to climb the tower from which he must fall in order to save, by his absurdity, the idea of depth as "the unchallenged locus of god or value" in the world.[28]

The humiliating literal enactments of dreams of innocent power paradoxically keep Ibsen's epic journeys from triumphant marriages or exclusions that would reconcile us to a world remade by art. His

27. See Nietzsche, *Will to Power*, 189, 317; Northrop Frye, "New Directions from Old," in *Fables of Identity: Studies in Poetic Mythology* (New York, 1963), 52–66.

28. Thomas Weiskel, *The Romantic Sublime: Studies in the Structure and Psychology of Transcendence* (Baltimore, 1986), 24. Weiskel assumes the genealogy of this dimension traced by Northrop Frye to the Romantic habit of transvaluating verticality.

would-be epic builders do not learn from the psychological sublime to educate the consciousness to loss and limitation; rather, their author must punish them with an irony that makes them dizzy. But they are also immune to the corrections of therapists like Otto Rank and Ludwig Binswanger who would convert *Verstiegenheit* (extravagant climbing) into the eager walk of Borghejm towards the future. If Solness does not have the necessary critical power to go continually up and down the Nietzschian ladder of fine spirits in search of problems, or the necessary humility, honesty, and responsibility to heed therapeutic warnings against the compulsive disproportions of the megalomaniacal creative temperament, and if he lives in a world hostile to climbers and to the striking of the artist's tent—still he helps to liberate from morality a space for mythical and psychological designs and desires.[29] It is a space he cannot live in, that Borghejm does not need, but it reminds us of both that accomplished exile from our natural medium and that demanded of our unnatural one.

If Hedda had the courage of Isabel Archer, she could have moved beyond her satiric sneers at specialization into the kind of personal power and freedom of consciousness that renders the Great World unnecessary. Her immature poetry dies in the world, for it has only opposed it as aesthetic conviction, not ethical choice; as slave resentment, not master creation. Yet, characteristically, it stays on the stage as value, once it is free from her body.[30] Even when those characters, like Nora, Mrs. Alving, Ellida, Allmers, and Rita, become places where longings are educated, not arrested, by fear, and where a new groping language pushes out the rehearsed phrasings of self-protection, they are never triumphant citizens of a Nietzschian republic of spiritual aristocrats. Ibsen's parody tenaciously keeps the Great World just beyond our reach.

G. B. Shaw seems to recognize the power of this transgression when he notes in his famous defense of Ibsen that "the idealist is a

29. Ludwig Binswanger, in *Being-in-the-World: Selected Papers of Ludwig Binswanger*, ed. and trans. Jacob Needleman (New York, 1963), 343. Binswanger borrows the phrase about the "artist's tent" from Hugo von Hoffmansthal, whose notion of spirit—which Paul de Man translates as "harassed confinement"—gives the philosopher a major pattern for his theory on *Verstiegenheit*. See Paul de Man, *Blindness and Insight: Essays in the Rhetoric of Contemporary Criticism* (New York, 1971), 45.

30. In "The Histrionic Hedda," *AIT: The Repertory Reader*, I (Spring, 1984), 2–3, Rick Davis suggests that Hedda seems theatrical because "she is in the wrong play."

more dangerous animal than the Philistine just as a man is a more dangerous animal than a sheep." Shaw's comparison rests upon the admission that "Ibsen's attack on morality is a symptom of the revival of religion, not of its extinction." Yet he gives too much conscious control of motive to our represented counterparts when he moralizes Ibsen's meaning: "Let everyone religiously refuse to sacrifice himself and others from the moment he loses his faith in the validity of the ideal." For our relationship to the ideal is never questioned except *through* the seduction of sacrifice and the psychic murder of self and other, and a life of changing ideals seems as impossible to bear privately as it seems hopeless to achieve publicly. The rabid temptation to sacrifice is a sign, to be sure, of an ideal that is profoundly guilty, but its pretense to climax and ultimate value, or ransom for bad parenting, must be disastrously played out in the drama so that we can catch a glimpse of the Great World beyond the scene that raises it by its ironies. No world-historical figures people Ibsen's major plays, and even tenuously achieved conversions of private frustration into public benefit—such as the new schools of Stockmann or Allmers and Rita, or the new marriage of Ellida and Wangel—are historically impotent and morally dwarfed by the stars and sea, by the easy evolutionary tolerance of ebb and flow, and by seasons and constellations of ambivalence and alternation.[31]

It might be useful to view the relationship between Allmers and Borghejm as a parodic version in a faithless world of that between Kierkegaard's Johannes de Silentio and Abraham. The longing that attaches the pseudonymous poet to the hero protects both the aesthetic and spiritual spheres against moral appropriation. Ethical confidence in a progressive future, lyric hope for a redeemed past, resignation to losses—none of these moods can master the scene, nor even promise us a world in which historically useful action and the long life of forgiving can be mediated or integrated into a com-

31. George Bernard Shaw, "The Lesson of the Plays," in *The Quintessence of Ibsenism* (New York, 1957), 183–84, 189, 191; Keith M. May, *Ibsen and Shaw* (New York, 1985), 121–23: "When Shaw falsifies, he does so, more often than not, because he wishes to minimise those elements in Ibsen that suggest how impotent beyond narrow limits, man's thought actually is. . . . Everything depends on whether one believes human nature to be the cause or the product of cultural conditions. Ibsen was rather of the first persuasion, Shaw emphatically of the second." David Rosengarten, "*The Lady from the Sea*: Ibsen's Submerged Allegory," *Educational Theatre Journal*, XXIX (1977), 474.

mon society. But the authenticity of their enunciation is an effective block against philistine morality's monolithic grammar, time,
and space. Kierkegaard's scene has value only because he keeps the
ethical realm, that most ambitious pedagogue, from absorbing either the aesthetic, which it loves to correct, or the spiritual, which
it loves to usurp. The refusal of Ibsen to close up spaces between the
Great World and small worlds, between practical progress and
aborted ascension, keeps the debased moral world from feasting off
a conflation of the spheres. When the literal ascent of the Master
Builder, rehearsed by visions of the impossible, refuses absorption
by the moral world that mocks its collapse, its absurd failure sus-
pends the ethical, like Abraham's faith, by its silly scorn of creative
responsibility that makes it so vulnerable to parody. Old Ekdal's forest may have its revenge, but not nice and cozy houses. Partly precipitated by the collapse of the identity between house and home in
Solness' public and private building, the Master Builder's climb
is engineered by a cooperation of fiercely autonomous realms—
the aesthetic, the psychological, and the mythical—constellating
against morality they would in the Great World be able to embrace.
Spirit's alliance with the aesthetic imagination is perhaps the most
important of Kierkegaard's strategies inherited in some way by
Ibsen. Although the lowest of the spheres for Kierkegaard, trapping
his figures in rhetoric and repetition, seduction and delusion, the
aesthetic realm can prepare the soul for the leap over morality. This
is the task of the playwright. He lets Hedda's absurd and destructive
addiction to beauty and nobility of gesture and deed ease the moral
stranglehold on value. She raises in a larger soil a flag that is lowered
neither by society's indifference nor Hedda's own cowardice—her
Romanticism, refused a moral scene of exercise, infantile. It waves
free, finally, through all its parodic pretense, from Brack's political
formula of moral control. "But people don't do such things" signals
a new kingdom even out of her unkindness and cruelty.[32] Hedda has

32. John Northam rightly notes of Hedda's poetry in "The Substance of Ibsen's Idealism," in Haakonsen (ed.), First International Ibsen Seminar, 12: "Fragmentary in expression
yes. But behind those absurd scraps of poetry we can surely sense an intensity of feeling
greater than the expression." See also Errol Durbach, "The Denouement of Rosmersholm,"
Educational Theatre Journal, XXIX (1977), 478, who notes that the "chorus" of Hedda Gabler
and Rosmersholm does not show up the heroines. Their fates show, rather, how stupid and
self-righteous are those who are left to utter banalities or superstitions.

been the catalyst for sending us beyond good and evil by her refusal of memorized goodness in a society devoid of spontaneous good, where her courage fails for that new morality Lawrence so desperately desired for her.[33] But it is in Nora, the greatest actress of bourgeois marriage, that we see most clearly the benefits of recruiting the aesthetic in the battle for free spirit. She comes closest of all Ibsen's heroines and heroes to embodying the tragic joy of becoming. At the end of her play, in fear and trembling, she actually goes forth into a deromanticized world of solutions to make problems.

The famous stocking scene of A Doll House remains the best and most moving illustration of the way in which the aesthetic helps to free spirit into a depth immune to the admonishments of tyrannical bourgeois morality. It is the first of the scenes in Ibsen's major period to drop us suddenly from the vulgar world of pretext to a deeper world in which we can roam unmolested by cause and calculation by the compulsion to perform. Until the trapdoor drops, under the feet of Rank and Nora who joke over the abyss of death, Nora cannot make her exit. And it is precisely what had seemed an enemy of self-knowledge—aesthetic and theatrical skills—that serves as an agent of spirit. The best appreciators have noticed how much Torvald sounds like the narrowest of Ibsen's critics when he censures Nora's dancing as "a bit too naturalistic. . . . It rather overstepped the proprieties of art" (I, DH, III, 180–81). When, after knowledge of his wife's "deceit," he snaps, "No more playacting," rejecting the aesthetics of self-sacrifice, as Krogstad had in an earlier scene with Mrs. Linde, we see how all the art that had once cooperated with moral stereotype by promoting the melodrama of furtive nobility now serves spirit in spinning Nora into a larger life, where the secret of macaroons and money opens into the fearful and beautiful mysteries of a world free from the stranglehold of Helmer morality.[34] Only the consciousness that belongs, as Nietzsche put it, to the higher type (that which *recognizes* conflict or, in Kierkegaard's

---

33. See Theodor Adorno, "The Truth about Hedda Gabler," in *Minima Moralia: Reflections from a Damaged Life*, trans. E. F. Jephcott (London, 1974), 93–94.

34. See Joseph R. Roach, "Ibsen and the Moral Occult," in *Telling Right from Wrong: Morality and Literature*, University College Occasional Papers, No. 5, Washington University (St. Louis, 1987); I, DH, 187, 178. In a draft of A Doll House, Krogstad says to Nora, "I dare say you have read in novels of villains whose only motive is revenge"; Archer (ed.), *Ibsen's Workshop*, 143. Krogstad, too, breaks down melodramatic barriers to join Nora on a deeper level.

lexicon, suffering) can finally spot the most treacherous cosmetic of Christian civilization: altruism. If it is not, as in Nietzsche's cynical transvaluation, sheer egoism, it is at least a sign of wanting to be more: "'And love'—What? Even an action done from love is supposed to be 'unegoistic'? But you dolts! 'And the praise of sacrifices?' But anyone who has really made sacrifices knows that he wanted and got something in return—perhaps something of himself in return for something of himself—that he gave up here in order to have more there, perhaps in order to *be* more or at least to feel that he was 'more'." The romance of self-sacrifice, in truth, *prevents* the Nietzschian ideal of self-overcoming by its parasitism, a secret urge to overcome another. The quotation marks that characteristically bracket moral terms of value deformed by bourgeois sentimental educations in the work of its critics of higher type, like Flaubert and Dostoyevsky, are suggested by Nora as she unhinges law and religion from life: "Oh, Torvald, I'm really not sure what religion is. . . . The law's not at all what I thought" (*I*, DH, III, 193). Now the art of play can serve the spirit by interpretation and help to release it from the morality of lower types into a liberated uncertainty. Ortega y Gasset reminds us that only when it does not itself have to be the sole support of life, as it does in Nora's marriage, can art be available to criticize it richly, and we feel this shift powerfully in the great stocking scene.[35]

Rank has made Nora promise that Torvald, allergic to life's ugliness, will not come to his sickroom. The doctor, too, would not ruin the aesthetic pleasure he shares with the Helmers in the "lunt og hyggelig" house where he is a daily witness to beauty and happiness. The exclusion of Torvald here and in the scene of Rank's leavetaking—when Nora and Rank talk right past Torvald's head about the deep and dark world of death through the imagery of masquerade—is necessary for the communion, which is only slightly undermined by the doctor's ignorance of Nora's suicide wish. The imperfection of the communion merely helps us to invest greater value in the space that is larger than any character or community. Against the exile of Torvald from aesthetic displeasure, Ibsen pits Rank's exile from aesthetic pleasure. He is dying from his father's

35. Nietzsche, *Beyond Good and Evil*, trans. Walter Kaufmann (New York, 1966), 148; Ortega y Gasset, *The Modern Theme*, trans. James Cleugh (New York, 1961), 82–83.

gay life without tasting the "asparagus tips and pâté de foie gras, truffles and oysters, port and champagne." The vulgar surface of se-duction, flirtation, and base motive, and the joking over death are aesthetic violations of morality's tyrannical game. The play that seems callous and cunning in Nora is, in effect, a cover for a power-ful need to travel with Rank through thoughts of death to the free-dom of a larger medium. The pretext is undermined by the fine crack between a common assent to the sadness of exile from com-munity and the common assent to a shared desire of release from moral repression:

> Nora. Why did you smile?
> Rank. No, it was you who laughed.
> Nora. No, it was you who smiled, Dr. Rank.
> (I, DH, II, 163)

The morality that separates us by legal judgment—the kind that cannot tolerate a wife that commits forgery or a friend in love with his friend's wife—is broken by the humor that unites us at a spiri-tual level. The childlike play, with the dying confession of love, blocks the vulgar way out of growth as it drops us into the world of timeless childhood, past guilt, a world of no demands and no dreams:[36]

> Nora. You know how much I enjoy it when you're here.
> Rank. That's precisely what threw me off. You're a mystery to me. So many times I've felt you'd almost rather be with me than with Helmer.
> Nora. Yes—you see, there are some people that one loves most and other people that one would almost prefer being with.
> Rank. Yes, there's something to that.
> Nora. When I was back home, of course I loved Papa most. But I always thought it was so much fun when I could sneak down to the maids' quarters, because they never tried to improve me, and it was always so amusing, the way they talked to each other.
> (I, DH, II, 166)

Where life is theater, above the servants' quarters, the desires of father and husband condemn her to games of plagiarized sentiments and opinion. The scene lowers us from those rooms to the quarter in which we can be ourselves and feel at home. It links the realms

---

36. This phrase is from a speech of Rosmer in I, R, III, 555.

of play and death, past and present, in an innocence of becoming—
the common air of the Great World. The moral world that would
appropriate spirit and art and put them through their paces is exiled
for a momentary spot in time.[37] That is why Act III can keep on
dropping us into the depths for longer and more fearful immersions,
in the icy waters of imagined suicide ("det bundløse") and profound
understanding ("tilbunds"). Set against Torvald's complaints about
being swept down into the depths of humiliation ("til grunde") and
against his terror of the psychological deeps, these depths can educate Nora beyond the moral theater of her husband. Her vocabulary
of depth dances on the edge between anxiety and expansion and,
therefore, is unfit as a vocabulary of evasion and peace. It reclaims
mystery in the name of a better morality, one opened by psychology
to spirit. The great mystery of being—a mystery generous enough
to allow full autonomy to spirit, rich competition between instincts
and morality, and growth to the psyche relieved of useless guilts—
blows Nora out the door with such poetic insistence that we forget
to ask, at least for a while, about the welfare of the children, the
cruel residues of her self-realization. We heard the wind all the way
back in Act I, when Nora muses on Mrs. Linde's losses: "How free
you must feel" (133). The line seems again a little vulgar and out of
place, almost childish, but it signals the dialogue of the "second degree," as Maeterlinck calls the conversation that drops us to depth.
It tends to rise out of a provisional somnambulistic trance Maeterlinck sees as the dominant atmosphere of The Master Builder, some-
where between life and death, stopping and spelling the time of
morality and letting us sense the time and freedom of the Great
World.[38] The reduced economic and social circumstances that Nora
chooses as the scene of her expansion seem an ironic host of liberation but effectively light up, in its difficult darkness, the nice and
cozy prison of compelled play she lived in. Nora's new circumstances prepare us, too, by useful suffering for the animated and
restless reality of our true medium. The abrupt separation of con-

37. Hermann Weigand, The Modern Ibsen: A Reconsideration (New York, 1960), 194,
misses the liberating intent of the scene, and Henry James might not have been able to convert vulgarity into moral release.

38. Maurice Maeterlinck, "The Tragic in Daily Life," trans. Alfred Sutro, in Toby Cole
(ed.), Playwrights on Playwriting, 34–35.

notative levels in the plays of Ibsen's major period disturbs the at-
mospheric harmony of the symbolist scene and is a negative herald
of the Great World. The acting body and the audience that experi-
ences it as a contested place between two grammars are almost unbearably strained between intense resistance to revelation and deep
desire for it.

Since the *Great World* is not a moral term, it cannot be fully
lived in until the day in which morality, itself, becomes good. As
dreaming symbolists, we project it as a place of poetry and peace, of
"cessation of all effort until the great 'sabbath of sabbaths.'" But it
is, in fact, naturally marked by the toleration of ambiguity and ambivalence in motive and desire, contradiction in thought, and dialectical play between the past, present, and future, between the
aesthetic, ethical, and spiritual spheres. Only the Grand Inquisitors
of patronage and protection and Nietzsche's enemies, self-pitying
thinkers, imagine that the Great World of spiritual value is a place
of peace. It is born of "personal distress, torment, voluptuousness,
and passion," rudely denied by moral pacifists.[39] Christianity has
willingly allied itself with bourgeois morality to find refuge from the
harrowing Kierkegaards who would keep it crucified against the
world, teleologically suspended from ethical absorption. Cleared of
the passions of both spirit and flesh, the "hallowed" rooms of goodness underwent the premature closing Paul Ricoeur calls "evil."[40]
Kierkegaard, Flaubert, Dostoyevsky, Nietzsche, and Ibsen were all
virulent in their protests against the kind of sentimental conflations
that seduced and deformed Madame Bovary. Doomed by her con-
vent synthesis of religion and romance, she yearns for peace of the
flesh in cheap versions of sainthood. The aesthetic is now positively
destructive of the spiritual, as it once threatened to be to Nora:

> So then, in place of happiness there existed greater felicities, above all
> loves a higher love, without end or intermission, a love that would

39. Nietzsche, *Birth of Tragedy*, 10–11; Nietzsche, *The Gay Science*, 284. Ibsen's Great
World much more resembles the recovered Nietzschian world of a future that includes the
conflicts of this life richly received and unrepressed than the Romantic paradise of lost oneness, the state of Edenic perfection, though neither is ever gained. The second design is
traced and analyzed by Errol Durbach in *Ibsen the Romantic*, esp. 15–18.

40. Paul Ricoeur, "Guilt, Ethics, and Religion," in Don Ihde (ed.), *The Conflict of Interpretations: Essays in Hermeneutics* (Evanston, Ill., 1974), 439.

grow to all eternity. Amid the illusions that her wishes prompted, she glimpsed a realm of purity, floating above the earth, melting into the sky, where she aspired to be. She wanted to become a saint. She bought rosaries, wore amulets, and asked for a little reliquary set in emeralds to be placed at the head of her bed, that she might kiss every night.

Flaubert's sentences reflect incessantly the antithetical provincial escapism of the modern age seeking peace in a fusion that devalues both terms: "Her soul, deformed by pride, found rest at last in Christian humility." Nowhere is the attraction of crude antithesis to conflation more exposed than in the final punishing view we have of the cliched opposition of enlightened atheist and sentimental Christian in the bodies of Homais and Bournisien. Sitting by the corpse of Madame Bovary they are indistinguishable from it, and, like the antithetical fantasies of Charles and Emma Bovary, of marriage and adultery lying side by side, they lose their identities to a common stupidity: "They sat opposite one another, bellies protruding, faces puffy and scowling, after so much discord united at last in the same human weakness; and they stirred no more than the corpse that seemed as if it were sleeping at their side."[41] This vengeful blending, teased out by Homais's notion of a progress that feeds on rehearsed antitheses, gains existential dignity only in the regressive post-Darwinian world of writers like Conrad and Brecht who, in the name of a larger consciousness, regularly collapse opposition.

The idealistic, abstract prosecutions of Dostoyevsky's Ivan Karamazov, like the utopian plans of the socialists, refuse to suffer the absurdity of life's disdain of logic and are set against the particular recognition by Alyosha of each face of each child, to the same purpose. Although later, out of fear of losing her son's love and his support of her lie, Mrs. Alving will, momentarily, echo Manders's moralizing that a child should love and honor his father and mother (I, G, III, 270), in her growing consciousness and courage, she snaps: "Oh, don't let's talk abstractions!" (I, G, II, 236) because she knows such imperatives evade the pain of the individual case. Wherever peace from the suffering of rich oppositions and ambigu-

41. Flaubert, Madame Bovary, 225, 344. In his book Flaubert: The Uses of Uncertainty (Ithaca, N.Y., 1985), 131, 169–71, Jonathan Culler links the process of binary ordering and undoing to the ambiguous value of the "stupidity" that attracts characters to meaning and author to its denial.

ity—so dear to Nietzsche—is the goal of longing, there will reign the tyrant morality, forcing love, stifled in its sexual and spiritual expression, into an inflation of duty. Freud singled out this attribute of moral Christianity when he railed against the "unpsychological proceedings of the cultural super-ego." The biblical imperative to love thy neighbor as thyself as "the strongest defense against human aggressiveness," *because* it is impossible to fulfill, lowers the value of love.[42]

This conflation of discourse, bodies, and values is precisely what Kierkegaard so savagely attacks in his diatribes against the immanent reconciliations of Hegel, the Romantics, and the theological establishment of his day. He deliberately tortures mediated forms like fairy tales, breaking their backs with moral weight and—against the young Aladdin of Oehlenschläger's poem and Sunday-school listeners who think that leaps of narrative logic in the story of Abraham can be smoothed out like fantasy—he launches version after version of the unfinished journey between the poet's wish and Abraham's faith. Not for the dialectical poet Emma's melting of body into ideal: "as she parted her lips to receive the Body of the Saviour, she swooned with celestial bliss."[43] Yet many a Pastor Manders makes a living from a poet-existence in Christian eloquence and thinks this is the same as living out spirit. Their righteousness is a rehearsed aesthetic truth. Christianity is no longer a problem because it has the aesthetic task, not of leaping over morality, but of keeping it in the hands of the priestly caste. In the sermons of Mynster, Christian restlessness becomes artistic serenity, and Kierkegaard's frontier disputes at each border of the aesthetic, moral, and spiritual are neutralized and painted out. Ironically, the preacher who wants a *separation* between daily life and religious hours is the very agent of fusion in discourse and sentiment, while Kierkegaard himself, who wants "the religious to be heard right in the midst of daily life," is the one who keeps the boundaries bris-

42. Nietzsche, *Twilight of the Idols*, 44; Nietzsche, *The Gay Science*, 335; Sigmund Freud, *Civilization and Its Discontents*, trans. James Strachey (New York, 1961), 90.

43. See comment of Georg Brandes in *Henrik Ibsen / Bjørnstjerne Bjørnson: Critical Studies*, trans. Jessie Muir; rev. William Archer (London, 1899), 15, who sees Heiberg as the source of the generic division between morality and fairy tale that Kierkegaard converted to dialectical relationship; Flaubert, *Madame Bovary*, 224–25.

tling.[44] Nothing could more effectively rebuke the easy appropriation of the language of life by Christian morality than Mrs. Alving's shocked response to Osvald's pathetic confession that Regina's "livsglede"[45] could be his salvation:

> Mrs. Alving (with a start). The joy of life—? Is there salvation in that?
> (I, G, II, 256)

So, it is war that is wanted by those subterranean poets against the reduction of our full dramatic medium and range, against the merging of the spheres of language and value. The Great World is renounced when we, like Ibsen's Aslaksen in his diplomatic moderation (I, EP, III 327), renounce warring on the contemporary small mind, demoted by Nietzsche the immoralist to the sterile sphere of a dead past: "Nothing has grown more alien to us than that desideratum of former times 'peace of soul,' the Christian desideratum." Flaubert might well have been parodying his own passion for peace in his Madame Bovary. This was not Ibsen's temptation, and we would have to agree with William Archer that in this respect he was more a Nietzschian spiritual warrior. Like Dostoyevsky and D. H. Lawrence, he worked for a reality that would honor the "teeming opposite elements" in our nature. Reversing the direction of Ivan Karamazov who insists that the lion lie down with the lamb, D. H. Lawrence returns the beasts to their natural cycle of attack, annihilation, and rebirth, for the battling creatures of the universe are perpetually constellated in magnetic opposition: "There is no peace of reconciliation. Let that be accepted for ever. Darkness will never be light, neither will the one ever triumph over the other. Whilst there is darkness, there is light; and when there is an end of darkness, there is an end of light. There are lions and there are lambs; there are lambs, and thus there are lions predicated."[46]

---

44. See Howard V. Hong and Edna H. Hong (trans. and eds.), assisted by Gregor Malantschuk, Søren Kierkegaard's Journals and Papers (6 vols.; Bloomington, Ind., 1967–78), VI, 371, 403. In Patterns in Ibsen's Middle Plays (Lewisburg, Pa., 1981), Richard Hornby applies Kierkegaard's distinctions between the aesthetic and ethical for both interpretation and staging of Ibsen's middle plays.

45. Ibsen's term used in all the plays for the sensuous and spontaneous gladness of living life in the present, and without guilt.

46. Nietzsche, Twilight of the Idols, 44; Thomas Postlewait (ed.), William Archer on Ibsen: The Major Essays: 1889–1919 (Westport, Conn., 1984), 109; phrase used by the Under-

The killer of life, nineteenth-century Christian humanism, in its antithetical fervor, "desires to dominate . . . beasts of prey," insists Nietzsche, and "its means for doing so is to make them sick."[47] The Ibsen landscape is littered with specimens. Solness, paralyzed by a conscience that both registers and invents sin and guilt, is one of Nietzsche's "sick, sickly, crippled animal[s], tame, aborted" and resorting to slave manipulation to keep his advantage. It is this creature who calls out Hilda, his "bird of prey" (*I*, MB, II, 833); conversely, Maja, who finds her animal instincts revived with Ulfheim, sarcastically calls Rubek "a tame bird of prey" (*I*, WWDA, III, 1086). It is not their art that renders the two builders impotent enemies of life, but the fact that it has capitulated to the terms of a culture governed by resentment and retribution. In *When We Dead Awaken*, spirit and sex are fighting against a morality that would suppress them, and the rabid divergence of heights from depths at the play's end is one sign of their long repression and abdication. Ibsen, Strindberg, Nietzsche, and Lawrence are together in revising Rousseau's great answer: morality has hurt rather than helped civilization. After two thousand years of deflected aggression, Ulfheim *needs* to be outrageously bestial against a world of infantile Hilmers taunting wild beasts in America from his provincial sanctuary (*I*, PS, I, 20–21). The strange creatures and gods of the forest, part of our original habitat, will have their revenge on the pretense of goodness by which they were banished. Morality's conspiracy of conflation and antithesis directed against the expressive desires of both body and soul has, in the name of a democratic Christian humanism, retarded the investigation of origins—an investigation that, in the hands of Nietzsche and his fellow underminers, would be the sword of humbling genealogy:

> Our inquiry into the origins of that other notion of goodness, as conceived by the resentful, demands to be completed. There is nothing very odd about lambs disliking birds of prey, but this is no reason for holding it against large birds of prey that they carry off lambs. And

ground Man in Fydor Dostoyevsky, *Notes from Underground* (in *Notes from Underground and The Grand Inquisitor*), trans. Ralph E. Matlaw (New York, 1960), 4; Lawrence, *Phoenix*, 691.

47. Nietzsche, *The Anti-Christ*, 132. In an earlier passage (124), Nietzsche calls the modern Christian the most *interesting* as well as the sickest animal, an evaluation supported by Ibsen in *Rosmersholm*.

when the lambs whisper among themselves, "These birds of prey are evil and does not this give us a right to say that whatever is the opposite of bird of prey must be good?" there is nothing intrinsically wrong with such an argument—though the birds of prey will look somewhat quizzically and say, "We have nothing against these good lambs; in fact, we love them; nothing tastes better than a tender lamb."[48]

If the origins of moral motives are hidden, then the ambivalence of all desire is concealed, consequence is taken for cause, and the languages of spirit and sex are yoked to a political morality. In a scene from *An Enemy of the People*, Stockmann's daughter refuses to translate an English story for the enlightened liberal newspaper because its moral stupidity offends all that the good cause supposedly stands for:

> *Petra.* It shows how a supernatural power, watching over the so-called good people of the world, arranges everything for the best in their lives—and how all the wicked got their punishment.
>
> (*I, EP, III, 331–32*)

But the journalistic Hovstad spots the advantage of using what the public wants in the back of the paper so that he can lead them "toward greater liberation and progress" in the front of the paper. His corrupt strategy exposes the pretense of superior morality that so infuriated the great demolishers.

Virtually all the plays of Ibsen's major period feature symptomatic conflations of language and value, but *Ghosts* and *Rosmersholm* are the richest reservoirs of this theatrics of self-preservation. With a shrewdness typical of the times, the peasant class, through Engstrand, politically parades and parodies religion's language of temptation for the sake of moral power before this language appears with a more deceptive dignity in the mouth of Manders.[49] This active exploitation prepares us for the pastor's delegating diction of special providential protection, intimately linked to the self-

48. Nietzsche, *The Gay Science*, 295; Nietzsche, *The Genealogy of Morals*, 151, 217, 178.
49. Inga-Stina Ewbank has done the most subtle and sensitive work on this language. See "Ibsen's Dramatic Language as a Link Between His 'Realism' and 'Symbolism,'" Haakonsen (ed.), *First International Ibsen Seminar*, 96–123, and "Ibsen and 'The Far More Difficult Art' of Prose," in Haakonsen (ed.), *Second International Ibsen Seminar*, 60–83. See also John D. Hurrell, "*Rosmersholm*, the Existentialist Drama, and the Dilemma of Modern Tragedy," *Educational Theatre Journal*, XV (1963), 123.

righteous rehearsal of his rejection of Mrs. Alving's passionate appeal in the past. That the failure to insure the orphanage against fire is a political decision, a manipulation of faith, accounts for the diffusion in our sense of cause and our lack of interest in pinning it down to Engstrand's cunning frame. The fire feels like spirit's revenge against its own cheapening. The displacement of psychological responsibility onto divine fate, carried by the perspective ("from our human viewpoint," I, G, I, 219) and the conflation of a defense and prosecution in the name of duty ("you're profoundly guilty as a mother," I, G, I, 227) are signs of that self-protective abstraction we recognize as the favorite philistine refuge. Like Nora and Rank, Mrs. Alving breaks the hold of morality with a playful allusion to elective affinities: "Osvald has more of a minister's look about the mouth" (I, G, I, 221). It joins art's particularity to an old rejected adulterous passion and by that alliance makes Manders a profoundly guilty human being. This counterattack is even more evident when Mrs. Alving fractures Manders's universal principle of love and honor for parents by the retort: "Why don't we ask, should Osvald love and honor Captain Alving?" (I, G, I, 236). Here again is the aesthetic sphere's service to spirit in the name of a higher morality, for it is art that names character and specifies husbands, wives, and their bohemian lovers in "so-called unconventional homes" (I, G, I, 223).

Manders stumbles into psychological insight from a blind morality: "You put your child out with strangers. And for that same reason you've become a stranger to him" (I, G, I, 227). Prosecuting universals can sometimes score psychological points, but they cannot educate those who hide behind them. The character of Kroll in *Rosmersholm* is an even more insidious agent of moral appropriation because he is such a shrewd psychologist. Ibsen's most cherished questions, coldly rehearsed and in no way pondered, fall from his mouth to be taken up only by those who have spirit. To Rosmer's question, in an early draft, "Have not radicals accomplished some good?" the Kroll figure replies, "That I will never admit as long as I live. They? What good should they accomplish? Can any good come from such an impure source?"[50] No wonder Rosmer worries

---

50. Archer (ed.), *Ibsen's Workshop*, 270.

the paradox of striving for purity through parties. *Unacknowledged* impure sources adore the antitheses of party and debate, the Homais game of playing at master of free discourse and thought when they are, in fact, their persecutors. Against this pretense of separation, Ibsen forces out through these words of Rosmer the deeper recognition that truly liberates psychology to examine origins: "Victory is impossible for any cause that's rooted in guilt" (*I*, R, III, 555). At once we have a denial of victory to the morality of idealized guilt in the higher types and political manipulation of spirit in the lower. In seventeenth-century England, great religious authority could protect the political design of its literature, but in Ibsen's age, the sphere and language of spirit can only be degraded by its political exploitation.[51] Brendel's attempt to invigorate the dialogue of liberation with spiritual fervor is booed off the stage. It is now the time, he naively claims, "to put on the new man," but he leaves with the biblical warning against building castles on shifting sand and with a new shirt and boots bought on borrowed money. Kroll is the master of a psychology more interested in power than truth; he blocks Rosmer's shift of the basis of morality to the blood by replying, in an early draft that is consistent with the final characterization: "To my mind faith and morality cannot be separated. And I know no other morality than our Christian one."[52] Kroll's version of Christian morality denies the individual for the sake of party and ardently prevents the teleological suspension of any ethical claim that can be used politically. The shrewd plying of morality to catch the sick conscience is, in fact, a tactic directly opposed to the mutual criticism of spheres. Mortensgaard, with the advantage of being free from ideals, is a difficult enemy; Kroll, defending against the rising liberal power of Norway and its publicity and press, must catch him in his sexual past through the Christian commandment:

> *Kroll.* Actually, I believe there's a commandment reminding us not to bear false witness against our neighbor—
> *Mortensgaard.* The headmaster hardly needs to instruct me in commandments.

---

51. See Steven N. Zwicker, "Lines of Authority: Politics and Literary Culture in the Restoration," in Kevin Sharpe and Steven N. Zwicker (eds.), *Politics of Discourse: The Literature and History of Seventeenth Century England* (Berkeley, 1987), 230–70.
52. Archer (ed.), *Ibsen's Workshop*, 296.

Kroll. Not even the seventh?
(*I*, R, II, 534)

Here is a more sophisticated version of the absurd contest between Homais and Bournisien, and surely Ibsen does more than imply that they resemble each other across party lines. His sister Beata's fate is the best bait for Rebecca, and Kroll plays it for all it is worth.[53] Ironically, his insinuation of guilty motives stimulates confession and liberation in his victim. His own family flaw is aired to catch conscience.

Like all political moralists, he demands a "unity of will" in his own house, a demand that traps Rebecca's political purpose and opens her to the awareness that "a person can be of two wills about something" (*I*, R, III, 567). Who could escape inclusion in the adage "There's always something in a family that isn't quite right" (*I*, R, I, 500)? But it is sounded as strategy by Kroll and received as insight by his victim. The public agitation carried by the liberal voice, one that affects the marriage question, has poisoned Kroll's private refuge:

> *Kroll.* Then you might as well know that this dissent and rebellion has infiltrated my own house. My own peaceful home. It's disrupted the harmony of my family life.
> (*I*, R, I, 505)

He shows how his vulgar confession is an instrument of entrapment when he adds, in his dollhouse mentality, "That sort of thing is best covered up" (*I*, R, I, 506). It does not surprise us that Kroll, like Manders, can suggest that Beata's trouble at one time might have been caused by Rebecca's books of advanced views of marriage and, at another time, by her instigation of Rosmer's sexual and political

---

53. In his book *Problems of Dostoyevsky's Poetics*, trans. and ed. Caryl Emerson (Minneapolis, 1984), 60, Mikhail Bakhtin comments on Dostoyevsky's suspicion of the arrogance of psychology that violates the mystery of another: "Truth is unjust when it concerns the depth of someone else's personality." See "To Damascus III," Scene 2, in August Strindberg, *Plays of Confession and Therapy: To Damascus I, II, III*, trans. Walter Johnson (Seattle, 1979), 193:

> *Tempter:* You happen to have effaced your own personality so you see with other people's eyes, think with other people's thoughts. In a word: you have committed psychic suicide.

Strindberg discusses psychic murder and psychic suicide, mentioning *Rosmersholm*, in *Vivisektioner*, trans. from the French by Tage Aurell (Stockholm, 1958).

33

apostasy. The public and private spheres have been hopelessly merged by the cunning provincial Iago. Watch him turn, by the tactic exposed by Nietzsche, nineteenth-century Christian humility to revenge in the name of justice—a deceit not too surprising in one who identifies religion exclusively with morality.

> Kroll. But then you've already read how these "defenders of the people" have gratified themselves by smearing me. . . . And now that I've tasted blood, they're going to learn that I'm not a man who just smiles and turns the other cheek.
>
> (I, R, I, 501)

No more than Hovstad or Flaubert's Rodolphe does Kroll gain privileged critical status by bracketing moral terminology, since he uses it politically for self-preservation and power.

Strindberg named as the major new understanding of modern drama the recognition that "an incident in life . . . is usually caused by a whole series of more or less deep-lying motives." As a hunter, Kroll raises this complex dimension, but as a receiver, he is like the spectator who "usually selects the one that he most easily understands or that he finds most favorable to his sense of honor." Rebecca, however, is deeply stirred as she descends the steps of motive down all the levels of consciousness offered by the playwright. Ibsen has given Kroll the word *liberation*, but the word undergoes the purgatory of definition in the blood of Rebecca. Kroll cannot, as Mrs. Alving puts it, listen to himself, but that is precisely what accusation helps Rebecca to do. She sees that she, too, under the pressure of an "alien law," had merged sex and spirit, deformed their desires by both bad and malicious faith. The marriage in death at the end of the play, in all its public uselessness, is the sad result of this strategy, but also a celebration of a vision freed from bodies that returns the spheres to their constellated autonomy, their *true* marriage. Where Mrs. Helseth sees demonic luring by the dead wife, Rosmer and Rebecca feel liberated from her corpse by a homeopathic blending with her in an almost ritualizing undoing of psychic parasitism, psychic murder.[54]

The democratic prejudice of progress fatally retarded the investigation of motive and morality Nietzsche called for because it po-

---

54. August Strindberg, preface to *Lady Julie*, in *Pre-Inferno Plays*, 75; Nietzsche, *Beyond Good and Evil*, 31.

liticized the past. It inevitably attracted Nietzsche's negative and narrower polemical revenge—the exposure of the preservation of priestly power behind the biblical imperatives thundered by Manders and his kind. But the philosopher opened up, as well, a positive possibility of multiple and unappropriated causes that returns us to our individuality. His psychology that could by regression to ambivalent desire lead us out of the reach of Kroll's ingenious and cunning seductions is the necessary antidote prescribed by Kierkegaard, Flaubert, Dostoyevsky, and Ibsen, as well. For too long, Nietzsche complained, psychology has been "caught in moral prejudices and fears" and has been unable to "descend into the depths," but that is where we have to go to undermine the morality that has closed off life's full and fearful dimension. By exposing the affective origin concealed by the democratizing of feeling into social laws, psychology could neutralize morality and scatter the crowd. Our individuality recovered, we cannot be threatened by that of another. It is only the small-minded, says Kierkegaard, who have made logic out of love, for whom "every individuality is a refutation."[55] Ibsen's Provost, the kind of Christian democrat despised by Kierkegaard, scolds Brand for making inequalities by his spiritual earnestness: "The surest way to destroy a man / Is to turn him into an individual" (M, B, V, 93). The Provost's morality, like that of Kierkegaard's orators, would "preach a sermon / On the duality of human nature / And . . . take a little light refreshment first" (M, B, V, 94). From the pulpit, he will appear a poet of goodness. But a liberated psychology could pose this paradox to progress: "What if the 'good' man represents not merely a retrogression but even a danger, a temptation, a narcotic drug enabling the present to live at the expense of the future?" Howells acutely realized that Ibsen was foremost among those moderns who make us "question the good" by using psychology to undermine majority morality.[56] If psychology can scarcely panic herds and formulas in Ibsen's plays, it certainly can, like Kierkegaard's, single out the individual for the agonies of spirit and reclaim for itself Aslaksen's motto, "A politician has to keep all possibilities open" (I, EP, III, 329). It makes

55. Nietzsche, Beyond Good and Evil, 31; Nietzsche, Will to Power, 148; Søren Kierkegaard, Works of Love: Some Christian Reflections in the Form of Discourses, trans. and ed. Howard Hong and Edna Hong (New York, 1962), 254.

56. Nietzsche, Genealogy of Morals, 155; Howells, "Henrik Ibsen," 14.

its raids on the *moral* world for the sake of the Great World, not to save lives, and it successfully leads us beyond bourgeois good and evil even if we are brought down from the climb that was too late, too timid, and too irresponsible.

All of Ibsen's plays in the major period stage the drama between psychology as prisoner of political morality and as liberator of spirit. The way in which Rebecca profits spiritually from Kroll's diagnosis is a fine example. But perhaps the most beautiful release is worked out in Acts II and III of *Little Eyolf*. At the end of Act I, Rita has begun the process of saddling psychological insight with reproach at the very moment of Little Eyolf's drowning: "If I'm vile and evil, Alfred, it's your doing" (*I*, LE, I, 893). The battling of mutual analysis and accusation slams at us like the sea. In the middle of Act II, the cruel jibes of Allmers mock Rita's displacement of personal guilt to haunting fate. "And were they evil, those eyes, Rita?" he asks, trapping her in acknowledgment of a projected original wish for the child's annihilation. Rita returns to the attack by fingering Allmers's own merging of Asta with Eyolf, an identification which continually "made someone stand in the way of the marriage" (*I*, LE, II, 907). The rhythms of attack, retreat, aggression, and self-doubt are relentless. For suspended moments, the two muse themselves back to desired innocence and forward to resignation:

> Rita (*stares desolately at him*). I think this can only end in despair—in madness for both of us. Because we can never—never make it right again.
> Allmers (*in a reverie*). I dreamed of Eyolf last night. I could see him walking up from the pier. He could run just like the other boys. Nothing had happened to him. Not the least harm. The ghastly truth was only a dream—.
> (*I*, LE, II, 910)

Rita's hostility resurfaces when she refuses to Allmers a god gracious enough to change pangs of conscience into existential grief, a move Allmers had already made on Rita. The language now intensely hounds its prey in short, snapping barks ("Dom over deg og meg") of retribution, still dependent on the assumption of some metaphysical order. In Act III, Allmers again personalizes Rita's evasive poetry of "sorrow and loss" (925) to "our gnawing pangs of remorse." The law of change—once, for Allmers, a strategy of sepa-

36

ration and contrast between the two "marriages," that of husband and wife and that of brother and sister—now is accepted sadly as a name for loss, interiorized into psychological expansion and healing:

> Allmers. Perhaps the law of change can still hold us together.
> Rita (nodding slowly). There is something changing in me now. It's such a painful feeling.
> Allmers. Painful?
> Rita. Yes, like something giving birth.
> Allmers. That's it. Or a resurrection. A passage into a higher life.
> (I, LE, III, 928)

Such rhetorical ascent is never without the heavy presence of irony. Rita is quick to mock Allmers's Kierkegaardian climax: "The loss— that's the heart of the victory" (I, LE, III, 929). "Fine phrases," she taunts, but psychology, by its recourse to indeterminate agents and objects, has nevertheless wriggled free, at least provisionally, from the politics of protection and prosecution to work for spirit. Allmers will not let Rita deny: "We've some part of the sea and the stars in us too." Earthbound, we are forced into dreams of innocence and purity and soon humbled. The mere work of charity, the projection of an ethical solution to remorse, cannot satisfy our aesthetic and metaphysical desires. Allmers poses us in between, for he looks straight at Rita when he says, "Upward." The final "thank you" of Rita is one of the most beautiful of Ibsen's closings, for it comes at the end of incessant accusation and self-doubt and testifies to some kind of deepening. Characteristically, Ibsen makes her words also renounce passion in life and high spiritual hope, while they drift, unheard by the gods, toward "that great silence" (I, LE, III, 936).[57] If only for a span, morality has settled into its sphere and allowed the full attraction of a place beyond good and evil.

The looming of the Great World, however inadequate we are to inhabit it, compels us to ask Ibsen's most persistent question: "At what height or depth can we live? Can we ever rise above the projections of bad conscience and the rationalizing designs of retribution, above the passion for purity and the regressive desire for perfect communion, long enough to find in our full medium a home? It

---

57. Compare Franz Kafka, Letters to Milena, trans. Tania Stern and James Stern, ed. Willi Haas (New York, 1953), 193.

is a question that refuses the therapeutic compromises of adjustment as much as it mocks willed ascent. In *Queen Christina*, Strindberg treats one of Ibsen's favorite early themes, that of a ruler unfit to rule, through whom both playwrights fruitfully explored their self-doubts. What appears outrageous immaturity or even silliness in a character like Queen Christina, Skule, or Lady Inger might well signal a false measuring standard in the world as it is:

> *Tott:* Yes, she's an eagle, born of air in the air, because she has such a hard time breathing down here! . . .
> *De la Gardie:* Doesn't she have any faults?
> *Tott:* No, because "faults and merits"—that bourgeois concept—doesn't cover her qualities.[58]

Hooked by the unpardonable sin of killing love in a human heart, Solness, Borkman, and Rubek still fly, at one time or another, beyond the adequate measure of philistine duty. Stranded in irony, these maimed modern titans can hardly be the heroes of overcoming that Nietzsche launches past bourgeois morality, since they are refused critical control and soar too close to the sun. Yet their trajectory leads us to the threshold of the Great World.[59] Even if we must remain behind, we might begin to experience guilt as the inevitable effluvium of a call to being that can never be fully answered.[60] Psychology takes as its ally for this release the major patterns of myth and symbol, a resource that moves us past morality into the mysteries of desire.

If moral melodrama radically separates Krogstad from Nora, the

58. August Strindberg, *Queen Christina*, in *Queen Christina; Charles XII; Gustav III*, trans. Walter Johnson (Seattle, 1955), 46–47.

59. See F. W. Kaufmann, "Ibsen's Conception of Truth," in Rolf Fjelde (ed.), *Ibsen: A Collection of Critical Essays* (Englewood Cliffs, N.J., 1965), 28: "Although Ibsen's plays seem to be mainly concerned with the opposite of truth, the 'life's lie,' the ideal of truth is never quite absent; it is represented in the struggle of the characters who even in their failure and because of their very failure point in the direction of that truth which is for Ibsen the creative response to life, originating in concrete situations and transcending them without vanishing in the lifeless realm of the abstract." It is interesting, in this light, to read Ibsen's poem "Stormsvalen," in *Ibsens Samlede Verker i billigutgave* (3 vols.; Oslo, 1977–78), I, 340. In his book *Henrik Ibsen*, trans. Helen Sebba (New York, 1972), Hans Georg Meyer tests the aborted selfhood of these heroes by the standards of Kierkegaard and Nietzsche.

60. Martin Heidegger, *Being and Time*, trans. John Macquarrie and Edward Robinson (New York, 1962), 333ff.

pair antithetically poised as villain and heroine, psychology leads them to a metaphorical unity (quite the opposite of the literal duplications Flaubert used for vengeance) as family forgers and would-be suicides, an identity of despair and survival. Torvald sees Rank, as Rank sees himself, as the "dark cloud setting off our sunlit happiness" (*I*, DH, III, 186), but his suffering and loneliness meet those of the deeper Nora, undoing the false conjunction of happiness and dollhouse:

> *Helmer.* Haven't you been happy here?
> *Nora.* No, never. I thought so—but I never have.
> (*I*, DH, III, 191)

What starts out as Nora's melodrama of political psychology, her strategy of seduction for money, quickly plays itself into an identity with Rank that leaves behind the crude antithetical structure of the world of blame and cause. The last words of *John Gabriel Borkman* unite feuding sisters at this level, and the low, deep, dark rhythm of authentic being, like Rita's final "takk," beats forth in the elemental language of the mythical realm:

> *Fru Borkman.* Vi to tvillingsøstre—over *ham* vi begge har elsket.
> *Ella.* Vi to skygger—over den døde mann.
>
> *Mrs. Borkman.* We two twin sisters—over him we both once loved.
> *Ella.* We two shadows—over the dead man.
> (*I*, JGB, IV, 1024)

At this depth, resignation touches the psychological sublime of *The Master Builder*; both the intense descent and ascent are conducted in words that reach beyond good and evil—though not with impunity—beyond the cause confused with consequence, most poignantly registered in the rejection of Hedvig by a father who assumes one origin. Moral control by cause is political psychology's defense against an investigation of origins.

Liberating psychology takes on the design of mythical thinking, as Ernst Cassirer describes it. "Whereas empirical thinking is essentially directed toward establishing an unequivocal relation between specific 'causes' and specific 'effects', mythical thinking, even where it raises the question of origins, as such, has a free selection of causes at its disposal. Anything can come from anything, because

39

anything can stand in temporal or spatial contact with anything."[61] Like the wild duck, Hedvig is protected from appropriation by the mythical time and space she carries in her. What she says about the duck's origin is true of her own as well: "Even the chickens have all the others that they were baby chicks with, but she's so completely apart from any of her own. So you see, everything is so really mysterious about the wild duck. There's no one who knows her, and no one who knows where she comes from either" (I, WD, III, 438). What a reproach to Hjalmar's hang-up on legal paternity! Mythical thinking is politically prodded by cause-mongering idealists, but in Hedvig's mouth, it shows up our morality as a fiction pitched against nature and gives us a pattern for the forgiveness Gregers rhetorically calls for and refuses to his own family. The freed psychology of Ibsen and his fellow seekers of the Third Empire posits, like myths, multiple beginnings and multiple gods. It yearns, like spirit, to recover the rich mythical forests of the universe and mind, lost with the moralizing of Christianity.

Because provincial morality rules by concealing origins behind cause to punish its children, it is a profoundly guilty parent. Yet even the genealogists of origins have some compassion for that proxy of a dead god. Like Nietzsche and Freud, Ibsen was well aware of the disastrous effects of too sudden a decompression of the metaphysical bubble. This warning of Manders might be impelled by self-protection but, like so many of the symptomatic admonishments from unacknowledged impure sources, it carries some general truth: "Don't demolish ideals, Mrs. Alving—that can have cruel repercussions" (I, G, II, 237). Of course, that act has brutal consequences mainly because the ideals were dead and deceitful baffles of painful truths. In fact, truth can be defined only against the ideals that deform necessary psychological recognitions of inevitable impurity. Nevertheless, Ibsen saw, with Nietzsche, the public pathos and pathology in the clinging to Christian morality as compensation for a fading divinity. It was a natural reaction to dying power, like that of the declining Norwegian bureaucrats who held on to moral authority for all it was worth.[62]

61. Ernst Cassirer, The Philosophy of Symbolic Forms, trans. Ralph Manheim (2 vols.; New Haven, Conn., 1965), 2, 46.

62. In Twilight of the Idols, 69–70, Nietzsche writes of George Eliot and English philosophers, "They have got rid of the Christian God and now feel obliged to cling all the more

The optimism of Feuerbachian humanism is provisionally trumpeted by Jacobsen's Niels Lyhne, in this enlightenment hope: "When heaven [is] a free infinite space instead of a spying, threatening eye," we will be at home on earth. It is met by the skeptical rejoinder: "Why, then, atheism will make greater demands on men than Christianity has done. . . . Where will you get all the strong individuals you will need to make up your atheistical community?"[63] It is a question that Ibsen probes through his sick consciences yearning to be joyous, robust, innocent.[64] The aggressive appropriation of spirit and sex by "the everlasting Truth" of Torvald is a defensive maneuver against the terror of weightlessness in a world devoid of God and bereft of epic heroes. The parodic imitation of what is left of a Christian god surfacing in the New Testament language of temptation in *John Gabriel Borkman* and *The Master Builder* is a protest against—or a symptom of—the anxiety of unsanctioned titanism. "Oh no, I pretty well got the idea that He wasn't pleased with me" (*I, MB, III*, 854), admits Solness in his need to have the order of God's disapproval, while Rosmer has to resign himself to "no higher judgment than ours" and to the necessity to "carry out justice ourselves" (*I, R, IV*, 583) without the assurances of legendary fate or martyrdom.[65]

What were the advantages of a strong investment in Christianity, asks Nietzsche?

1. It granted man an absolute value, as opposed to his smallness and accidental occurrence in the flesh of becoming and passing away.
2. It served the advocates of God insofar as it conceded to the world, in spite of suffering and evil, the character of perfection—including "freedom": evil appeared full of meaning.
3. It posited that man had a *knowledge* of absolute values and thus *adequate knowledge* precisely regarding what is most important.[66]

---

firmly to Christian morality." On the political defensiveness of Norwegian bureaucrats, see B. J. Hovde, *The Scandinavian Countries, 1720–1865: The Rise of the Middle Classes* (2 vols.; Ithaca, N.Y., 1948), II, 558.

63. J. P. Jacobsen, *Niels Lyhne*, trans. Hanna Astrup Larsen (New York, 1967), 145–46.
64. This yearning is especially powerful and obsessive in *Rosmersholm* and *The Master Builder*.
65. See Inga-Stina Ewbank, "Ibsen's Dramatic Language" in Haakonsen (ed.), *First International Ibsen Seminar*, 104–10.
66. Nietzsche, *Will to Power*, 9–10.

This is a great consolation. Despite the fact that this faith gives only the illusion of adequate knowledge, it has over the centuries—instead "of making us modest," as Robbe-Grillet puts it—concealed from us "the weakness of our resources when it comes to essentials." While the higher types are caught between the inability "to esteem what we know and not to be *allowed* any longer to esteem the lies we should like to tell ourselves" the Manderses and Torvalds must brace themselves against the terror in the thought—often expressed but not anxiously felt in the Enlightenment—that, in Stockmann's words, "truths aren't at all the stubborn old Methuselahs people imagine. An ordinary, established truth lives, as a rule—let's say—some seventeen, eighteen, at the most, twenty years" (*I*, EP, IV, 356).[67] When Osvald's agitated "enlightened" mother, fearing the loss of her son's love, ironically is backed into Manders's corner of everlasting biblical universals, she says, "Surely a child ought to feel some love for his father," and the son retorts, "It's one of those ideas that materialize in the world for a while, and then become relentless ghosts" (*I*, G, III, 269–70). Both Stockmann and Osvald realize, with Nietzsche, that it is when ideals are dying that the majority clings to them most exclusively and fanatically (*I*, EP, IV, 357).

If the beyonds, behinds, and belows of religious projection have been brutally exposed to suspicion by antimetaphysicians of science, philosophy, and criticism from the Enlightenment on, still, as Ibsen's Julian admits, we cannot ever be free of Christianity. Even Hjerrild laments, in Jacobsen's novel *Niels Lyhne*, "Let us be honest! No matter what we call ourselves we can never quite get that God out of heaven; our brain has fancied him up there too often, the picture has been rung into it and sung into it from the time we were little children." Flaubert's resistance to socialist optimism rests on its neglect of the necessity to suffer, a legacy of "the blood of that Christ that stirs within us." It is not surprising, then,

---

67. Robbe-Grillet, *For a New Novel*, 20; Nietzsche, *Will to Power*, 9–10; Weigand, *The Modern Ibsen*, 128. Commenting on ironies implicit in Stockmann's idealism in the name of realism, Weigand writes, "[His] insight into the relativity of values is his own *logical* undoing." In a comment of 1887, Ibsen, *Speeches and New Letters*, trans. Arne Kildal (Boston, 1910), 57, contends, "I am a pessimist in so far as I do not believe in the everlastingness of human ideals. But I am also an optimist in so far as I firmly believe in the capacity for procreation and development of ideals."

that the subterranean poets and prophets transvaluated and turned by irony New Testament phrases and sacramental designs. They yearned for all the gods to come out of the forests, off the crosses, and into a community of numinous presence. If morality's crucifixion of spirit and sex could be undone, Nietzsche's Dionysus, Lawrence's Pan, and a new, living Christ might harrow the modern world into freedom. Lawrence gives us our prayer: "I worship Christ, I worship Jehova, I worship Pan, I worship Aphrodite. But I do not worship hands nailed and running with blood upon a cross, nor licentiousness, nor lust. I want them all, all the gods. They are all God." We have been reminded by ancient tragedy of the close relationship between living communal ideals and conventions and the rich presence of conflicting gods.[68] The sexual and spiritual quarantine must be lifted, and physical and metaphysical aspiration together reclaim the world killed by a sterile present, chained to a dead past, and bereft of living fathers.[69] When Brand scorns the bourgeois God as an old man, claims Shaw, "that was the first time it suddenly flashed on Europe that, after all, supposing God were to be conceived as a young man?"[70]

Brand, like his model Kierkegaard, has a need for something majestic to love. Was there ever a world so large, they both wonder, in which love for the absolute and for the family were not at crosspurposes, not scored by tragic irony? Could we still, muses the nineteenth-century prophetic imagination, "suckled in a creed outworn" see God great and strong?[71] The draining of power from both divine and human love by a democratic Christian humanism jealous of majesty and terrified of the unknown and the collapse of Kierkegaard's transcendental climax of passionate misunderstanding between God and man—this was the loss registered by Flaubert, Dostoyevsky, Nietzsche, Ibsen, and Lawrence. If Christianity were

68. Meyer, *Ibsen*, 399; Jacobsen, *Niels Lyhne*, 282; Gustave Flaubert to Louise Colet, September 4, 1852, in *The Selected Letters of Gustave Flaubert*, 141; Lawrence, *Phoenix*, 307; Martha C. Nussbaum, *The Fragility of Goodness: Luck and Ethics in Greek Tragedy and Philosophy* (New York, 1986), 81.

69. The general image of being chained to the dead is one Ibsen used more than once in his plays: *Ghosts, Rosmersholm,* and *The Master Builder.* See the ending of Dostoyevsky, *Notes from Underground,* and Nietzsche, *Ecce Homo,* 133.

70. Bernard Shaw, "Modern Religion," in Dan H. Laurence (ed.), *Platform and Pulpit: Bernard Shaw* (New York, 1961), 123.

71. See *Brand,* Act III, and Wordsworth's sonnet "The World Is Too Much with Us."

a *living* thing, laments Bjørnson's king, the corruption of institutional power could not be tolerated. But in the absence of a faith in which morality could come into contact with reality, the priestly castes and civil servants of a slave ethic rule by concealing under the language of duty a "politics of vengeance" and under pacifying pictures a dying god. "What could equal in debilitating narcotic power the symbol of the 'holy cross,' the ghastly paradox of a crucified god, the unspeakable cruel mystery of God's self-crucifixion for the benefit of mankind?" We can, with Lawrence's Romain Rolland, look back to the Christian democratic epoch and see only the limp sorrow of Gethsemane. Appropriate the miracle, mystery, and authority of such a death, and you have a monarchy of morality dedicated to the suppression of any ascending movement of life. Even Hardy's impressionable Tess is able to recognize the ugly parasitism of modern morality on theology, which "in the primitive days of mankind had been quite distinct." [72]

In Lawrence's Michael Angelo, we see the beginning of that passage from the classical worship of might and glory to the modern epoch of service, equality, and humility, which now, in its decadence, must be abandoned so that power can once again come to us from beyond. "When power enters us, it does not just move us mechanically. It changes us. When the unseen wind blows, it blows upon us and through us. It carries us like a ship on a sea. And it roars to flame in us, like a draught in a fierce fire." [73] This is the awakening to divine power in life that we dead await. The splitting of power and love—richly married in pagan, Old Testament, and even gospel story and diction before the priests managed to divorce them by fixing morality and identifying love with the romance of sacrifice—is a curse posing as a cure. [74] It has forced the will to bully the known and fear the unknown. That is why the poets and prophets are willing to risk the anxiety of demolition for the sake of a

72. Bjørnstjerne Bjørnson, *Kongen* (*The King*), Act IV; Nietzsche, *Genealogy of Morals*, 169; D. H. Lawrence to Lady Ottoline Morrell, April 7, 1916, in Diana Trilling (ed.), *The Selected Letters of D. H. Lawrence* (New York, 1958), 131; Nietzsche, *Twilight of the Idols*, 45; Thomas Hardy, *Tess of the d'Urbervilles* (New York, 1965), 274.

73. D. H. Lawrence, *Phoenix II: Uncollected, Unpublished, and Other Prose Works*, ed. Warren Roberts and Harry T. Moore (Harmondsworth, Middlesex, 1981), 456.

74. See G. Wilson Knight, *Henrik Ibsen* (New York, 1962), 115: "Like Byron, he was a regular reader of the Bible. He is a prophetic dramatist striving for the union of love and power; or, put differently, for the advent of Christ *as* power."

higher morality that would once again be in love with life. By killing life, modern Christianity has *demoted* morality. Strindberg views it as the murderer of authentic virtues, as "the killer of reason, of the flesh, of beauty, joy, all the purest affections of humanity. The destroyer of virtues: honesty, valor, glory, love, and pity." [75]

The severe irony inherent in Borkman's self-deceiving titanism, brutally bounding past love in its greed for the "shining aura of power and glory" in the depths and darkness of an inexhaustible kingdom, cannot altogether devalue the passion that wants it all, wants intimacy and integrity in a world dead to spirt. Borkman's "rage for power" (*I, JGB,* II, 987) and Solness's hunger for the innocent strength of youth (*I,* MB, II, 833) have been stimulated by democratic Christian humanism's systematic repression of natural aristocracy, the noble ethic. That is what makes the striving, Christian part of mankind "suffer from megalomania." The language of temptation in *John Gabriel Borkman* and *When We Dead Awaken,* the promise of the glories of the world, are evoked out of a longing and half-conscious envy of the old god's guiltless binding of power and love, which the satanic aesthetics of theology have split apart. Though he punished the will by his ceaseless irony, no one asked with more personal passion than Ibsen why it must in the modern world feel guilty for desiring their communion. The Great World promises love and will a "new power in life" but one of which we are as yet "incapable." [76] We are condemned to sense it only through the failures of our full and foolish extensions and through the disequilibrium brought on by morality's bullying of the spheres and our vulnerability to its imperative commands and laws. The gap between power and love in Borkman's play is at least as impressive as a sign of cultural loss as one of personal failing. The Third Empires of Ibsen, Nietzsche, Flaubert, and Lawrence, all breaking out of dualism, will be ruled by men like them: true aristocrats "seeking out . . . contraries only in order to affirm themselves even more gratefully and delightedly," the "noble, good, beautiful happy ones," standing together after standing alone against the ma-

75. August Strindberg, *Inferno, Alone and Other Writings,* trans. and ed. Evert Sprinchorn (Garden City, N.Y., 1968), 273.

76. Archer (ed.), *Ibsen's Workshop,* 186; Ibsen, speech at the banquet in Stockholm, September 24, 1887, in *Speeches and New Letters,* 56–57.

jority.[77] We may not be ready for Stockmann's new school, however seriously we are attracted to his comic naïveté, but his Darwinian correction of the politics of the majority, his selection of mongrels for the new education, is a satisfying if also absurd reminder that nineteenth-century Christianity had, as a natural enemy of evolution and life, selected out for moral praise the weakest, whose secret power is sacrifice, producing a species bent on self-preservation through dependency. What Nietzsche calls "the solidarity of the weak, this hampering of selection" is as unnatural and deforming a party as could be imagined.[78] No wonder its schools have produced Madame Bovarys with dollhouse fantasies of perfect love.

All the subterranean tunnelers, then, rail against the democratic Christian myths of equality which are, to Nietzsche, the masks of spite, or to Lawrence only "the negative form of power."[79] The justice that recognizes natural inequality and anatomizes the leveled provinces grown fat on grace, cuts with Flaubert's secular scalpel.[80] As Flaubert's letters are filled with the rage to dissect Christian democracy and his novels relentlessly level the levelers, his demolishing materialism prepares the way for the rule of spiritual mandarins. In the age of bourgeois monarchies, even great pretenders to superior morality, devoid of spirit, democratize to control. We are not surprised that Rodolphe's reduction of women "to a single level of love where all were equal" elicits from his author a rare defense of his heroine. Against that negative democracy, the subterranean prophets set the aristocracy of the singleness of the self, a higher democracy in truth, since, as Kierkegaard and Dostoyevsky view it, spirit rescues the individual from the fantastic fate of the abstract category.[81] Ibsen takes up the weapons of anatomy and psychology

77. Nietzsche, Genealogy of Morals, 171; see also Gustave Flaubert to George Sand, April 29, 1871, in The Selected Letters of Gustave Flaubert, 238–39.

78. Nietzsche, Will to Power, 142.

79. See D. H. Lawrence, Apocalypse (New York, 1960), 28ff. Lawrence is here at his most Nietzschian. See also Phoenix, 709, and an essay on aristocracy in Phoenix II, 475–84.

80. This is a metaphor of Charles-Augustin Sainte-Beuve, Causeries du lundi (15 vols.; Paris, 1852–62), XIII, 363: "Fils et frère de médecins distingués, M. Gustave Flaubert tient la plume comme d'autres le scalpel." Flaubert, himself, spoke often of his desire to write anatomy, a term that deliberately sharpened fiction to surgical justice.

81. Flaubert, Madame Bovary, 213, 203, 236; Kierkegaard, Works of Love, 282–83.

to liberate the individual to an inequality that prepares for the democracy of spirit.

This critical aristocratic radicalism, as Brandes sympathetically calls it,[82] necessarily assumed by the generations of diagnosticians persecuting the dead ideals of the Enlightenment and Revolution, marshals its attacks against outraged reviews of plays like *Rosmersholm*: "Love, truth, religion, and self-respect have still some hold upon us, and it is hardly likely that Ibsen's gloomy ideas will be generally accepted." Morality, claims the reviewer, must look after its own mission when art betrays it. The formulas of egalitarian individualism launched by Rousseau against the conventions and cabals of a society apparently intent upon quenching his "burning love for the great, true, beautiful," have been harnessed by a later morality to rein in the apostles of life. Democratic Christian humanism had absorbed the promises of both the Revolution and Apocalypse, ecstatically bonded in the recent past of early Romanticism. Nietzsche notes the appropriation, leveling, and cheapening of the legacy: "the rule of the poor in spirit, the curse on voluptuousness, the curse of the morality of self-sacrifice, on master morality, the curse of philosophies of the 'happiness of all.'" Foucault sees through Nietzsche's eyes when he calls Christian humanism "a whole series of subjected sovereignties." In this inversion of strength and spirit, the bodies of the children of believers in eternal ideals will suffer anxiety, the Kierkegaardian despair of not being a self. And they, as Ibsen's parents, kill their children.[83]

D. H. Lawrence asks what could stop ventriloquists of the Hydra head of Equality, Liberty, Fraternity from babbling the formulas that mute and level the raging and ragged origins and evolutions of

82. Georg Brandes, "An Essay on Aristocratic Radicalism," *Friedrich Nietzsche*, 106–107. Brandes quotes from a letter from Nietzsche: "The expression *Aristocratic Radicalism*, which you employ, is very good. It is, permit me to say, the cleverest thing I have yet read about myself" (64). To Nietzsche, Brandes wrote, "I find much that harmonizes with my own ideas and sympathies; the depreciation of the ascetic ideals and the profound disgust with democratic mediocrity, your aristocratic radicalism" (63).

83. Review quoted by Archer in *Archer on Ibsen*, 38, 45; Jean-Jacques Rousseau, *The Confessions*, trans. J. M. Cohen (Harmondsworth, Middlesex, 1954), 233; Nietzsche, *Will to Power*, 58; 1971 interview of Michel Foucault in *Language, Counter-Memory, Practice: Selected Essays and Interviews by Michel Foucault*, trans. Donald F. Bouchard and Sherry Simon (Ithaca, N.Y., 1977), 221; Foucault, "Nietzsche, Genealogy, History," in *Language, Counter-Memory, Practice*, 147.

desire? To scotch the resurrection of "the beastly Lazarus of our ide-alism," the favorite bourgeois denial of death, he pleads for the re-covery of natural miracle and wonder:

> The ideal of love, the ideal that it is better to give than to receive, the ideal of liberty, the ideal of the brotherhood of man, the ideal of the sanctity of human life, the ideal of what we call goodness, charity, be-nevolence, public spiritedness, the ideal of sacrifice for a cause, the ideal of unity and unanimity—all the lot—all the whole beehive of ideals—has all got the modern bee-disease and gone putrid.[84]

The post-Revolutionary disappointment of Ibsen's age is regis-tered no longer in noble depression, but in anarchic disgust against morality's murderous arrest of the cycles of spiritual struggle towards Freedom. Ibsen writes to Brandes in 1870:

> The old France of illusion is broken in pieces . . . so that we suddenly find ourselves at the start of a new era. How the ideas tumble about us now! And indeed it is time. All that we have been living on until now is but scraps from the table of last century's revolution, and that gristle has been chewed and re-chewed for long enough. The ideas need to be scourged and re-interpreted. Liberty, equality, and fraternity are no longer the same as they were in the days of the lamented guillotine. That is what the politicians refuse to understand, and that is why I hate them.[85]

Those politicians call for "the living truth" (*I, EP,* III, 325), in the words of Billing, but in his language of moral manipulation, this great spiritual value becomes a formula to protect the majority. The distance between the good and the useful is so wide that the Rousseau in Dina who burns for the great, true, and beautiful must sigh: "Oh, if I were far away, I could be good too" (*I, PS,* I, 29). Like that of Mayor Stockmann, the moral authority of Bernick de-pends on his ability "to reel off the whole speech" (*I, PS,* II, 43) of community service and public altruism—the rhetoric that so effec-tively conceals egoism, greed, cowardice. Bernick, no less than Flaubert's Rodolphe and Deslauriers, is interested in using his lan-guage of moral superiority to level all competition. Against a claim

---

84. D. H. Lawrence to Bertrand Russell, July 15, 1915, in *Selected Letters,* 112; Law-rence, *Aaron's Rod* (New York, 1961), 271.

85. Henrik Ibsen to Georg Brandes, December 20, 1870, trans. Michael Meyer, in *Ibsen,* 346; see full letter in *Correspondence,* 205.

for progress by his workman Aune, he turns defense into offense, problem into prosecution: "Yes, for your own narrow faction, for the working class. Oh, I know you agitators: you make speeches, you stir people up—but as soon as there's some real progress at hand, like this with our machines, then you won't go along with it" (*I*, PS, II, 43). By this time the word "real" has been corrupted so radically that it actually means its opposite, and this divorce between morality and reality is the target of Nietzsche's sharpshooters.

It is psychology that must break through its own misuse to the living language of desire by forcing morality into the air of spiritual inequality, of a higher reality, where it will confront the unknown it can no longer pretend has been colonized and is identical with the known. Political psychology, as Flaubert and Kroll (at different levels of consciousness) use it to punish, confines us to the *known* world—the thoroughly known, hence stupid, provinces of language and mind, where there is no outlet for the suffering of body and thought. The unconscious has been anxiously confined by duty to a paralyzing guilt in the higher types, as the natural world is subjugated by the known world's pathetic fallacies of Providence and retribution. Jung, among others, charts these instinctive strategies of self-protection and their unfortunate consequences:

> The daemonism of nature, which man had apparently triumphed over, he has unwittingly swallowed into himself and so become the devil's marionette. This could happen only because he believed he had abolished the daemons by declaring them to be superstition. He overlooked the fact that they were, at bottom, the products of certain factors in the human psyche. When these products were dubbed unreal and illusory, their sources were in no way blocked up or rendered inoperative. On the contrary, after it became impossible for the daemons to inhabit the rocks, woods, mountains, and rivers, they used human beings as much more dangerous dwelling places.[86]

Solness sees himself as the chief dwelling place of trolls, and the materializing of his fears in Hilda, a daemonic server and helper, may be the wished-for chance to break the spell of stultifying public and private guilt fostered by bourgeois morality's aggressive hostility

---

86. Gustave Flaubert to Louise Colet, September 4, 1852, in *Selected Letters*, 141; Carl G. Jung, *Psychological Reflections: A New Anthology of His Writings, 1905–1961*, trans. R. F. C. Hull, ed. Jolande Jacobi and R. F. C. Hull (Princeton, N.J. 1978), 232.

to spontaneity of character and expression. The eruption of the repressed, seeking relief from the twin wardens of sophistic moral
knowledge and political psychology, is more unambiguously met in
the fiction of D. H. Lawrence, where the redaemonizing of the
world is positively related to the respiritualizing of the universe.

In one of *The Rainbow*'s most difficult scenes, Ursula confronts
the horses in the rain only after she has allowed herself to see
within her own darkness "points of light like the eyes of wild beasts,
glowing, penetrating, vanishing." Unlike the white horses haunting the guilt-ridden Rosmer and Rebecca, Ursula's animals are free
from service to domestic superstitions and can, by their very autonomy, stir the soul to a higher marriage with life. Her soul "had
acknowledged in a great heave of terror only the outer darkness,"
but now she knows she must have the courage to let "strange
gods . . . come forth from the forest into the clearing of [the]
known self, and then go back," otherwise, the forest will surely
have its revenge. This recognition is raised to a stage of faith when
it shows us, in the language of spirit, "the unknown in ourselves"
that answers the God that receives what "exceeds the mind of man
in all directions."[87] That which the Master Builder acknowledges as
something "deep within me I'm so much hungering for" might be
what John Knox calls the "unassuageable hunger or loneliness" of
the secular world bereft of God but still needing Him. The yearning
for a mythical release into innocent creative power, given childish
expression by Hilda's claim, "Nobody but you should have a right to
build" (*I*, MB, II, 821) is, in all its pagan dress, as much spiritual
as psychological, a deep calling unto deep when "we are unable to
separate one deep from the other, the deep of our need of God and
the deep of the God we need." Solness's stranded spirit, gasping in
the shallows, both longs and fears to live in a pluralistic universe
full of strange gods. Nora and Ellida, going in opposite directions,
confront the murderer in their own hearts, confined by the laws of
their untrue marriages; only then can Ellida make creative "the

87. D. H. Lawrence, *The Rainbow* (New York, 1967), 316, 437; D. H. Lawrence, *Studies
in Classic American Literature* (New York, 1972), 16; Thomas Merton, *New Seeds of Contemplation*, 136–37. On the staging of the relationship of the conscious to the unconscious,
the known to the unknown, see Rolf Fjelde, "*The Lady from the Sea*: Ibsen's Positive World-
View in a Topographic Figure," *Modern Drama*, XXI (1978), 379–92, and in the same issue,
M. S. Barranger, "*The Lady from the Sea*: Ibsen in Transition," 393–403. Of related interest
is Barranger's article on *The Master Builder*: "Ibsen's 'Strange Story' in *The Master Builder*: A
Variation in Technique," *Modern Drama*, XV (1972), 175–84.

mystery in her marriage—which she scarcely dare[d] acknowledge" and raise the necessary Lawrentian Holy Ghost between husband and wife. That mystery is the longing that can never be domesticated, for an old, naked, dancing, universe of gods that Zarathustra dreams of, forever athwart gravity: "the world unrestrained and abandoned and fleeing back to itself—as many gods eternally fleeing and reseeking one another, as many gods blissfully self-contradicting communing again and belonging again to one another." That is the dream of the Great World, in which necessity and freedom seek each other like mythical lovers. To Ibsen, as to Nietzsche and Jung, the vision of these gods invites us to court the conflict in ourselves, the claims of inequality between desires and responsibility, the rich mix of "discord and tribulation which should not be squandered by attacking others." [88] Whether Bolette will ever be able to bring her passion for the wide world face to face with her terror of the unknown remains to be seen, for Ibsen is never as exuberant as Nietzsche about this terrifying task, though quite as willful.

All might admit in their hearts that with so much Christianity in our bones, "even on the highest peak we shall never be beyond good and evil," but it is Ibsen who would feel most acutely the comic pretense of that ascent. He does not believe we can redeem the "fiasco" we have made "both in the heroic and lover roles," and these are the roles most ardently recovered, the first by Nietzsche, the second by Lawrence. In his plays, only irony can sanction the necessity to climb. His comic exposure of the psychological ethic of adjustment, clearly evident even in Jung, is paraded by the evolutionary boast of Ballestad, the jack-of-all-trades in *The Lady from the Sea:* "But people, human beings—they can acclam—acclimatize themselves" (*I, LS, V,* 688). His stutter suggests our amphibian hang-up, but Ellida soars out of Ballestad's range when she adds "once they're free," for that is not a state, but a struggle: "What I call the struggle for liberty is nothing but the constant, living assimilation of the idea of Freedom." [89]

That is why avalanche, millstream, frost, and quarry so often rise

88. John Knox, *Myth and Truth: An Essay on the Language of Faith* (Charlottesville, 1964), 8, 40; D. H. Lawrence, *Phoenix II,* 432; see an early draft of *Lady from the Sea* in *Ibsen's Workshop,* 331–32; Nietzsche, *Thus Spoke Zarathustra: A Book for Everyone and No One,* trans. R. J. Hollingdale (Harmondsworth, Middlesex, 1969), 215; Jung, *Psychological Reflections,* 221.

89. Jung, *Psychological Reflections,* 245; Henrik Ibsen to Georg Brandes, September 24, 1871, in *Correspondence,* 218; Ibsen to Brandes, February 7, 1871, in *Correspondence,* 208.

to meet us on our climbs, on our goings forth to preserve the living ideal of Freedom. Some readers might feel, with John Hurrell, that in Ibsen's world, most markedly in a play like *Rosmersholm*, "ideals cannot be detached from man—and more importantly, from man's knowledge of himself. The ideals and hence the idea of a tragic death as assertion of the ideals, fall with the man." We might well wonder what is left of the ideal of ennobling mankind after its politicizing by Kroll and Mortensgaard, its cynical abandonment by Brendel, and its appropriation by the communion of suicide of Rosmer and Rebecca. The brutally ambiguous endings of Ibsen's plays might tempt us to identify his passion for punishing the world that disappoints him with that of Flaubert. The Great World would then be only a pale projection of provincial sentimentality: "They were tunes that were heard elsewhere—tunes played in the theatre, sung in drawing rooms, danced to at night beneath lighted chandeliers—echoes reaching Emma from the Great World outside.[90]

Ibsen was certainly one who wanted to recover idealism, even self-sacrifice, as the driving force of a vigorous community and rescue it from having to serve as the major symptom of a lost and perverted one. We feel the full irony of Hjalmar's assessment of Gina: "She has no feeling at all for the ideal phase of these complications" (*I, WD,* V, 485). We are grateful for her, but the ideal dimension, however deformed, needs to be exercised. When Don Quixote, on his death bed, pulls his body away from belief, he leaves around him a motley world stirred to spirit and adventure, in love with the invisible. Like the first man, he has named reality by his story: "Children finger it; young people read it; grown men know it by heart, and old men praise it. It is so dogeared, in fact, and so familiar to all sorts of people that whenever they see a lean horse go by, they cry: 'There goes Rocinante.'" Unhampered by a sobered host, Mambrino's helmet remains more real to us than the barber's basin; the freeing of the convicts seems as necessary an act as their capture. If no modern imagination is as pure as that of Don Quixote, no modern world as eager to incorporate it, it must still be recognized that the Great World, the ideal medium of our full becoming, is as stubbornly aloft and alive as the Golden Age, and that both

90. John D. Hurrell, "*Rosmersholm,* the Existentialist Drama and the Dilemma of Modern Tragedy," 120; Flaubert, *Madame Bovary,* 78.

are preserved by precisely what seems to destroy them, the relentless assaults of parody against the idealizing will.[91] In his attack
on contemporary Christendom, Kierkegaard used *Don Quixote* to
support one of his favorite notions, that all developments end in
parody.[92] By Ibsen's day, the deformation of spirit by bourgeois moralists, unconscious parodists of Christianity, seems to coax out a
countering parody, one that cannot be overcome by its victim's
beauty of character. But its cruel and relentless exposure is precisely
what guarantees, against immanent absorption, the autonomous
presence and permanence of the Great World, which is never dependent on an absurdly authentic birth in the mind of a knight of
chivalry or faith, or on a motive generous enough to overcome its
silly or self-justifying origin.

All parody, of course, pays tribute to the ideal. But with no an-
chor in Paradise, no Waiting Father to save it from the vagaries of
evolutionary rhythms, no Hegelian *Geist* to embody those rhythms
as climax, Ibsen's parody, like modern parody in general, cannot,
after distancing, lead us home to inherited value, to Mansfield Park
or Shandy Hall. Modern parody leads us into exile where, most
often, art's ravens feed us in the wilderness. By refusing to use art as
a refuge from a perverted home and homeland and, at the same
time, refusing to let us come into the incessantly receding Great
World, which is on the stage before we make our entrance, Ibsen
forces us to feel the Great World's essential call and authority *only*
through dishonest, impure, and perverse missions in the name of an
ideal. The plays are strewn with those who sell out a version of the
Great World by dreaming it for others—those who use it to gain
power over others, to evade the terror of self-realization, or to escape the suffering of love. The appropriated ideals are pathetic
agents of the Great World immune to their absolute and rational-
ized nature which can be mocked into daemonic service. Parody
liberates longing from its human parasites.

91. Miguel de Cervantes, *Don Quixote*, trans. J. M. Cohen (Harmondsworth, Middlesex, 1963), 490; Johnston, *The Ibsen Cycle*, 202. Johnston makes this claim, which might be
made of Joyce as well: "Ibsen's demolition work is so ruthlessly thorough because he has
building plans to justify the devastation. For this reason, his return to the past is totally different from the more sentimental revivalism of the Celtic, Classical, Viking, or Medieval twi-
lights so typical among artists and writers of Ibsen's times" (202).
92. See, for example, Kierkegaard, *Journals and Papers*, II, 274.

Hedda, Gregers, and Allmers of the first acts of his plays are great perverters because the last thing they want is to accept the struggle toward Freedom that brings with it the insecurity and anxiety of moral relativity and social, economic, and spiritual misunderstanding. The Great World that Hedda crowns with vine-leaves is actually only a world of vengeful victory against the necessity of her marriage and her exclusion from the forbidden world of Løvborg's dissolute life. While Løvborg, himself a parasite on the will of others, talks of a "hunger for *life*" (*I*, HG, II, 739), Hedda, terrified to leave the dutiful world she torments, throws back a sister phrase to those last words of Brack: "That's no way to think!" If, as Foucault suggests, transgression is the sole manner of discovering the sacred in a desecrated world, it might seem that Hedda is a justified transgressor. But because her fearful spirit yearns not for self-power as much as for "power over a human being" (*I*, HG, II, 745), she really can be only the murderer she is afraid to meet on the way to a higher reality.[93] Not only Thea's action but also Brack's words can show up her resistance to the Great World of becoming by insinuating what she must deny—that with pregnancy, something great might stir in her (*I*, HG, II, 730). Gregers and Allmers invest in missions that destroy the hosts they parasitically infect, the children who expose so vividly the communal impotence of the Christian ethic of self-sacrifice when it has degenerated into an inversion of self-realization. The humanism that Borkman, Solness, and Rubek yoke to their passion for power is clearly a cover for violations of higher love and the need for social dominance. The metal sings itself free only to procure for Borkman the means to "subjugate all the riches" held by nature, to "carve out a kingdom for himself," while it pretends to hymn the "well-being of so many thousands of others" calculated and converted into financial security (*I*, JGB, II, 986).[94] What a parody this is of Ibsen's advice to Brandes: "There is

93. Michel Foucault, *Language, Counter-Memory, Practice,* 30. In her discussion of Hedda's character from the actress's point of view ("*Hedda Gabler*: The Play in Performance," in Durbach [ed.], *Ibsen and the Theatre: Essays in Celebration of the 150th Anniversary of Henrik Ibsen's Birth* [London, 1980], 89), Janet Suzman relates the need for power over others to the hatred of pregnancy.

94. See Aslaug Groven Michaelsen, *Ibsen's "Bygmester Solness" som tidsdiagnose* (Tangen, 1982), 1–30, for a discussion of a socialist critique of *The Master Builder*. Michaelsen exposes the oppression of Solness's family and colleagues under the mission to build homes. Harald Beyer, *Nietzsche og Norden,* II, 38, points out that John Gabriel Borkman is apparently Nietzsche's higher type, but reallly the "overskurk" he accuses Hinkel of being.

no way in which you can benefit society more than by coining the metal you have in yourself."[95]

The man for whom misunderstanding is a self-justification against the small world instead of a given of the great one becomes, in Ella's words, a "double-murderer" of the strange gods in the forests of his soul and in those of others (*I, JGB*, II, 986). The psychic murder of Beata is clearly linked to the dream of power over others for their own sakes, and it is this messianic tyranny that stirs Gina, the cool realist, to sound like Ibsen's critics exasperated over the symbolic investment in the wild duck: "Oh that sacred duck—there's been crucifixes enough made for her" (*I, WD*, III, 440). It might well be questioned whether or not these messianic impositions can have anything but negative value in showing us what the Great World is not, yet, however trapped in an inferior social ethic, however brutal the family consequences or impure the motives, each attempt to rise towards it testifies to its everlasting presence which Ibsen will neither relinquish nor reduce. We do not feel that Relling's cynicism or Gina's literalism have the last word, though they certainly are valuable critical agents.[96] And we remember that Relling's philosophy of the necessary life-lie assures his social power over others and testifies to an impoverished spiritual and erotic expectation. His scope and selfhood are too small for Ibsen's vision. Gina is busy keeping Hjalmar's fiction alive, so her chastisement of the idealizing tendency helps us to understand why we need it. We sense that parodic deformations of the Great World—especially when they are shamed by the knowledge of the world as it is, the kind that comes in with a Mrs. Linde as she patronizes Nora's secret romance of sacrifice—are the necessary helpers and servers of strange gods.

Nora's departure is into a greater world than that which afflicted Mrs. Linde, because it joins necessity to spirit fed on romance. The remainder of spiritual space that opens up between Mrs. Linde's quite admirable recovery and Nora's new determination is a positive and permanent presence for us, but this distance is no less kept clear by those who can only develop into death, retreat from, or pervert, the ideal.[97] This space of parody marks the limitation by

95. Henrik Ibsen to Georg Brandes, September 24, 1871, in *Correspondence*, 218.

96. See the discussion of Errol Durbach, "On the Centenary of *Vilanden*: The 'Life-Lie' in Modern Drama," *Scandinavian Studies*, LVI (1984), 328ff.

97. This makes misleading the claims of G. B. Shaw and George Steiner that Ibsen is an anti-idealist. Steiner writes, in *The Death of Tragedy* (New York, 1961), 293–94: "In Ibsen's

which we feel and desire, fear and yearn for, the great mystery of uncertain evolution that opens up around unhappy marriages. We ought to be able to "possess ourselves of the sea . . . learn to harness the storms and weather," writes Ibsen in notes to *Lady from the Sea*. Some day the body, will, spirit might move with the seasons in a greater world, but then "we shall not be in it! Shall not live to see it!" The Great World, as far as we are concerned, retains its value only by moving ahead of our impetuous abbreviations of the struggle towards Freedom. To imagine the realm as a future world for a spiritually developed species seems a cruel abuse of our hope, but the paradox that Ibsen holds so dear is this: the more intense the struggle for Freedom and depth, the more limitation will be forced into the role of catalyst for the realm that waits, in the distance, for its citizens. The limitations felt in the parody of the impure will to self-realization precipitates the plays past a melancholy pathos Ibsen dreaded as much as self-pity and into communication with a distant world that is not mere longing. This is how Ibsen describes the peaceful life disturbed by the struggles of the *The Lady from the Sea*:

> Life is apparently bright, easy and lively up there beneath the shadow of the mountains and in the monotony of seclusion. Then the idea is thrown out that this kind of life is a life of shadows. No energy; no struggle for liberation. Only longings and desires. Thus they live through the short, light summer. And afterwards—into the darkness. Then awakes the longing for the life of the great world outside. But what is to be gained by that? With surroundings, with spiritual development, demands and longings and desires increase. He or she, who stands on the height, yearns for the secrets of the future and a share in the life of the future and communication with distant worlds. Everywhere there is limitation. The result is melancholy like a hushed, wailing song over the whole of human existence and over the deeds of men. A light summer day with the great darkness to follow—that is all. [98]

---

vocabulary, the most deadly of these cancers is 'idealism,' the mask of hypocrisy and self-deception with which men seek to guard against the realities of social and personal life." But see Brian W. Downs, *Ibsen: The Intellectual Background* (New York, 1969), 78: "If he directed the full force of his critical intelligence . . . against ideals, it was to subserve a higher and more comprehensive ideal, that of freedom, the freedom to develop the human personality to the limit of its capabilities."

98. *Ibsen's Workshop*, 331, 330.

The challenge is to keep growing evolutionary consciousness from a fateful passivity that would make parody itself the climax, rather than the agent, of life.

Lukács, among others, has named the burden of modern tragedy a disequilibrium between ethics and aesthetics brought on by the collapse of the secure relationship between character and destiny. We recognize this in the self-consciousness of all modern art:

> So long as tragedy did not become ethically problematic, either inwardly or outwardly, the pure aesthetics of structure functioned quite naturally: from a given beginning only a single given result can follow, since the ethical structure is a given precondition known to the poet and public alike. But when ethics ceased to be a given, the ethical knotting with the drama—thus, its aesthetics—has to be created; whereupon ethics, as the cornerstone of the artistic composition, move necessarily into the vital centre of motivation. In this way the great and spontaneous unity of ethics and aesthetics within the tragic experience, commences to be the problem.[99]

Only if the problem can be forced into a critical pathology can characters like Osvald and Rank become dramatically and symbolically active. Ibsen's vision and his art remain true to the determination of Kierkegaard and Nietzsche to create problems out of solutions as a countermove against modern artificial mythologies. The difficulties are not finessed; they are brought aggressively to consciousness. What still seems to many an inherited modern weakness in *A Doll House*—a lack of adequate transition between the first and second Nora—is, in fact, a deliberately breached transposition from inherited aesthetic morality, melodrama, up to a life of moral subtlety and uncertainty. Ibsen's simultaneous connection and separation by parody of the small and great worlds is reminiscent of the workings of Kierkegaard's irony, patrolling the border between a repeated morality and a chosen one.[100] We need to stretch ourselves in the bodies of those visited by the dissonances and disequilibriums stimulated by their solutions and who are,

99. Georg Lukács, "The Sociology of Modern Drama," trans. Lee Baxandall, in Margaret Herzfeld-Sander (ed.), *Essays on German Theater* (New York, 1985), 162–63.

100. See Errol Durbach, *Ibsen the Romantic*, 84: "In asserting a Kierkegaardian form of absurdity, Ibsen's transcendentalists succeed only in creating the 'absurd' condition of modern existential anxiety." This is true for the characters themselves, but not for the Great World they stimulate.

therefore, not entirely "acclimatized." Parody assures the conversions to problems and keeps them energetically enacted, even through paralyzed conscience, so that by distance it protects the Great World and by imitation it keeps us longing for it.

Parody, too, revives the critical dialectical energy between appearance and reality deadened by an absorption that modern theoreticians lament. Our ideals, by this aggressive device, can never be exhausted by debased political and psychological applications, any more than the wild duck's mystery is exhausted by her use for greedy definition. While she sits brooding in our midst, her mysterious beginnings tempt and trap projections that try to deny the distance and death opened by parody.[101] Because Hedvig, like the duck, lives between origins and worlds, she is a thorough realist about their distinctions, and never a willful prosecutor by mixed and poetic discourse: "When all of a sudden—in a flash—I happen to think of that in there, it always seems to me that the whole room and everything in it is called 'the depths of the sea'! But that's all so stupid" (I, WD, III, 438). Driven in part, perhaps, by a subliminal sense that the guilty origin that could make her his half-sister must be redeemed by myth, Gregers wants her *not* to make this separation, to fuse the spheres of discourse and value by raiding Hedvig's formula, and Hedvig is astonished at the cheat.[102] In a play shadowed by the Last Supper, the perverted Christian romance of sacrifice is put in its place, not only by the final suicide, but by Hedvig's refusal to destroy the duck as she senses what we consciously see—the outrageous arrogance of equating fantasy with the real world, a persistent strategy of adult self-protection.

> Gregers (approaching Hedvig). I can see by your face that it's not
>   fulfilled.
> Hedvig. What? Oh, about the wild duck. No.
> Gregers. Your courage failed you when the time came to act, I suppose.
> Hedvig. No, it's not exactly that. But when I woke up this morning

101. For a sound discussion of the parabolic passion in the play, see Janel Mueller, "Ibsen's Wild Duck," Modern Drama, XI (1969), 349. Errol Durbach maintains in Ibsen the Romantic, 28, that the fear of death in Ibsen's characters stimulates their search for symbols of permanence.

102. See discussion of John Northam, Ibsen, 140–42; also Joan Carr, "'The Forest's Revenge': Subconscious Motivation in The Wild Duck," Modern Language Review, LXXII (1977), 845–56.

early and thought of what we talked about, then it seemed so strange to me.

Gregers. Strange?

Hedvig. Yes, I don't know—Last night, right at the time, there was something so beautiful about it, but after I'd slept and then thought it over, it didn't seem like so much.

Gregers. Ah, no, you couldn't grow up here without some taint in you.
(I, WD, V, 477)

The conversation is a parody of that deep communion sought by all the idealists in the plays. Unfortunately, tainted by devotion to Hjalmar, Hedvig is not entirely immune to the idea of crucifixion from despair.

But it is through Gregers's body that we move in order to make Hedvig's recognition a dramatic and persuasive agent of the Great World. As an enabler of Hjalmar's fictions, Hedvig is not altogether innocent, but the absence of critical responsibility, of the rage to judge, renders her a better carrier of wonder than of longing for the Great World. She can, for example, remain open to the mystery of the duck and refuse the habit of definition and blame. She can also prevent language from prematurely closing over motive. Of Gregers's self-identification with a hunting dog, bringing truth to light in his plunge after dying wild ducks, Hjalmar says, "I can't follow a word you're saying," tempting us to make the application. But Hedvig teaches us better how to read Ibsen when she muses: "I don't know—but it was just as if he meant something else from what he said, all the time" (I, WD, II, 428–9). By opening up the possibility of multiple motives and origins, she helps us to identify Gregers's obsessive use of metaphor as a self-protective taboo against a deeper reality.[103] Nevertheless, it really is through the negative body, the one in love with the idea of Truth for all the wrong reasons, that we are stimulated to convert solutions to problems, for it

103. Jose Ortega y Gasset, *The Dehumanization of Art and Notes on the Novel* (Princeton, N.J., 1948), 33ff. The importance of the mysterious origin of Hedvig and the duck for the sacred and mythical atmosphere they carry might be illuminated by Cassirer's explanation of the attraction of myth to genesis: "All the sanctity of mythical being goes back ultimately to the sanctity of origin. It does not adhere immediately to the content of the genesis, but to its coming into being, not to its qualities and properties, but to its temporal genesis in the past. By being thrust back into temporal distance, by being situated in the depth of the past, a particular content is not only established as sacred, as mythically and religiously significant but also justified as such" (*The Philosophy of Symbolic Forms*, II, 105).

makes us want to get rid of the world's habit of making "true" marriages a refuge from the rich and teeming opposites of our psychological, moral, and spiritual needs. From his earliest play, Ibsen knew that the Great World badly dreamed would abandon dreamers and still grow fat on their desire.[104] When Catiline kills Aurelia, he says to Furia:

> It seemed to me that when she sighed her last
> My heartstrings snapped. I feel so ill-at-ease,
> As though the whole wide world had all at once
> Become one great enormous wilderness
> And in it none but you and I remain.
> (O. 1, C, III, 106)

By the time of Love's Comedy, parody openly exploits the conflict continually scrutinized by Ibsen between marriage and self-realization, and Falk's release into celibacy is draped in characteristic ambiguity. The brutal parody that hangs on negative missionary ascents to the Great World is the only way Ibsen can save that world from the fate of the body, protect its autonomy, its integrity, and secure its dramatic interest.

In order to keep the requirements of the Great World nourished by the limitations of the small one, Ibsen, like only the most powerful writers, sets the table on every level—geographical, political, cultural, psychological, moral, spiritual, sexual, aesthetic. His parody, like Kierkegaard's irony, forces inadequate versions of faith to work for the fuller one. He continually evokes the credo of the Great World that "all is possible" by letting us hear the formula of duty, that "nothing is permitted" (and its parasitic Voltairian challenge that "if there were no God, everything would be permitted"). He refuses us secure standpoints, loosens the stranglehold of cause and blame by surfacing multiple beginnings and motives. Werle Sr. might be called by Gregers at the beginning of The Wild Duck "a kind of providence" to Hjalmar (I, WD, I, 400). Straight irony

---

104. See Nietzsche, Will to Power, 314. This separation is what really lies behind Ibsen's apparently anti-Romantic attitude towards the far and the foreign, as embodied in Hilmer Tønnesen's absurd references to America; see Horst Bien, Henrik Ibsens Realismus: Zur Genesis und Methode des klassischen kritisch-realistischen Dramas (Berlin, 1970), 129. It is, to my mind, the protective instinct of parody that mediates and liberates the indignation that Hermann Weigand hears as "the pathos of disillusioned idealism" in Ibsen's tone (The Modern Ibsen, 125).

would have its way when Hjalmar later seems to rebel against this patronizing image, or Gregers finally finds it immoral. But the motives of Hjalmar and Gregers are mixed at least as much as Werle's, and the whole desire for moral security is undermined by bad faith. By the end of the first act, there is not one safe standpoint of authority, conscience, providence, state, because it is precisely the "dead maintenance of a certain given standpoint of liberty that is characteristic of the communities which go by the name of states." How many light years there are between the flimsiness of Gregers's comment on his father's motives, "It's almost a kind of conscience" (*I*, WD, I, 398), and the solidity of Diderot's complaint to Rousseau: "I know that whatever you do, the testimony of your conscience will always speak in your favor. But is that testimony alone sufficient?"[105] Gina is eager to remind us, before Hjalmar hides his failures behind the bastion of blame, of what we often forget, that Hjalmar's mother had bad eyes (*I*, WD, II, 421). This is a crucial qualification of Hjalmar's uncomfortable doubts in Act II when he is asked to match Hedvig's age and the years of his marriage. This might well be a motive for the insistence with which he plays at family. Outside the family, the limitations of social and political revolutions whose promises are always impure and whose ideals are always vulnerable to manipulation, like the causes of political psychology, provoke the only revolution that really matters, the revolution of individual consciousness.

The emphatic distinction between public and private revolutions, of the country and of consciousness, was one made with increasing insistence by all the passionate lovers of the great world of Freedom, primarily the subterranean poets, as the nineteenth century wore on in the wake of failed political promises. The determination was boosted, for Ibsen, by the contrast between appearance and reality in the trumpeted intellectual, political, and social liberal breakthrough in Scandinavia, particularly Norway. Ibsen noted in 1882 that technically Norway is a free country, but it is inhabited by unfree men and women.[106] This distinction is particu-

---

105. Henrik Ibsen to Georg Brandes, February 17, 1871, in *Correspondence*, 208; Rousseau, *Confessions*, 442. Unsure standpoints make persuasive the kind of reading John S. Chamberlain gives in *Ibsen: The Open Vision* as he regularly takes into account the disturbance of fact by projection.

106. Henrik Ibsen to Olaf Skavlan, January 24, 1882, in *Correspondence*, 355.

larly painful in light of the Storthing envy of Norway's neighbors who viewed post-1840 Norway as the happiest and freest of lands. It was a lament that was to be only more stimulated by the failure of the Sverdrup ministry to grant a pension to the writer Alexander Kielland, a rejection that underlined the impotency of liberalism in the second half of the nineteenth century to carry through the promises and proposals of its propaganda. In one of his most famous speeches, Ibsen warned in 1885:

> There is still much to be done in this country before we can be said to have achieved full freedom. But our present democracy scarcely has the strength to accomplish that task. An element of aristocracy must enter into our political life, our government, our members of parliament and our press. I am of course not thinking of aristocracy of wealth, of learning, or even of ability or talent. I am thinking of aristocracy of character, of mind and of will.[107]

Though the speech was delivered to the Workers' Association of Trondhjem, it is not, Ibsen insisted, by political reforms that freedom will come. However, it is *through* the worker's question and the woman's question that the need for a higher freedom might begin to be felt. Ultimately, Ibsen was extremely zealous about keeping the question of social freedoms *separate* from that of higher Freedom, for, typically, it is only by treating the lower questions as preparatory parodies of the higher that they could be useful. At the banquet of the Norwegian Society for the Woman's Cause in 1898, Ibsen reminded his audience of the distance between those who want "liberties" and those who want "liberty." To keep the Great World free from the degradation of political language and manipulation, which neither Brandes nor Bjørnson could quite manage, Ibsen had to insist upon a breach between private and public freedom that was already our given condition.[108] Not even his most authentic carriers of social ideals, Nora and Stockmann, can have absolute advantage in Ibsen's global market, negotiating between "liberties" and "liberty," for the Great World, always ahead, is draped in uncertainty and mystery, and there is always something a bit theatrical, comic, or disproportionate about the reductive clarity of absolute and intellectual claims.

107. Meyer, *Ibsen*, 572; the full speech is in Ibsen, *Speeches and New Letters*, 53.
108. Henrik Ibsen to Bjørnstjern Bjørnson, July 12, 1879, in *Speeches and New Letters*, 84–86.

In an early draft of A *Doll House*, Ibsen has Mrs. Linde and Nora initiate a discussion of the rights of divorced women. When Nora complains about the injustice of the law, she cannot resist this insight: "It's easy enough to see that it was made by men." And Mrs. Linde replies, "Aha! you are beginning to go in for Woman's Rights." Nora quickly retorts, "No, I don't care about them at all."[109] The demotion of public by private battles for rights is a clear indication of Ibsen's impatience with the language and purpose that would reduce the Great World's beckoning Freedom, use it up by utilitarian applications. To settle for that level would be equivalent to settling for Manders's reduction of the Great World to a providential higher will: "It was your proper role to bear with a humble heart that cross that a higher will saw fit to lay upon you" (*I*, G, I, 226). Would not the Great World, like the great liberal breakthrough, dwindle to the kind of world-historical paragraph Kierkegaard scorned as "system" in the history of Scandinavia? The necessary separation refutes the eager identity of spirit, ethics, aesthetics, interested in avoiding the suffering passage through the terrible irony that prepares faith for Kierkegaard, the parody that prepares Freedom for Ibsen. To Bjørnson, who could never resist political participation, however high-minded he remained, Ibsen wrote in 1884: "I admit, however, that in politics, too, I am a pagan; I do not believe in the emancipatory power of political measures; nor have I much confidence in the altruism and goodwill of those in power." This is a sign of Ibsen's tendency to link political with theological deformations. But it also means that his drama cannot suggest the Great World without referring to social liberties. The systematic repression of the robust conscience of the past (*I*, EP, I, 295) was recognized as a point of social protest by the feminists who remembered they had more freedom as Vikings than as nineteenth-century mothers and wives. It is not surprising that Stockmann's son, a child of the future, blurts out in a society babbling of progress and parading the goodwill of those in power, the liberal press, that he wants to be a Viking, a pagan—a regressive wish we meet in one form or another in all of Ibsen's later plays, remembering the early ones with a longing trapped in a world of political self-protection and appropriation of virtue. While Nietzsche was persistently exposing the egoism behind the altruism of those in power, Ibsen was busy representing the

109. *Ibsen's Workshop*, 140.

slavery practiced under the flag of freedom. Theodor Adorno has explained the contemporary critic's quick dismissal of A *Doll House* as a political battle already won as a symptom of suppressed guilt over the secret knowledge that the real liberation never had come to fruition. Perhaps that accounts for the general underreading of Ibsen, the refusal to yield to his subtle profundity of dimension and value.[110]

The mere presence of the social questions that found their way into Ibsen's plays to this day obscures their dialectical relationship to spirit. Though Ibsen surely stands behind Dina's remark, "I hate making promises. Things have to go their own way" (*I*, PS, IV, 99), as a reproach to moral and political machinations, he is pressed by his jealous sons into the role of willful reformer. How is it possible, we ask, for Knut Hamsun to attack, in his lectures of 1891, Ibsen's "coarse and false psychology, good only for writing about social problems and freedoms?" How could he accuse Ibsen's social subject matter of formal sterility? And how could Pär Lagerqvist say of the master, "Ibsen, who was long the modern writer *par préférence* because he exhaustively plodded through all the social, sexual, and mental-hygienic ideas and ideals which happened to come up for discussion, merely weighs us down with his perfectly consummated and fixed form, impossible of further development"?[111] Few seem to make this mistake about a writer of social questions like Turgenev, but then his surface, unlike Ibsen's, was so immediately poetic and subtle. What is more important, any will is muted by pathetic irony, as it is diffused by the metaphors that serve consciousness in James. But we are always in the presence, through parodic forms, of the willful drive in Ibsen that translates itself as "the constant, living assimilation of the idea of Freedom."[112] It is this will towards Freedom in the plays that is caught and shackled by social fervor in the minds of his misreaders. The appeal to anarchy that so troubled

110. Henrik Ibsen to Bjørnstjerne Bjørnson, March 28, 1884, in *Correspondence*, 379; Theodor Adorno, *Minima Moralia*, 93. The feminists' independence and energy are manifest in *The Vikings of Helgeland*.

111. Even Strindberg recognized Ibsen's availability to misinterpretation in the preface to *Getting Married*. Meyer, *Ibsen*, 708–709; excerpt in James W. MacFarlane (ed.), *Ibsen: A Critical Anthology* (Harmondsworth, Middlesex, 1970), 141–45; Pär Lagerkvist, "Modern Theatre: Points of View and Attack," trans. Thomas R. Buckman, *Tulane Drama Review*, VI (1961), 22.

112. Henrik Ibsen to Georg Brandes, February 14, 1871, in *Correspondence*, 208.

Brandes is, in fact, an appeal to "free will and all that is spiritually akin to it," and when Ibsen imagines society liberated from State, he is really imagining Freedom of the spirit and senses loosed from imprisonment in parodic forms and bodies. That is the risk Ibsen takes by putting Freedom in a dialectical relationship with freedom, as Kierkegaard put aesthetic seduction in a dialectical relationship with faith.

The abortion of Ibsen's Great World through the assigning of ultimate value to intellectual and social freedoms in discussions of the plays is typical of a long history of defense against his passionate depth. The layers and levels of language and silence between the low consciousness of political slavery and the high consciousness of spiritual desire are spanned only by the Nietzschian ladder of problems. The bohemian life that Osvald admires in Paris, of free living, thinking, and loving, must not be taken as a solution to the guilty and inhibited life of Norway's provinces.[113] As the freer life casts suspicion on the "exemplary husbands and fathers" (*I, G, I,* 224) who raid the virtuous houses of the continent in reactive debauchery, it disturbs the life of Manders solutions, thereby preparing it for use by the Great World. The relationship is repeated more economically in the tension between ideals and the Truth:

> *Manders.* Isn't there something that tells you, as a mother, not to destroy your son's ideals?
> *Mrs. Alving.* Yes, but what of the truth—?
> *Manders.* Yes, but what of his ideals—?
> *Mrs. Alving.* Oh—ideals! If I only weren't the coward I am.

The identity of the two would represent, like an identity between the two freedoms, a premature closing out of the inner revolution, just as if Rebecca had stopped with her hope for a new great world of political freedom "pioneering the future" (*I,* R, III, 564). If we stop our development at ideals, we are likely to use them as absolutes, noble concealers of life. But it is, we recall, impossible to get to the place of Truth without journeying through this temptation. When Osvald clasps his head and moans, "Oh, that the beautiful freedom of life—could be made so foul," Manders, mistaking sick-

---

113. See a discussion of the double nature of the life of joy in Evert Sprinchorn, "Science and Poetry in *Ghosts:* A Study in Ibsen's Craftsmanship," *Scandinavian Studies,* LI (1979), 361.

ness for sin, cannot understand him, for the pastor refuses life to lower freedom and cannot imagine a higher one (*I*, G, I, 224).

Mrs. Alving's own early impulsive flight from marriage to Manders, closed off by rejection and a failure of courage, is the secret of her self-education. From the beginning of the major period, Ibsen regularly prepares for the movement into the Freedom of depth by a preliminary refusal or cutting off of the possibility of social freedom. Freedom is a transposition of freedom's loss to gain, somewhat like the relationship between repetition and Repetition in Kierkegaard's vision, though Ibsen's climax is always plagued by parody. Osvald and Lona are used to living in the global world, though neither could have a normal family life there, so at their return they stimulate the original spasm of social defiance in Bernick and Mrs. Alving to a higher pitch. When Lona has it out with Bernick, she claims that his declaration of love could hold up only "as long as you were living out there in the great, free world that gave you the courage to think great, free thoughts yourself" (*I*, PS, II, 62). Thea has no problem with the word *love*, while Hedda, trapped in domestic slavery, does. But Thea's social freedom, jealously assaulted by Hedda, precipitates the explosive and bitter climax of Hedda's frustrated poetry of Freedom.

Lona's reminder, like that of Hilda, of a moment in the world of free thought and free love is linked to her desire to have her "childhood hero standing free and true" (*I*, PS, IV, 116). But her preaching qualification of Bernick's notion of freedom at the end of the play seems symptomatic of a desire, still, on Ibsen's part to mediate freedoms and Freedom—a desire he will deliberately disappoint in future plays. Freedom thrives on the *frustration* of social liberties because the journey to depth cannot then be aborted. Martha's longing for the Great World is kept at an aesthetic level of rhetoric by Rørlund who asks: "And do you really place such value on the life you hear 'rushing and roaring' by outside? Look down there in the street. There goes sunstruck humanity sweating and haggling over its petty affairs. No, the truth of it is, we're better off sitting here, in the cool of this room, and turning our backs on the source of all that distraction" (*I*, PS, I, 18–19). The renunciation of a picture of life in its highest social form, as against Rørlund's preservation of the sacred life of the provincial family, is precisely the way in which we feel the power and imperative value of the idea of Freedom, starving in the small world of Martha's family fate. The dream of "the sky wider, the clouds higher than here, and the air more free overhead" will be lived out, if it can be, by Dina in America. But we will never see her, for America must remain for Ibsen essentially a punishing perspective aimed at provincial morality. His lack of belief in political virtue and his dialectical use of political freedom kept him from Dickens's immense disappointment in a materialized America: "This is not the republic of my imagination."[114] Out of the cynicism of collapsed idealism Dickens drew the cartoon of an obsessively political America, an allegory of the weak and patronizing self of rhetorical morality he had caricatured in Pecksniff. Out of disgust with the provincial mind, Ibsen called upon an America free of the politics he chastised in Scandinavian provincial society. Even Stockmann, suspecting that "it's probably no better in the free, United States," where there is perhaps a "plague of solid majorities and liberal public opinions and all the other bedevilments," pictures the dispersion of political evils in the immensity of territory as an antidote to the evils confined by the pillars of Norwegian society (I, EP, V, 368).

That is why Ibsen lets Lona say: "All this moral linen reeks of decay—like a bundle of shrouds, I swear. I prefer the air off the prairies, I can tell you" (I, PS, I, 38). Most of all, its wildness could house those strange gods Lawrence hoped to find coming out of its forests, insufficiently repressed by a young civilization. So could the world from the mountaintop of Rubek's biblical promise: "You said you'd take me with you up on top of a high mountain and show me all the glory of the world" (I, WWDA, I, 1037). Since this place is offered to both Maja and Irene, we understand that it is tainted by its use for erotic and spiritual manipulation. Ibsen could never materialize a mountaintop, an America that we could really live in, for Freedom must always remain in front of us, while parodic journeys from the small world sanction it as an imperative goal. Maja's taunting descent into a new sensual life, liberated from the sterile spirit of regret in her husband, is a negative version of the climb that both humorously and powerfully affirms the absurd validity of the ascent of Rubek and Irene. From the castle in the air, Hilda and

114. Charles Dickens to William Charles Macready, March 22, 1842, in F. W. Dupee (ed.), *The Selected Letters of Charles Dickens* (New York, 1960), 67.

Solness can look down on the dollhouses of Europe. But the climb must be made literal in order to keep that perspective from being absorbed by lower liberties: free thought, free love, equality in marriage, equality in education. We need greedy, flawed, and foolish transgressors of the small world, like Solness and Borkman, to raise us over a civic version of the Great World.

Foldal's minor talent for poetry has elicited too small a vision of Freedom. Musing on his daughter's departure for a new life, he consoles himself: "So really, it hasn't come to nothing that I've been a poet. For now she has her chance to go out in the great, wide world that I once dreamed so hopefully of seeing" (I, JGB, IV, 1017). If Foldal is no poet, Brendel almost defeats his reduction with humor, slouching "homewards" to the "great world." Bankrupt of ideals, he still cannot vault into the Great World, but he anchors it for us by his retreat. A life without ideals can be exploited by the Mortensgaards of Scandinavia, "lord[s] and master[s] of the future" (I, R, IV, 578, 579). But Brendel—by leaving behind him his ominous reminders of castles on shifting sand, the sacrifices of mermaids, the fearful fancy of castration of finger and ear—can preserve for us the distant world in which revelation and myth receive our terror and desire without guilt. The scope of value Ibsen opens for us can never be enacted, and, perhaps, that is what gives us the sense both of its immense theatrical difficulty and its powerful pattern of hope against hope. No divine call can sanction anymore the struggle to our full medium, the working our way out, as Mrs. Alving and Borkman call it, to freedom. Death and exile have to bear their cross of absurdity and foolishness, narcissism and immoral arrogance. But the bodies of those who are driven from the small world successfully punish the "bully boys of virtue" (I, R, I, 512) (Brendel names Kroll "en av hine dydens drabanter). The uselessness of modern sacrifice is the very attribute that underlines the consequences of our severance from the Great World.

Kierkegaard rebuked Rousseau for practicing all the Christian collisions without the necessary humility and faith; Ibsen keeps the parody of those collisions in the service of protecting the Great World from Romantic seduction or philistine appropriation. Agnes dies from her glimpse of the Great World, but her sacrifice does more than Brand's reprimand to keep Ejnar from successfully shrinking that world for us:

You would reduce God's Kingdom,
A Kingdom which should stretch from pole to pole.
(M, B, I, 29)

Brandes was particularly interested in this notion of Nietzsche, that the repression of aggressive instincts and free expression by state and society emerged as the impulse to self-sacrifice instead of self-realization.[115] Though Brandes would, characteristically, work out such a recognition on the lower levels of liberties, he continually fed Ibsen's own interest in spiritual revolution. Literal death, in Ibsen, is always the fruit of a guilty conscience or, in children, of the sense that something is wrong in the family. As such, it can still only be a parody of the union of power and love. Yet, as a negative version of the Great World's innocence of becoming, it protests its deformation in the small world. Death, in the Great World, is taken into the rhythm of life; down here, a ferocious antithetical enemy of the morality it has already infiltrated, it tempts us to fictions of nobility (it is our walking companion), or to peace from ambivalent feelings. It cuts short the necessary absorption of the unknown into life and cancels the mysterious marriage with strange gods in our midst.

Ibsen splits the Christian relationship between self-sacrifice and self-realization by killing the children (Hedvig, Little Eyolf) of parents who hide behind noble ideals, felt in the flesh of the offspring as a goad to that sweet sleep in the sea (I, LE, I, 877) The Rat Wife's fearful and fascinating allurement gains power because it responds to Allmers's descent from the mountain, a new mission of self-sacrifice. The deformed Christian ideal is disturbed by a pagan force carrying the whole range of desire that must die in this world because, like rats, it is persecuted by aesthetic morality. The Rat Wife's ferociously amoral poetry haunts the scene of useless suffering, of evasion from the work of spirit and instinct. Ibsen and Nietzsche open the scene to an atmosphere out of the control of Providence and retribution as they press on "to remove the concept of guilt and the concept of punishment from the world and to purge psychology, history, nature, the social institutions and sanctions of them."[116]

115. Brandes, *Friedrich Nietzsche*, 39.
116. Nietzsche, *Twilight of the Idols*, 53.

To this purpose, they set against the forgetting of the small world that manifests itself as repression the forgetting of the Great World, which releases us to mythopoeic power and robust consciousness and deed. Typically, in Ibsen, the negative version of forgetting is a parody that both opposes and prepares the higher one. Allmers is master of forgetting as an escape from seeing suffering through. He probably never grasps what we suspect—the identification between the Little Eyolf who died "on the threshold of a spiritually aware existence," as a "being with such infinite possibilities" (*I*, LE, II, 897), and his own life, arrested at the stage that preceded the suffering conflicts of sex and desire, of authorship and self-realization. So it is particularly ironic, but not surprising, that he should confess to Asta, in a crucial conversation of Act II, that instead of mourning for the boy, he has "been sitting here, living in memories. And he wasn't there" (*I*, LE, II, 900). Asta's consolation is more prescient than she knows: "Oh, but Alfred—little Eyolf was behind everything." Allmers, still the self-protecting literalist of safe identity, protests, "No, he wasn't. He'd slipped out of my mind. Out of my thoughts. I lost sight of him a moment while we sat talking together. Totally forgot him that whole time." His guilt in the face of the boy's depth, "where he lies drifting down" (*I*, LE, II, 901), is not yet ready to rise beyond retribution. We feel the aesthetic nature of a guilt that confesses, "I caught myself wondering what we were going to have for dinner today."

In the middle of the most intense battle of blame between Rita and Allmers, Rita counterpunches accusation of sexual seduction with this searing reminder: "Oh, let's say instead, you forgot the child and everything else" (*I*, LE, II, 909), again, not consciously linking sexual guilt with death. In Act III, Allmers relates his fantasy walk with death in the mountains where he forgot, for a time, wife, son, and sister (*I*, LE, III, 931). Lifted out of the trap of sexual guilt and the longing for innocence into a companionship with death that might lead him, by rich forgetting, into the fullness of love and communion, he aborts and perverts the experience by refusing to pass through the terror that makes us cling to self-preservation: "I felt his terror in everything. In all that we still don't dare to give up." He comes down with merely a displaced mission and, even at the end, with the hope of freeing himself from the demands of marriage. Like Mrs. Alving, he still wants to ease in his son what cannot be cured (*I*, LE, I, 882), but the spur is cowardice, not love. No wonder the Rat Wife supplants Allmers as doctor to the sick and leaves to him the ghosts of the deep. Allmers plays with them at the edge of the sea, but when Asta, close to departing, pulls up lilies that "shoot up—from the farthest depths" (*I*, LE, II, 917) as a "last greeting" from both her and the child, we are as close as we ever get, in Ibsen, to the entrance of the Great World. Even out of water, the metaphor survives the blasts of moral prosing. That the stems must be broken prevents us from making the Christian connection of salvation between Little Eyolf and his parents, but once again, limitation—the brutal deracination from the Great World that marries life and death—preserves it. We are *not* cradled in the great prophetic vision of Wordsworth:

> Hence in a season of calm weather
> Though inland far we be,
> Our Souls have sight of that immortal sea
> Which brought us hither,
> Can in a moment travel thither,
> And see the children sport upon the shore,
> And hear the mighty waters rolling
> Evermore.[117]

Because Ibsen insisted on chastening his prophetic powers and hopes through parodic versions of what he wanted to be, what he wanted the world to be, he cuts himself off from the consolations of poetic privilege. It was his deepest conviction that even in exile, a man who feels "within himself a contradiction between word and action, between will and task, between life and teaching" is a man who "shares the responsibility and the guilt of the society to which he belongs."[118]

---

117. Wordsworth, "Ode: Intimations of Immortality from Recollections of Early Childhood," Stanza IX.

118. Henrik Ibsen, Speech to the Norwegian Students, September 10, 1874, in *Speeches and New Letters*, 50; Ibsen to Ludwig Passarge, June 16, 1880, in *Correspondence*, 334.

TWO

Exile

Like Strindberg and Kafka, Ibsen
might have taken from Schopenhauer and Swedenborg the notion
that we are *born* into exile, into a penal colony of original and ignorant suffering. Since the whole of life is a psychic Hell, it "resembles nothing so much as the consequence of a false step and a
guilty desire." Or he might have anticipated the Camus who speaks
of our fate as that of exile, strange and alien "in a universe suddenly
divested of illusions and lights." From this perspective, we are without remedy since, unlike Abraham and Moses, unlike the Romantic
poets, we are "deprived of the memory of a lost home or the hope of
a promised land." We could see Allmers, finally forced to forget the
myth of his childhood, as one stranded like this. Brandes, who
viewed Ibsen as a brother in exile, identifies him with the Nietzschian hero of consciousness who calls for a nobility detached from
love of country, nourished by exile from the fatherland, in love
with a future that will redeem the past. Ibsen could well have asked
the question: How is it possible for us, as orphans, "children of the
future," to be at home in Europe? He could have answered it in
Nietzsche's words: "We feel disfavor for all ideals that might lead
one to feel at home even in this fragile, broken time of transition;
as for its 'realities', we do not believe that they will *last.*" We might
say he applied himself to the task of breaking the ice of "these all
too thin 'realities'," or we might ally ourselves with the psycho-

analysts who deem his kind of leavetaking a necessary expression of the "will to separation," strongest in the creative type but "as biological and human a principle of life as the will to union." Attendant guilt is the stimulant to artistic growth.[1]

That we can picture Ibsen in alliance with these thinkers and writers is certainly not surprising. But it should not lull us into a vague assent to a common temper for, though Ibsen would never entirely detach historical from ontological condition, he could not be comfortable neutralizing the problem of guilt and exile by philosophical or psychological diffusion and displacement. The absurdity of Aslaksen's fear of local politics in both *The League of Youth* and *An Enemy of the People*, when taken out of its parodic context, is not so stupid a resistance to the palliative urge to universalize away responsibility. Ibsen would agree that personal motives and mistakes of alliance can hide better behind a national politics, can get lost, in fact, in a more complex bureaucracy (*I, EP, III, 329*). This kind of parodic deflection of psychological truth, enacted over and over in the plays, pins Ibsen to his personal pain of a divided determination, to leave home for the wider world and to refuse to that exile a guiltless release from impure motives. Brand's lament at the endless legacy of guilt passed from father to son is his: "Where does responsibility/For man's inheritance from man begin?" (M, B, II, 43). But its philosophical dignity is not allowed to neutralize the endless personal struggle towards justification. The most powerful tendency of Ibsen's art, its parody of all that was "great and beautiful," "stirring vividly" within him at his "best moments," might be viewed as a homeopathic strategy he shares with Kierkegaard— what Camus calls "an intentional mutilation of the soul to balance the mutilation accepted in regard to the absurd."[2] What makes the comic parody of Ibsen in Stockmann seem rather shallow in relation to the parody surrounding the nobility of a character like

1. Arthur Schopenhauer, "The World as Will and Idea," in Richard Taylor (ed.), *The Will to Live: Selected Writings of Arthur Schopenhauer*, trans. R. B. Haldane and J. Kemp (New York, 1967), 207; Albert Camus, *The Myth of Sisyphus*, trans. Justin O'Brien (New York, 1955), 5; Durbach, *Ibsen the Romantic*, 85; M. H. Abrams, *Natural Supernaturalism: Tradition and Revolution in Romantic Literature* (New York, 1973), 164ff.; Brandes, *Friedrich Nietzsche*, 47; Nietzsche, *The Gay Science*, 338; Otto Rank, *Will Therapy*, trans. Jessie Taft (New York, 1950), 83.

2. Ibsen, Speech to the Norwegian Students, September 10, 1874, in *Speeches and New Letters*, 50; Camus, *Myth of Sisyphus*, 29.

Rosmer is that the doctor's mutilation is not self-inflicted on Ibsen's behalf, unless one were to reckon political naivete as sickness, for Stockmann does not really have to fret about a guilty origin. In fact, his return *from* a northern limbo to his own town, his mission—compatible, it would seem, with home—is a scathing exposure in its shocked innocence of the necessity to attack from a distance the society whose guilts one shares.

Ibsen's own consciousness of absurdity begins as the terrible misunderstanding in the place made for perfect understanding—the family, uncharacteristically happy and generous in Stockmann's case. That family does not have to be set right, but Ibsen's does, and it is the guilty urge behind the desire to set society right that makes all missionary efforts subject to such fierce parody. No one except Stockmann could get away with a robust and justified prosecution of the majority without severe crippling, though no writer more than Ibsen wanted to punish majority morality. Ibsen may have agreed with Nietzsche that "Christianity has been a misunderstanding, like all moralities of improvement," but only because he so acutely felt his culture's spiritual, moral, and erotic disequilibrium through his own family romance which stirred and blocked his young desire to "achieve nothing less than complete fulfillment 'in greatness and love.'" [3] His plays reveal again and again how impossible it was for his powerful will, like that of Kierkegaard, to make peace with the disappointment experienced as both guilt and frustration. In 1867 he writes: "Do you know that I have entirely separated myself from my own parents, from my whole family, because a position of half-understanding was unendurable to me?" [4] In life and literature, he chose a situation of counterexile against the exile he inherited, of self-justification paid for by self-parody. It is no wonder if we hear in the words to his brother the concern of the majority's Mayor Stockmann: "I have to confess, it sounds very mysterious. Is anything wrong? Something I'm excluded from? I would assume that I, as chairman of the board of the municipal baths—" (*I*, EP, I, 290).

The whole of Ibsen's art expresses the persistent dream of an innocent communion between desire and will, blessed by the family,

3. Nietzsche, *Twilight of the Idols*, 34; Meyer, *Ibsen*, 74.
4. Henrik Ibsen to Bjørnstjerne Bjørnson, December 9, 1867, in *Correspondence*, 146.

and the passionate need to parody its pretensions, in order to keep it. Foldal, the failed poet, and Borkman, the failed banker, share the grand yearning for perfect understanding and justification:

> Foldal. . . . But Frida was the only one that understood me a little. (*Shakes his head dolefully.*) The others can't understand me at all.
> Borkman (*somberly, staring into space and drumming his fingers on the table*). No, that's a fact. That's the curse that we, the exceptional, the chosen human beings have to bear. The masses—all the gray average—they don't understand us, Vilhelm.
> (*I*, JGB, II, 971)

The alliance will be broken by Borkman's scorn, and the wish by Ibsen's, but they re-form as the memory of a murdered communion with Ella, sacrificed for a selfish marriage:

> Borkman. . . . It's the eye that transforms the action. The newborn eye transforms the old action. (*Breaking off.*) Ahh, you don't understand that.
> Mrs. Borkman (*brusquely*). No, I don't understand it.
> Borkman. Yes, that is the curse, exactly: that I've never found understanding in any human soul.
> Ella (*looking at him*). Never, John Gabriel?
> Borkman. With one exception—perhaps. Long, long ago, in the days when I didn't think I needed understanding. But since then, never, with anyone! I've had no one attentive enough to be near at hand, encouraging me—rousing me like a morning bell—urging me on once more to do inspired work. And confirming to me that I've done nothing irretrievable.
> (*I*, JGB, III, 998)

This is a particularly interesting exchange in light of Ibsen's marriage, a model of spousal encouragement and protection, but it was not in marriage that Ibsen felt the first and irretrievable exile. The jealous trinity of author Henrik, with wife Suzannah and son Sigurd as privileged listeners of each new play, resembles nothing so much as a counterexclusion against the past. Despite the maternal legacy of theatrical interest and personal unselfishness, Ibsen gives to Olaf Liljekrans these words spoken on the heights, looking down (an often repeated position and an image of family rejection in the poems and plays): "Did I not become a stranger in my mother's house . . . ?" (*O. 1*, OL, III, 530). Though he ascribes the cause to his new young love, the feeling will be attached in future plays to a guilty family that produces children who are as passing strangers.[5] In the midst of his passionless marriage, what Borkman wants is the maternal conversion of all flaws and failures into occasions for love, communion, and the maternal sanction of creative will, cruel in its neglect of others, but blessed in its innocence. And it is this that Rubek wants from the original family:

> Rubek (hesitantly). What I now feel so powerfully—even painfully—that I need, is to have someone around me who can reach my inner-most self—
> Maja (interrupting him tensely). You mean, I don't, Rubek?
> Rubek (hedging). Not in this particular sense. I need companionship with someone who could fulfill me—complete me—be one with me in everything I'm striving for.
> (I, WWDA, II, 1062)

Is it any wonder that Ibsen most cherishes in Brandes a maternal spirit that can recognize his errors without reducing his greatness? "There is something both in his praise and in his censure that does me an indescribable amount of good; and that something is—that I am understood."[6]

The dissolution of the dialectical relationship between a fated and chosen exile is a constant temptation for Ibsen, and Ludwig Binswanger, the first and most astute analyst of his separation from the family, was entirely justified in prowling around that early scene. The fierce indictment of the society Ibsen left might well have been displaced resentment against a home economically bankrupt, then socially and emotionally depressed. Stirred by the need for original and secondary redemption, the passionate will vents its guilts in scorn.[7] The double misunderstanding of a creative will trapped in the romance of maternal communion and paternal shame stimu-

---

5. The best discussion of the sister/brother relationship as screen for the mother/son relationship is in the important article by James E. Kerans, "Kindermond and Will in Little Eyolf," in Travis Bogard and William I. Oliver (eds.), Modern Drama: Essays in Criticism (New York, 1965), 203.

6. Henrik Ibsen to Frederick Hegel, December 14, 1869, in Correspondence, 180.

7. See first pages of Ludwig Binswanger, Henrik Ibsen und das Problem der Selbstrealisation in der Kunst (Heidelberg, 1949); see also Harald Noreng, "Henrik Ibsen som Komedie-dikter—med Konsentrasjon om 1890 arene," in Harald Noreng (ed.), En ny Ibsen: ni Ibsen-artikler (Oslo, 1979), 46, on the relationship between self-knowledge and aggression against society.

lated Ibsen's characters persistently to mouth the mission of redemption, and just as persistently provoked their author to mock
the arrogance and deceit of trying to make it good again. The author remembers the feeling of Mrs. Borkman about her son's future
as his own filial hope: "He, with his great mission to fulfill!" Then
he spits back through Ella's disdain: "Oh, come, his mission—!" (*I*,
JHB, I, 955). The line between the two moves is the same as that
which separates imposed from chosen exile, a line of guilt that testifies to the necessity for self-realization and the necessity to punish it
for punishing the family and world that obstructs it. In this way,
Ibsen makes conscious the parody of that original pose of society
and family as standard and authority, whether in political or spiritual claims of power.

The feelings of being misunderstood became identifed, in Ibsen's
mind, with a fall in social status suffered between the ages of seven
and fifteen, but if we feel from the plays that the fall screened an
earlier one, it would help us to account for the intense resentment
against the reduction of space and class that surfaced in a lifetime of
hyperconscious social vanity. In the disclaimed *St. John's Night*,
Birk notes: "My life has been divided into two sections. What happened to me before I left my childhood home I have practically entirely forgotten. I was only 9 or 10 then and soon after that I had a
serious illness" (O. 1, SJN, I, 225). But Ibsen cannot forget: "My
parents both belonged to the most respected families of the Skien of
their day. . . . In writing *Peer Gynt* I had the circumstances and
memories of my own childhood before me when I described the life
in the house of the rich Jon Gynt."[8] He could never mute the division which was all the more radical for repeating the earlier separation of child from mother. The worm of guilt would gnaw on the
hope for complete fulfillment in greatness and love for the rest of
his life. The will to artistic expression would need to be represented
as lonely, and whenever it would think it had found understanding
and consummation, it would have to be killed. The creative will
wanted more than anything else to be in league with the mother,
who had stimulated it, but the desire itself betrayed the father who
then betrayed the family. We recognize this dilemma of the life in

8. Henrik Ibsen to Georg Brandes, September 21, 1882, in *Correspondence*, 361.

77

the literature. Here is a confession of Peer Gynt's mother justifying her affections for her son:

> We clung together in want and sorrow—
> for I must tell you, my husband drank,
> roaming the district with foolish chatter,
> wasting and trampling our wealth underfoot
> while I sat at home with Little Peer . . .
> What could we do but try to forget?
> I was too weak to face the truth—
> it's a terrible thing to look fate in the face,
> so you try to shrug your troubles away
> and do your best to keep from thinking;
> some try lies, and some try brandy,
> but, ah, we took to fairy tales
> of princes, trolls, enchanted beasts,
> and stolen brides. . . . But who'd have thought
> those devil's tales would stay with him?
> (W, PG, II, 58)

The art is characteristically parodied down to fancy, but its mission of redemption from shame is first projected and then imposed upon the sloping shoulders of Ibsen's many immature idealists, most notably Gregers, whose purpose makes his father feel lonely (I, WD, I, 409). The misunderstanding Ibsen ascribes to his father in a letter of 1869 to his sister Hedvig, countered by her understanding, feeds the yearning for communion remembered by Allmers with Asta and by ambitious missionaries with bad consciences; because of this, it must always claim some origin in his own desires and disappointments.

The disappointment might have included his mother as well. Would the strong-willed child feel such a legacy of guilt if he had been fully loved, fully understood? In a drafted exchange between Asta and Borghejm, Ibsen has Asta call the brother/sister love the deepest and most innocent one. She confesses that she missed that communion with her parents and asks whether Borghejm had that love. His envied answer resonates through all the plays of Ibsen, in one way or another: "Yes, both a mother's and a father's. And I believe that is what has made me so light-hearted and happy."[9] It

---

9. *Ibsen's Workshop*, 502; Henrik Ibsen to Hedvig Stousland, September 26, 1869, *Correspondence*, 178; see also Robert Brustein, *The Theatre of Revolt: An Approach to Modern Drama* (Boston, 1964), 73, who notes the sharp paradox that it is "in trying to follow Ib-

must have been a relief for Ibsen to say to his mother, through a character he scorned, "You put your child out with strangers. And for that reason you've become a stranger to him" (*I*, G, I, 227).

It is not surprising that, in a letter to Bjørnson, Ibsen linked his fury at the reception of *Peer Gynt* both to society's misunderstanding and to the necessity of leaving home because of the *family's* misunderstanding. His fierce indignation greatly eases the early guilt: "I will not spare the child in the mother's womb."[10] The design of the anger might seem to justify the great motif of *kindermord* in the plays, but Ibsen well knows how multiple and double-jointed causes are. Rubek is not excused for his betrayal of love and art by his belief that "the world knows nothing! Understands nothing!" (*I*, WWDA, I, 1035). Ibsen's suspicion of his own illegitimacy is bound to his guilt over actually making, like Peer, an illegitimate child, and this haunts Ibsen's stranger-children belonging to neither parent, perhaps a wish for self-invention, for the mysterious origins of the Wild Duck, necessarily maimed. It also haunts his justification for exile and the origin of his art. Northrop Frye gives a historical framework to this sensation that certainly helps us to account for the obsession, in modern art, with impure sources: "But from Rousseau's time on a profound change in the cultural framework of the arts takes place. Man is now thought of as a product of the energy of physical nature, and as this nature is subhuman in morality and intelligence and capacity for pleasure, the origin of art is morally ambivalent, and may even be demonic."[11] Feeling this, Ibsen blasts by ambivalence Solness's dream of building warm homes where children and parents can belong to each other (*I*, MB, II, 825), and blasts, too, his fatherhood, by a bad conscience and transcendental scorn. In a letter of 1877, in which Ibsen tries to explain why he could never return to Skien, he refers to "certain spiritual trends then prevalent, with which [I] could feel no sympathy."[12] Though, in fact, the pietism embraced by his mother and sister came most strongly into his house after his departure for Grimstad (an eco-

---

senite principles" that "Gregers is . . . excoriated so mercilessly that he almost seems a scapegoat."

10. Henrik Ibsen to Bjørnstjerne Bjørnson, December 9, 1967, in *Correspondence*, 146.
11. Northrop Frye, *Fables of Identity*, 187.
12. Henrik Ibsen to Christian Paus, November 18, 1877, in *Correspondence*, 313; the translation given here is by Michael Meyer, *Ibsen*, 74.

nomic and educational necessity experienced as exile), it marked the upbringing and disturbed the sense of mission. The early religious atmosphere may have tempted the creative ambitions of the author to identify spirit and power. As a boy, says Solness, "I came from a pious home out in the country. That's why the building of churches seemed to me the noblest thing I could do with my life" (*I*, *MB*, III, 853). But it was obvious also that it was instrumental in rendering guilty the desired communion of the erotic and artistic will. Rosmer's sexual inhibitions are clearly related to his inability to act publicly. Where there is emphasis on the personalizing and democratizing of spiritual conscience, self-judgment serves a passive acceptance of God's will. The creative ambition to chastise and change the world would be in torment. The vagueness of ascription to the religious problem indicates that Ibsen could never climax his complaint by reference to universal or even cultural tendencies for long. He could not ease the guilt of personal ambition through diffusion into global guilt, as Strindberg's Indra describes it: "a breakdown in its orbit, perhaps something else, a rebellion accompanied by crimes that had to be suppressed."[13] Yet on the personal plane, this is a fair picture of what happens in the plays, and it is not, of course, unrelated to the repressed character of the culture.

Ibsen's plays ruthlessly expose homes as refuges that human beings do not know how to use for happiness (*I*, *MB*, III, 855), as poisoned places of untrue marriage, but the criticism is not appeased by raising them, in the manner of Strindberg, to an allegory of the child's Hell: "supposed home of all the virtues, where innocent children are tortured into their first falsehood, where wills are broken by tyranny, self-respect killed by jostling egos. The Family!"[14] Complaint, pity, fatalism cannot serve the struggle of Ibsen's will trapped between two exiles. The parody of his desire is callous so that it can rise above pity to the Great World. Those who, like Borkman and Allmers, burden children with their missions, are undeserving of the child's lament they appropriate: "I am misunderstood in my own house." Gregers passes on as child-torture his

13. Strindberg, *A Dream Play*, in *A Dream Play and Four Chamber Plays*, trans. and ed. Walter Johnson (New York, 1975), 21.

14. Strindberg, *The Son of a Servant: The Story of the Evolution of a Human Being, 1849–1867*, trans. and ed. Evert Sprinchorn (Garden City, N.Y., 1966), 24.

own sense of misunderstanding with his father. The split between the child's victimization and the parodied complaint against misunderstanding in the wounding adult, the maimed artist or prophet, marks the crucial difference between the self-pity of Strindberg's "Father" and that of Hjalmar, Solness, Borkman, and Rubek. Ibsen was as terrified of pity as Nietzsche and, like him, raised relentless rationalizations of his culture to a power murderous enough in its consequences to call out the "*aggressive* pathos" of the subterranean soldier.[15] His indignation made for him, as for Nietzsche, a clear moral identity for which he would have to take responsibility as it absorbed the high consciousness of ambivalence in all its affective origins. If he had been unable to accept ambivalence as a source of his creation, Ibsen would have been, like Solness—who converts his desire for innocent power to guilt over his wife's apparently blasted talent for building souls—a paralyzed builder still vulnerable to the myth of free creation. To God, the Master Builder vainly vows: "From this day on, I'll be a free creator—free in my own realm, as you are in yours" (*I*, MB, III, 854). He would not plead with Strindberg the motley makeup, the patchwork nature of author and character that deflected responsibility. Strindberg's Tekla, wondering what degree of guilt we must assume for the mess of our marriages, asks, "Aren't we innocent?" And Gustav answers: "Yes, to a certain extent. But there is a margin of responsibility all the same; and the creditors appear sooner or later! Innocent but responsible! Innocent before Him, who doesn't exist anymore, responsible before oneself and before one's fellow men."[16]

It is this kind of recognition that leads to the Baron's words at the end of *The Bond*, "We're both to be pitied," or to the *Dream Play* chorus, "Human beings are to be pitied."[17] The innocence Strindberg speaks of derives from a sense of fatality which inevitably reduces responsibility to a kind of moral good-sportsmanship. Responsibility is not yoked to will, which is always guilty, but to its sacrifice. Ibsen's muscular irony severely splits responsibility from fatality and innocence when Rosmer says with determination:

15. *Ibsen's Workshop*, 237; Nietzsche, *Ecce Homo*, 47.
16. Strindberg, *Creditors*, in *Pre-Inferno Plays*, trans. Walter Johnson, 185.
17. Both translated by Walter Johnson in *Pre-Inferno Plays* and *A Dream Play and Four Chamber Plays*.

"There is no higher judgment than ours, so we have to carry out justice ourselves" (*I*, R, IV, 584).[18] Even more is responsibility unable to free itself from self-protective guilt in Allmers's persistent reversion:

> *Allmers.* Well, you have to remember I'm responsible for Asta. For her life's happiness.
> *Rita.* Responsible—come on! Asta's grown up now. She's capable of choosing for herself, I should think.
> (*I*, LE, I, 886)

If Ibsen concentrated on punishing his desire for innocence, for being understood on the deepest level of love, it was perhaps that, like Kierkegaard, he had to justify a refusal to renounce the drive towards self-realization that makes the will unhappy. Strindberg longs for happiness, harmony, and peace, in spite of the will; Ibsen knows the will cannot have that if it wants the Freedom of the Great World. For the self-judgment of Ibsen's will must not only take guilty cognizance of its toll on the lives of others, but be responsive to the call of the Great World that, in Strindberg's cosmos, is lost between heaven and earth.

Brustein is doubtless right to shift our attention from Ibsen's social indignation to his creative ambition: "For Ibsen's deepest quarrel is probably less with those pillars of church, state, and community who dominate his plays than with the supreme authority figure, God himself. Behind the demand for a new beginning for mankind, one can glimpse his half-hidden desire to fashion a New Creation more in keeping with the logic of his poetic imagination."[19] But it is crucial to see how passionate Ibsen is to keep the Great World free of his artistic domination, beyond his power to control. His will would not relinquish the responsibility that bound him to historical and personal guilt, even if he recognized the ontological aspect of our bad beginning. The desire is to bring into being the world we can imagine from our own deformities, a world in which morality and mythology are dialectical, not antithetical, categories. This is,

18. See comment of Rank, *Will Therapy*, 21: "The perfect understanding of the analyst is like an all-pardoning of the parents; constructive understanding on the contrary is a self accusation in Ibsen's meaning, 'holding court' over one's own ego."

19. Brustein, *The Theatre of Revolt*, 40. On the troubled and perverse relationship between the Master Builder and God, see Michael Hinden, "A Reading of *The Master Builder*," *Modern Drama*, XV (1973), 403–10.

like Kierkegaard's Christianity, the real world we have relinquished and reduced, not the world dreamed by poets in competititon with God. In fact, Solness's challenge to the Creator is, for all its great and absurd dimension, a deformed and deforming defiance because it has polluted the necessary act of self-judgment, out of which genuine creation rises, with resentment and misreading. The Master Builder ends by aggravating the division between creation and responsibility already set by personal and social history. Yet Ibsen uses this extension, this mutilating of the absurd, to free the larger medium from our grandiose projections. The withering irony of Kierkegaard, Ibsen, and Nietzsche is always propelled by the need to overcome their own and the world's weakness without escaping the suffering of shared guilt. This is quite a different purpose from that of the German Romantics which allows, through its poetic world-humor, an escape in life and literature to an alternative atmosphere, mediating the divisions of spirit, morality, and flesh by acknowledging creative limitations with the good cheer of its broken form.

In his most quoted adage, Ibsen calls art a judgment on the self, but the judgment is executed by a parody of dreaming.[20] Without this parody, Ibsen might well have been the impotent and continually deluded Borkman, retrying, for years on end, the "whole case—all to [himself]": "I've re-opened the proceedings again and again. I've been my own prosecutor, my own defender, and my own judge" (*I, JGB*, III, 996). While Flaubert parodies what is worst in him in order to exorcise it, Ibsen parodies what is best in him in order to deserve it and preserve it for the Great World. While Flaubert's parody releases a lyric prose, into "elsewheres," from ethical responsibility, Ibsen's historically and psychologically binds his attributes to the perversions of his age to release a world of ethical spontaneity and equilibrium. His experience of the split between power and love, sanctioned by a modern morality he calls aesthetic and theological, is hooked to his own guilty desires both aired and punished in the yearnings of his sick idealists. This helps us to realize what Ibsen meant when he said that the willful Brand "is myself in my best moments," as well as what is behind Rubek's words to Maja, "I've really had only one model . . . for everything

20. See Ibsen's poem "Et Vers," *Ibsens Samlede Verker*, I, 404.

83

I've done" (I, WWDA, I, 1041), even though he seems to be referring to Irene. In a speech of 1874 to Norwegian students, Ibsen asserts: "Nobody can poetically present that to which he has not to a certain degree and at least at times the model within himself.[21] Despite the fact that no character in Ibsen is ever completely free from projection, the opening of the Great World by this parody helps us to grant authority to Irene when she judges the impotence of Rubek's self-assessment:

> You're soft and lazy and full of self-forgiveness for every sin of your life, the acts you've done and the thoughts you've had. You killed my soul— and then you model yourself in remorse and penance and contrition— (Smiles.)—and you think that settles the score.
> (I, WWDA, II, 1073)

She loses stature by hanging onto retribution, but Ibsen uses her as an agent for the kind of active art that would work for the full orchestration of desire, spirit, morality, and myth in the larger world that hangs in the air of every play.

Rubek is seduced unto death by the ideal of the pure origins of his masterpiece, while Flaubert's Frédéric lives on, stopped at the level of sterile reverie, ransom for the high reverie of his author— a sign that Ibsen is not after the aesthetic innocence that lured Flaubert, but the innocence of becoming in the Great World. This world is, we must remember, the opposite of the Christian beyond that has served as a refuge from the responsibilities of spiritual nobility. Nietzsche calls for an art that will recover the "pathos of distance" lost to Christian culture, that will courageously detach the rage for equality from the transcendental projection that drains off our best attributes. Ibsen's parody, his most painful exile, achieves this distancing. Its relationship to self-judgment is one that keeps all values from being leveled by morality ("the lie of equality of souls")[22] and closes all escape routes from guilty power. It forces the will to charge past sacrifice, to desire and demand clear action, and to accept its deformation and isolation. Hjalmar the dreamer is easily vulnerable to Gregers the missionary, for neither can use judgment for anything but prosecution and excuse, and Relling's

---

21. Henrik Ibsen to Peter Hansen, October 28, 1870, in Correspondence, 199; Ibsen, Speech to the Norwegian Students, September 10, 1874, in Speeches and New Letters, 50.
22. Nietzsche, The Anti-Christ, 156, 157.

cynicism is a sell-out as well. As teachers, they are herded into equality. But parody distances them for us and prepares them for the judgment that opens us to a higher world of value.

Without this goading of our virtues back to their impure sources, how could we keep out of our gardens what Nietzsche calls the "petty weeds of grief and chagrin"? The strong artist needs not "confession, conjuring of souls, and forgiveness of sins"; what he needs is "a new *justice.*" To conceive of art as a kind of justice was a favorite strategy of many writers of the second half of the nineteenth century, helping them to separate themselves from the bourgeois class and climate they shared. But Ibsen, by binding together judgment of his society with parody of his best reforming instincts, gained by exile a complex and generous scene for his guilt. His refusal to disentangle himself from the idealizing rationalizations of his characters in heroic exile is probably what deceived Nietzsche into thinking he was unable to distinguish between freedoms and Freedom: "For all his robust idealism and 'will to truth' he did not dare to liberate himself from the illusionism of morality that speaks of 'freedom' without wishing to admit what freedom is: the second stage in the metamorphosis of the 'will to power'—for those who lack freedom." [23] Whether or not we allow to Nietzsche any more positive recognition of what makes Freedom than to Ibsen, we can affirm that by charting the multiple perversions of both political and aesthetic idealism, Ibsen released ahead of us the thrilling and fearful atmosphere of the world of full possibility which, for the sake of its autonomy, he would only meet, not possess. It seems ironic that Nietzsche, who with Kierkegaard was most intent on the value of being misunderstood, should accommodate Ibsen in his recognition, shared by Jacobsen's Niels Lyhne, that "Those who are in opposition must not expect to be attacked for what they really are or really want, but for what the party in power is pleased to think they are and want." [24]

It has been suggested that Ibsen's political anarchism, so troubling to Brandes, might have given him the freedom to judge so-

23. Nietzsche, *The Gay Science,* 231–32; Arnold Hauser, "The Origin of Domestic Drama," in Eric Bentley (ed.), *Theory of the Modern Stage: An Introduction to Modern Theatre and Drama* (Harmondsworth, Middlesex, 1968), 418–19; Nietzsche, *Will to Power,* 53. When Nietzsche calls Ibsen a "typical old maid" (*Ecce Homo,* 76), it is clear he does not understand the revolutionary power of Ibsen's self-parody.

24. Jacobsen, *Niels Lyhne,* 144. See also Nietzsche, *The Gay Science,* 343.

ciety from all points of view.[25] In this way, his irony, even more than Nietzsche's, steered clear of political temptations since in Ibsen's plays we never see a robust leader handing down the new tablets of stone. But nowhere in the plays is there a character who does not *want* to be understood by the society whose guilts he shares. This is what makes the privilege of judging honest, for Ibsen cannot separate himself from Solness's unattractive retort to Brovik: "Lord—don't you understand me either?" (*I*, MB, I, 787). What keeps the complaint from heroic sanction is precisely the honoring of Nietzsche's insistence that no motive is unambivalent, especially the most personal, the most cherished. Ibsen's scorn, like that of Solness, has to pay for its privilege of judging by letting us see it as a balm for guilt, a defense against the envy of the young. Doctor Herdal is at a loss to understand Solness's pleasure in "letting Aline do [him] an injustice" (*I*, MB, I, 798) in thinking he is interested in Kaja, but, in truth, she respects him too much and herself too little to think he would flirt for any other reason. When Hilda comes upon the scene, she seems to liberate Solness into the guiltless cruelty of self-realization, releasing him from slavery to the past by forcing his generosity to the young. But Aline continues to stand between the first ascent and the second, just as Ibsen's childhood guilt stands between his first and second exile. Ibsen does not need Solness's version of Aline to "discover some sly, hidden meaning in the most innocent thing" he says (*I*, MB, II, 817), because he could never say as guiltlessly as Hilda: "I'm never going home again" (*I*, MB, II, 831).

Like Dickens, Ibsen would forever walk the line between rage and guilt from the double ejection from paradise in psychological and economic disappointment. His exile into the "great world" of "liberty of thought and a wide view of things" was surely necessary for his own "spiritual emancipation and purification," but the early desires and unsanctioned ambition haunt his separations like Mrs. Alving's ghosts. That is why Ibsen had to tie so closely, by means of self-judgment, that emancipation to the "responsibility and guilt of the society to which he belongs."[26] Peer Gynt's return to comfort

25. See Janko Lavrin, *Ibsen and His Creation*, 95.
26. Henrik Ibsen to Christian Paus, November 18, 1877, in *Correspondence*, 313; Ibsen to Ludwig Passarge, June 16, 1880, in *Correspondence*, 334. Like his revered Ibsen, James Joyce, through Stephen, continually suggests that sentimentality in love and language occurs when the artist refuses to pay the debt for his exile.

his dying mother does not redeem the exile from neglect of personal and national guilt; Brand's refusal to return does not sanction his mission. This keeps Ibsen's exile hostage to his original home. The obsessive return to childhood in the plays belies the refusal to return, in life, to Skien, and is both nostalgic and murderous. There Nora could be herself, at least in the servant's quarters, and Allmers could be beyond desire, as Rosmer puts it: "Our life together began the way two children fall in love, secretly and sweetly. No demands, and no dreams" (*I, R, III,* 555). Provisionally released from sexual conflict by a brother/sister communion, Asta shares Allmers's myth of the "really . . . beautiful time . . . the two of us alone" (*I, LE,* II, 899). Rebecca also sheds the guilt of sexual turbulence when she converts to Rosmer's ascetic nobility and evokes this strikingly imaged scene of purity: "A profound inner peace descended on me—a tranquillity, like an island of sleeping birds, up north, under the midnight sun" (*I, R, IV,* 575). Even Mrs. Sørby imagines the retreat to innocence and the release from villainy as she speaks of restoring Werle: "Now, he can sit and talk to me as freely as a child. He's never had that chance before. He, a healthy vigorous man, had to spend his whole youth and all his best years hearing nothing but sermons on his sins" (*I, WD, IV,* 463).[27]

That both the nostalgia for a lost paradise and the projection of a better future generally accompanying it are so regularly parodied by Ibsen is a sign of the uniqueness of his utopian moves. He knows that these retreats screen out a profound conflict between desire and will, and that is one reason the return to childhood is most often paid for by physical mutilation and death. Parents are punished for having the kinds of marriages that never "leave the child in peace" (*I, WD, IV,* 460).[28] The regularly experienced grief of marriage in Ibsen's plays is a secondary manifestation of the original gulf between parent and child. What opens up between Torvald and Nora was already there between Nora and her father; what opens up between Werle and the unmarriageable Gregers the redeemer was already precipitated by the son's inability to separate from the mother whose bitter, ailing character is charged to his father (*I, WD, I,* 409). Asta, like Allmers, finds it difficult to give herself to another "whole and undivided" because Asta's mother

27. We might compare the case of Arthur Clennam in Dickens's *Little Dorrit.*
28. See Lawrence, *Phoenix,* 620; compare *Little Eyolf,* I, 883, in which Allmers announces his plans for the child.

"wasn't always what she ought to be" and Allmers "never noticed anything like that" (*I, LE*, III, 923; II, 903).

It is Ibsen, in his counterexiling art, who cannot leave children in peace, any more than he can leave the parents in peace. In play after play, inadequate parents are spiritually frustrated spouses who burden their offspring with the task of redeeming the past and justifying a future for which adults cannot take responsibility. In this devious way, the untrue marriage tries to join what Ibsen will insist must be split asunder: innocence and responsibility. Because Ibsen, the child of the first marriage, could not have innocent power in his family, the child's dream of creative joy is estranged in the second marriage by parental displacement of self-realization onto the children, who, in turn, are displaced in the family, belonging neither to their parents nor to themselves.[29] That is the terrible disequilibrium visible behind Hjalmar's defense against his denial of his father in the opening scene of *The Wild Duck:* "Oh, if you were in my place" (*I, WD*, I, 403). No more than Gregers is Hjalmar in his own place, especially when he pretends to be: "So what if we skimp and scrape along under his roof, Gina—it's still our home. And I'll say this: it's good to be here" (*I, WD*, II, 420). This sentimental, literary, and idealized picture is purchased at the price of reducing Hedvig's illustrated dreams to basket-making—a preparation justified on the surface for her possible coming blindness, but a fine example, with the parasitic dependence of the family on the invention-fantasy, of paternal maiming of aesthetic ambitions which must remain exiled in the home. It is this deceit that makes the family vulnerable to the displaced idealism of Gregers. Ironically, while the child is the sacred future, she cannot be allowed, without leaving home, to develop further than the psychic past of the parent. Since Ibsen would have died to expression without the capability of counterdisplacement, Hedvig must pay for the author's creative and constructive exile. Where the ego is not master in its own house, it stunts those of the children.[30]

29. Adma d'Heurle and Joel N. Feimer, in "Lost Children: The Role of the Child in the Psychological Plays of Henrik Ibsen," *The Psychoanalytic Review,* LXIII (1976), 46, discuss the way in which the lives of Hedvigs and Eyolfs are lost because they have to depend on the psychological readiness of parents to receive them. See Joan Carr, "'The Forest's Revenge': Subconscious Motivation in *The Wild Duck,*" 845–56.

30. James E. Kerans, "Kindermord and Will in *Little Eyolf,*" 206; Sigmund Freud, "One of the Difficulties of Psycho-Analysis," in *Collected Papers,* trans. under supervision of Joan Riviere, ed. Ernest Jones (London, 1950), IV, 355.

The conflict between the bourgeois family and spiritual self-realization is radically emphasized by Kierkegaard who saw, as did Ibsen, though from a celibate perspective, the inevitable collision between the child's ambitions and desires and the collective misunderstanding of the parents. By setting up the choosing of Christianity against the inheritance of it, the Christianity of self-concern against that of the welfare of children, Kierkegaard justifies the biblical breaking of relationships and bonds, exile from home: "It is an unchristian kind of love (it is, in fact, only race love) for parents to be unwilling to understand that to become a Christian is a decision which defines the single individual as spirit, that in this respect one person can do nothing for another."[31] Where parents displace their self-realization onto the mission for others, the children have guilty individualities. The irony in Allmers's desire to develop every side of Little Eyolf's individuality has opened the door to the Rat Wife.[32] With his abdication of self-realization, Allmers abandons the human responsibility that was the subject of his book. The child Ibsen, like the child Kierkegaard, willed more than anything the identity between expressive ambition and the love of parents, of the world that would sanction that bonding. But it could not be, so both turned to the positive uses of separation and misunderstanding and charted all the abuses of their deepest motives in order to legitimate them as agents of a more authentic reality. Ibsen's most poignant strategy is to free his missionary drive by assigning it to the parents who torture the children into being its objects. The assumption of full responsibility for the mission and for the individualizing of children (the opposite of turning them into sacred symbols) is a task Ibsen seemed to accomplish fairly well in life, but in his art, the failure of the necessary distinction, like the failure of figures in Kierkegaard's literature to *choose* Christianity, pays for the guilty exiles and the sacrifice of any hope for unity between eros and will.

The close bonding of the child's future to the developed parent marks Ibsen as a profound psychologist, but he would not stop at the therapeutic presumption of adequacy. In *Pillars of Society* he

31. Kierkegaard, *Journals and Papers*, II, 32.
32. *Ibsen's Workshop*, 476; see also Kerans, "Kindermord and Will in *Little Eyolf*," 203. We could also profitably compare with this harmful displacement the abdication of will of Marcel's mother who kisses the crying son, an act so desired and, later, so regretted, in Proust's *A la recherche du temps perdu*.

could attach Lona's praise of Bernick, "At last, you've found your-self" (*I*, PS, IV, 114), not only to Mrs. Bernick's claim, "Now I know that you never were mine—but I'm going to win you" (IV, 115), but also to Bernick's recovery of the son and childhood that "never really belonged to me" (IV, 105). In most of his plays, how-ever, he cruelly opposes the urge to self-realization and the nurtur-ing of children. (Even the Stockmann family has to be unhoused by a hostile society, and Ellida has to be estranged from the family be-fore she is accepted by those who will soon be leaving to look for the Great World.) Ibsen could not honestly work out his dream of an innocent and joyous ambition *in* the family. The threatened par-ent cannot risk the child's freedom *in* marriage, without distortion. Mrs. Alving recognizes the pathos of the Captain's confinement when she remembers "he *was* like a child" (*I*, G, III, 266), an in-sight that binds his frustrations to hers and to those of Ibsen him-self. To make a creative nobility out of his double resentment and guilt, he had to give himself the "pathos of distance" which is parodically played out as the killing of titanic ascents towards self-realization and of the child in the family, apparently on "the thresh-old of a spiritually aware existence" (*I*, LE, II, 897)—a place too long closed to the parent.

It is precisely the uncertainty, thrill, fear of the larger world that Allmers had tried to evade. Writers of the second half of the nine-teenth century regularly blasted the children of the future, but for Ibsen, one grim positive residue of the deaths could be enforced re-placement of the parents in relation to each other and themselves. The devastation of children in Ibsen is never mere punishment though it avenges creative frustration and mutilation. It can never signal recovery but is not utterly meaningless.[33] It is not allowed, finally, to serve as symbol in the ritual of Christian compensation, as it did so often in the actual mourning ceremonies of the popu-lace, nor in the cheap versions of this, named providence and retri-bution. But the killing of the child has the power, even if only pro-visional in a character as shallow as Hjalmar, to force self-judgment after blame, so that there is something positive in the quiet recogni-tion that now the child belongs to both.

33. Though Durbach, *Ibsen the Romantic*, 101–102, cogently identifies *kindermord* with the counter-Romantic half of Ibsen—the half that, with Gina, despises pretentious mytholo-gizing—I cannot accept his reduction of Little Eyolf's death to absurdity. This claim leads inevitably to compensatory overestimation of the ethical value of the final resignation.

The art that aestheticizes and deforms life to climb over its spiritual responsibilities is also reminded, by its identification with dead children, that it must come back to the perilous place of double exile. Irene tells Rubek she would have killed their "child" had she known how much public ambition and fading idealism would have disfigured it. Rubek had cheapened art's necessary task of misunderstanding by hiding his satire behind animal faces and revising his masterpiece for motives that served neither his spiritual life nor that of society. Regret and scorn need to be set free from their slavish dependence on the enemy to the exclusion of their dialectical partner, the creative work of the will in exile. Both Irene and Rubek suffer from their slavish dependence on prosecuting rage and satire, which, without the term of self-judgment, are as monolithic as the morality that pits itself against the life they mourn as lost. In all its unavoidable impurity, Ibsen's missionary dream that used art to redeem honor, his aesthetic boldness standing in for personal cowardice, his spiritual imperatives covering personal ambition, had to be punished like the child, like his own childhood in two families, in order to belong to him.[34] But even Irene's killings "in hate and revenge" are shadowed by "agony," an agony that opens up possibilities past retribution and penance to a liberating creation she could not live (*I*, WWDA, I, 1047). Squeezed between Irene's aggressive, murderous sickness and Rubek's passive ailing conscience, the double deformity that served as its origin, Ibsen's art arose out of manifold misdirections and motives, misunderstandings confessed, felt, and chosen. The monolithic homes of bourgeois morality could not house the creative will it made guilty, and the Great World could not yet receive a will that was working its way through its malformations. Ibsen's art did its work energetically in the corridor between the family and the Great World.

Ibsen refused to abandon the home for an undeserved personal transcendence. But he insisted, too, on charting the kinds of crippling he would have endured if he had stayed or gone back. Short of exile, his situation might have become a version of that of Captain Alving, pressed into licentiousness from a sexually inhibited marriage and a socially superfluous situation. Osvald's return *necessi-*

---

34. While Meyer can speak of Ibsen's well-documented cowardice face to face (*Ibsen*, 577), Joyce can say to him, "You walked in the light of your inward heroism" (James Joyce to Henrik Ibsen, March 1901, in Richard Ellmann, *James Joyce* [New York, 1959], 90).

tated an unbearably punitive blow against Mrs. Alving's last hope of recovery:

> *Mrs. Alving.* Oh, I could almost bless this illness that forced you home to me, because it has made me see you're really not mine, you still have to be won!
> (*I*, G, III, 270)

> *Osvald.* And what is this life you gave me? I don't want it! You can take it back!
> (*I*, G, III, 274)

The art is forced homeward, but never to stay in Kafka's helpless realm of the Father's laws. Despite appearances, Osvald's death, un-like that of Gregor Samsa, is a punishment that really gets us some-where and rises above its determinism. It gets us to the depth that stubbornly stays as value against the morality of self-preservation, the denial of suffering. There *kindermord* gives birth to the primor-dial child that ferries us through death and renders irrelevant a long history of perverted parenthood. So antiutopian is the promise of Ibsen that we are forced to ask at the end of *Ghosts*, who can bear to gain what has been gained?[35] And suffering might often seem as useless as it is in Kafka. Rosmer and Relling are both cynical about the possibility of being "ennobled from the outside" (*I*, R, IV, 576; WD, V, 476). In Mrs. Alving's house, the last room, freed of its sick secrets, springs open its sealed doors to a place in which we are ennobled from the inside, a place of depth. Locked up with that pain, Mrs. Alving can at last leave home. We have to want the fullness of consciousness opened by suffering. Ibsen's rhythms leave us panting for the cruel freedom from our lies; it is where we need to go. Stephen Whicher maintains that the haunting presence of "the wide eyes of the dead children—all the sacrificed lives," including Ibsen's own, finally cuts off the realm of redemption, but that can be overcome by the knowlege that we feed a future of mythical ex-pansion into our full medium, past our own lives.[36]

---

35. In "The Death of the Artist's Father," *British Journal of Medical Psychology*, XLVI (1973), 138, D. Russell Davis discusses the identity of Ibsen and Osvald, Grimstad and the Paris of *Ghosts*; compare Kafka's story "The Judgment," as well as "The Metamorphosis"; James Hurt, *Catiline's Dream: An Essay on Ibsen's Plays* (Urbana, Ill., 1972), 112. Hurt sug-gests that sending Osvald away is the renunciation of one side of Mrs. Alving's own character.

36. Stephen Whicher, "The World of Ibsen," in Fjelde (ed.), *Ibsen*, 172. G. Wilson Knight, *Henrik Ibsen*, 114, claims that creative dying opens up a "cosmic trust."

Ibsen's chosen exile enables his parodies of the will to Freedom to serve as catalysts to the third realm Kafka denies: "No third place exists for mankind."[37] Josephine and the Hunger Artist are defeated, like all Kafka's heroes, by the world whose laws are an unbeatable enemy since, backed by parental authority, they repress more by arbitrariness than by consistency. This reflects both the impossibility of coming through the family without guilt and the infantile refusal to choose it. Ibsen's figures of released will, falling from towers and under avalanches, or freezing on benches, can be defeated only by themselves in that they set Freedom and family guilt against each other as antithetical enemies instead of dialectical partners. They sink into the gulf opened by the nineteenth-century moral education between duty and desire. The third realm binds family guilt to Freedom through the energetic uses of irony. By this action, both the ontological and historical origins of our division are converted into stimulants to the creative will. Kafka, like Strindberg, seeks happiness and peace through comic pathos, while Ibsen thrills to the struggle for a Freedom that can be born only out of choosing misunderstanding in the family as in the world.[38]

By remaining alive while he is "chained to the dead" Ibsen uses his psychological determination to convert escape into exploration, aesthetic wandering into spiritual depth.[39] To some extent, the yoking of his own successful exile to its parody in the plays—mountain and steeple ascents, attic confinement—keeps the world from seeming arbitrary and weightless in meaning and value, keeps the orphaned artist savior from being overwhelmed by the irreverence and indifference that greet Kafka's Country Doctor. While Ibsen could no longer feel the clear victory over history Rousseau could claim by the literal removal of his body from the salons of Paris, he has far more gravity than Kafka, who, like his doctor, is mindful of the right to expect more while spinning nakedly in the wilderness. The deaths of children in Ibsen's plays pull us past the desire to

37. Franz Kafka, *The Diaries of Franz Kafka: 1914–1923*, trans. Martin Greenberg with Hannah Arendt. ed. Max Brod (2 vols.; New York, 1968), entry for January 28, 1922, II, 214.

38. Charles Lyons, in *Henrik Ibsen: The Divided Consciousness*, and James Hurt, in *Cataline's Dream*, see value as inevitably enslaved by the delusions of the will whose projects are deformed; they miss the dramatic emergence of the autonomous Great World, the impersonal original medium that opens up beyond projections and defeats.

39. This lament of Solness (*I*, MB, III, 845) is heard in various versions throughout the plays.

make the beginning right again, a possibility only mournfully surrendered in the last lines of Kafka's story. The alternately dying and undying patient of that Country Doctor, perhaps his own wounded childhood, prepares us only for a universe in which traditional modes and words of salvation hang in the air and do not apply to us. He cannot assume the power to connect parents and children, and this very powerlessness is what keeps his art, from Adorno's point of view, constructive as dialectical criticism.[40]

Ibsen's authorial anger at Allmers's pretense of curing the child in order to avoid curing himself allows him to spare the connection between his mission and the future of humanity, between his creative will and moral responsibility. The children, by their maiming, break through the identification of moral custom with moral health. Kafka's helpless heroes, stranded between the morally arbitrary public sphere and the guilty private one, might stimulate a criticism of the modern world but not a possibility beyond it. This refusal is the source of his humor and pathos. But Ibsen's anger generates unappeased ghosts between duty and desire to signal that the broken connection between past and future, between history, psychology, and spirit might be resumed in a life that waits for us. Someone stands between all that should be married in Ibsen, and stands there in every major play. The readiness to answer the appeal to being is experienced in Ibsen as Heidegger's *choosing* to have a conscience, an act that connects moral responsibility to the past with spiritual possibility in the future. Typically, Ibsen represents this appeal parodically in his plays, for there is no apparent mediation between the call to self-realization and bourgeois self-preservation.[41] This keeps personality from appropriating the state of mind by which the playwright so unsentimentally captures us. By remaining chained to the dead world of democratic Christian morality, Ibsen's art, with its double-faced parody, exorcises the ghosts between slave morality and master creation. It testifies that in this way, at least, Rosmer is wrong: victory can be rooted in guilt, and some good can come out of impure sources.

Exile has been called the nostalgia of the religious man for the

---

40. Theodor Adorno, "Reconciliation Under Duress," trans. Rodney Livingstone, in Ronald Taylor (trans. ed.), *Aesthetics and Politics: Ernst Bloch, Georg Lukács, Bertolt Brecht, Walter Benjamin, Theodor Adorno* (London, 1977), 160–70.

41. Heidegger, *Being and Time*, 334.

perfection of the beginning. For Ibsen, it was a choice of distance from which the imperfection of the beginning could be viewed as a source of creation. To answer the call to being means assuming impure origins as a natural and inevitable byproduct of imperfection and disequilibrium, caught as we are between moral imperatives and mythical imaginations. The complete erosion of any metaphysical or historical authority for the call to save others while saving the self increases the possibilities of bad faith in the mission and the need for shrewd self-judgment. The collision between the call to self-realization and community is economically exploited and arrogantly appropriated in self-defense by John Gabriel Borkman because he will not admit responsibility to love. But his situation of homelessness, parodically staged as imprisonment in the attic of his home, as social humiliation posing as choice, justifies Ibsen's calculated distancing of the creative will from the community. To Brandes he writes:

> But I believe that it is better for you to go without leaving friends at home. Friends are an expensive luxury; and when a man's whole capital is invested in a calling and a mission in life, he cannot afford to keep them. The costliness of keeping friends does not lie in what one does for them, but in what one, out of consideration for them, refrains from doing. This means the crushing of many an intellectual germ. I have had personal experience of it; and there are consequently many years behind me during which it was not possible for me to be myself.[42]

Literal dispossession, "living like a foreigner in a foreign land," is tested as displacement in the plays. The Ibsen who complained, through Brand, that his father and mother loved and understood him inadequately, who never revisited his home and, even "when he [was] a wealthy man . . . [felt] no longing to possess a house and home and still less a farm and lands, like Bjørnson," certainly does have an "idea of what a home is like," though through these words of Manders he uproots its definition and strands it in uncertainty (*I*, *G*, *I*, 222). And that is precisely why he must live away from it, like Osvald, who finds real morality in the bohemian houses of Paris artists and can refrain from investing a moral mission in a characteristically deformed household of the homeland, a tableau of domestic

---

42. Mircea Eliade, *Le Sacré et le Profane* (Paris, 1965), 80; Henrik Ibsen to Georg Brandes, March 6, 1870, in *Correspondence*, 183.

bliss. We can imagine how much Ibsen liked in Dickens (who regularly *unites* innocence and responsibility) the parody of the missionary mother in Mrs. Jellyby, evangelically intent upon saving the lives of distant natives, ennobling herself from the outside by "telescopic philanthropy." At the sight of Mrs. Jellyby's children scattered in filth and disorder around her missionary work, it is no wonder that Mr. Jellyby finally must manage this warning: "Never have a Mission."[43] A mission and the family torture each other. By mocking the missionary urge when it stays at home, Ibsen saved its power in exile for service to the Great World.

If his mission is to serve men and women, the poet-savior cannot patronize from a position of authority either without or within the play that elevates him beyond the guilts of his society. What Ibsen does with the doctor figure to keep him from the role of privileged raisonneur is instructive. In a draft of A Doll House, it is Rank who, musing with Nora, says of a longed-for journey to the sea: "And then, to see your home from a distance, in a new light." This is a particularly poignant projection in light of Rank's approaching death, and he would seem to be set apart by distance from those he loves. But, in fact, Ibsen keeps Rank, like himself, an impure lover of Nora and in a position of half-understanding.[44] The mutual bantering over Torvald's head in his last scene does not sanction his last words, for he is thoroughly seduced by the theatrical role he has been assigned in the Helmer household. This is all the more apparent if we remember that he almost made it as raisonneur in the first act when he spouted his scorn of moral cripples.[45] Wangel is forced by Ellida's exile to yield to a healing evolutionary regression against the enlightened progression of standard and overconscious cultural controls. In Stockmann, his comic counterpart, Ibsen sacrifices his prophetic authority by leaving him absurd and unhoused, stripped of friends and brother, and unable to get published. In a revision of

43. Meyer, Ibsen, 578; I, MB, III, 856; Georg Brandes, Henrik Ibsen, 43; Charles Dickens, Bleak House, ed. George Ford and Sylvere Monod (New York, 1977), 374. The speechless Mr. Jellyby gives that parting advice to his daughter Caddy. Dombey and Son is, of course, the fullest exploration of the disastrous effect of Mission on the child.

44. Ibsen's Workshop, 134; see discussion of the identity of Rank and Ibsen in Arild Haaland, Seks Studier i Ibsen (Oslo, 1965), 22–28.

45. For a discussion of the authority of the "raisonneur" in the drama of the Second Empire, see Maurice Valency, The Flower and the Castle: An Introduction to the Modern Drama: Ibsen and Strindberg (New York, 1963), 73–88.

the tragic hero as polluter, there is no society, no chorus to receive the Truth, only a political majority intent on self-preservation. Dr. Herdal, in *The Master Builder*, is impotent in the face of Solness's hunger and gives us no spiritual measure for the uses of madness. The dialectical closeness of the idea of home and exile in the plays, the price of critical and creative authority, keeps Ibsen from the kinds of moral preaching of which he is wrongly accused, indulged in by Stockmann who falls into the same antithetical pattern of prosecution practiced by the majority as he rejects the guilts of his culture.[46] The same is true of Relling who, himself, rants about the national disease, "moralistic fever" (*I*, WD, III, 451). By these parodies of the doctor-savior, Ibsen salvages the idea of the dramatic poet as "a doctor tending to the body of his times" and keeps his own body, like that of Rosmer, shy of political and social frays, but immune to escape and primed for creation.[47]

Carl Sternheim speaks of the homeopathic skill of the artist-doctor who heals his heroes by lacerating them: "He can place a finger on the diseased part of humanity and have his hero oppose that ill with eager and militant defiance at the risk of his life (this is the nature of tragedy), or he can inject the moribund quality into the hero and have him be fanatically possessed by it (this is the essence of comedy)." In fact, Ibsen could be said to reverse this identification in his impure figures, for we could place Stockmann in the first category and the heroes and heroines of sick conscience in the second. This impression derives primarily from the double construction of exile in one who shares the guilts of his society, the double use of parody to distance and punish the small world while preparing and preserving the great one. Otto Rank speaks with many analysts of modern culture when he assumes that before the creative man can be "therapist for other sufferers," he must, in the absence of metaphysical authority and the presence of moral tyr-

---

46. Michaelsen, *Ibsens 'Bygmester Solness' som tidsdiagnose*, 33; on Stockmann's naïveté, see discussion of Helge Rønning, "Individualism and the Liberal Dilemma—Notes Towards a Sociological Interpretation of *An Enemy of the People* by Henrik Ibsen," in Daniel Haakonsen (ed.), *Contemporary Approaches to Ibsen: Proceedings of the Third International Ibsen Seminar, 1975* (Oslo, 1977), 104, 110: "His inadequate understanding of economic laws leads to an incomplete insight into the connection between economic and moral power. Dr. Stockmann regards power and justice as being synonymous."

47. Carl Sternheim, "Thoughts Concerning the Nature of Drama," trans. Joel Agee, in Herzfeld-Sander (ed.), *Essays on German Theater*, 165.

anny, become "first of all his own therapist." Ibsen's uses of comedy and tragedy are symptomatic not only of the generic impurity of the age's art, but of the difficulty of playing out the drama of his personal struggle to liberation, a continual and unfinished act, when it is dialectically implicated with that of all men and women. The drama must use all the aesthetic tricks to make itself ethically honest enough to serve others without suspicion of bad faith.[48]

Like Kierkegaard and Nietzsche, Ibsen knew that "becoming well is of more value than being well," and very much more dramatic. Creation is, in a favorite image of the nineteenth century, a continual convalescence, typically parodied in Lyngstrand; in Ibsen the disease was the radical and unmediated breach, ontological, historical, personal, between the family of man and self-realization.[49] The paradoxical treatment was an exile bound to home by a parody of countless scapegoats, misguided idealists. The gulf is felt through the layers of bad connections between frustrated powerful wills and the society that houses them. The deaths of Hedda, Rosmer, Rebecca, Solness, Rubek, and Irene suffer the humiliation of isolation, the impossibility of symbolic representation in the name of universal order and the future.[50] Their disappearance does not even elicit the relief brought on by the death of Kafka's bug. The ancient bindings between polluted heroes and land, great gains in the individual consciousness and public restoration, are parodied by the endings of *Hedda Gabler* and *The Master Builder*, by Maja's childish chant of freedom at the end of *When We Dead Awaken*. What kind of mediation could hold together the space, resonant with ambivalence, between Ragnar's words ("How horrible this is. And so, after all—he really couldn't do it") and Hilda's ("He went straight, straight to the top. And I heard harps in the air. *[Swings the shawl up overhead and cries with wild intensity.]* My—my master builder!"). The design of this radical split between a parodied myth of expansion and bourgeois myth of duty, each inadequate to produce new consciousness in *this* world but able, on the same stage, to generate the presence of the Great World, anticipates Brecht's dialectical distancing that Althusser praises as the stimulus to a new produc-

48. *Ibid.*; Rank, *Truth and Reality*, 289.
49. Rank, *Will Therapy*, 153. The concept of creation as convalescence is particularly evident in writers like Baudelaire and Nietzsche, who so closely bound image and philosophy to the body.
50. Brian Johnston, *The Ibsen Cycle*, 100–102.

tion of consciousness *in* our world. When, with Nietzsche, Ibsen helps the tragic "age of moralities and religions" to become conscious of itself, he prepares us for the comedy of collisions in the endlessly deferred future world.[51]

The emphasis upon the possessive pronoun keeps Solness from fusing with the Great World; the prosaic assessment of the scene by Ragnar keeps the ascent from significance in the small world. The impossibility of separating the affective and ambivalent evaluation from the universal and world-historical forces the fall into a parody of ancient catharsis and recovery of public balance. Yet the gulf between interpretations is emphasized by the staging—the tiered views in the conversation of Act II between Hilda and Solness are as spiritually symbolic as the split scene of *The Wild Duck*. Hilda looks at both the garden and Solness while sitting in his house; he points to the new house on the site of the old one. The stunning levels in the exterior scenes after Little Eyolf's death that separate Allmers and Rita and collapse towards the end chart the topography of misunderstanding as dramatically as the homeless idealism tramping off the stage in the guise of Brendel. The aggravation of the inherited split between duty and desire convinces us that no body in Ibsen can carry the Great World. The communion of castle builders can never found a new community. Yet, the fact that none of these can be split entirely apart, in that they are held together by the art, even as they fail to listen to each other, forces us to move value into the gap we sense as depth, our abdicated medium.

And in this way, just as Ibsen had validated his own struggle for Freedom by linking it to a guilty past and pressing it towards creation, so too, by crossing ascent with misunderstanding, he authenticates the independence of the Great World, waiting for us in exile and rich in the unmastered dialectical rhythms of attraction and conflict between the spheres. The gulf between creative possibility and life in the homeland both reflects the misunderstandings of Ibsen's childhood and prepares us for the terrifying crossing of the wilderness. Attacking provincial sterility in *Love's Comedy*, Falk complains that "love has to cross the desert to get here these days" (O.2, LC, II, 157). Perhaps, as Rosmer suggests, it has never, in its purest form, made the journey (*I*, R, IV, 576). The ironic qualifica-

---

51. Louis Althusser, "The 'Piccolo Teatro': Bertozazzi and Brecht," in *For Marx*, trans. Ben Brewster (London, 1979), 129–51; Nietzsche, *The Gay Science*, 74.

tion of Falk's celibate setting forth to self-realization at the end of the play throws suspicion of any possible alliance between art and epic action—shows how early Ibsen needed to preserve an exile between understanding and his mission. That exile continued to refuse to serve as escape from a family and society that wounds the will that has wounded it and gave imperious weight and authority to the distant world of possibilities. His diseased carriers cannot be society's doctors, but through them, Ibsen could find a standpoint halfway between Rousseau's wilderness and the borrowed homes of the abusing missionaries like Gregers, of dispensers of domestic daemonism like Relling. The thick texture of his art derives not only from the constant dialectical rhythms between guilt and indignation as it struggles towards creation, but from the fact that the author has parody as an *activating* agent while his characters do not.

The epic dream of leading the homeland to a new destiny is present from the earliest plays. In a version of *The Burial Mound*, Blanka, on the eve of her return, imagines a great and heroic North from the distant South: "So the hearts of Norway's sons are also filled with fervent longing and with secret dreams!" (*O. 1*, BM, I, 137). It is mocked in the bodies of Hjalmar and Gregers, Brendel and Stockmann, who return because they have not embraced self-judgment. In ignorant exile, "distance and deprivation and memory [throw] a kind of enchantment over the town" (*I*, EP, IV, 353). But the parody of aesthetically dreaming ethics, started in a sustained fashion in *Peer Gynt*, stimulates a voracious hunger in the judging faculties that keeps the Great World protected from the deformity of our wishes. Against nothing is the parody more vigorous than the hope of the artist, spotted by Brandes as one shared by Mme. de Stael and her exiled heroine Corinne, that the "growing fame will bring her recall to the native land, reinstatement in her rights." The Ibsen that his family remembers standing apart as a child becomes the Brand who brutally rejects the invitation to claim his rights at home, rights that cannot be made innocent.[52] Ejnar initiates this exchange:

> [You] always kept to yourself and never played
> With us.
> *Brand.* No, I was not at home

52. George Brandes, *Main Currents*, I, 128; compare the picture of himself Kierkegaard barely disguises in *Works of Love*, 195.

Among you southerners. I was
of another race, born by a cold fjord,
In the shadow of a barren mountain.
Ejnar. Is your home in these parts?
Brand. My road will take me through it.
Ejnar. Through it? You're going beyond this?
Brand. Yes, beyond; far beyond my home.
(M, B, I, 27)

The creative will, punished by the death of the new family, by the death of Brand himself, by returning home in the mind can find compensation for not, in the pathetic words of Frida, joining in the dance. Borkman's response to her, arrogant and ironically resonant in its context, nevertheless is Ibsen's: "What evens it up is that you've got ten times more music in you than all the dancers put together" (I, JGB, II, 969). By refusing to his art an escape from home, painfully registered in Osvald's return from distance, Ibsen makes of his exile a door to the Great World of depth. He believed in nothing so fervently as these words to Brandes:

> What I chiefly desire for you is genuine, full-blooded egoism, which shall force you for a time to regard what concerns you yourself as the only thing of any consequence, and everything else as non-existent. Now don't take this wish as an evidence of something brutal in my nature! There is no way in which you can benefit society more than by coining the metal you have in yourself.[53]

Distance freed from the past or enslaved by its guilt, by its public purpose, could never serve that medium.[54] Depth and distance, dialectically entwined, prevent theological aestheticism from reductively solving our rich oppositions in the manner of modern Christianity. Ibsen was early ready to revise Svanhild's underestimation of exile for spirit's sake:

> Oh, nothing is so easy as to follow
> the Bible's bidding, forsake hearth and home
> and seek the love that leads forward to God."
> (O.2, LC, III, 184)

For Ibsen, nothing was so difficult, so necessary.

As the struggles for social freedoms both blocked and prepared

53. Henrik Ibsen to Georg Brandes, September 24, 1871, in *Correspondence*, 218.
54. See Jung, *The Basic Writings*, 9, and Gaston Bachelard, *Poetics of Space*, trans. Maria Jolas (Boston, 1969), 205.

the way for the struggle for Freedom in Ibsen's plays, so too the question of rights, in the call to spiritual authority, screened and justified the retrogressive passion to make the childhood right. That the call had become more and more suspect since the Romantic age made it more and more imperative that Ibsen shackle it to guilt. Kierkegaard had settled for the epithet "no authority" attached to his authorship and exposed the perils of spiritual individuality gone wild in his *Book on Adler*. In the modern, reflective, self-conscious age, notes Kierkegaard, "the extraordinary has the dialectic not only of being the supreme salvation but also of being the worst corruption." Because of this dual beginning, so much like Ibsen's, the prophet must be as attentive as possible that "no one is harmed by a direct relation to his extraordinariness."[55] This warning is, of course, clearly appropriate for Brand. But it also backs Borkman into self-protective confession: "It's not easy to remember motives from the past" (*I, JGB, II,* 983). Indirection is Kierkegaard's humane and selfish shield as parody is Ibsen's. It was the only way the will could create instead of die through guilt. Like Kierkegaard, Ibsen had to raise misunderstanding from the domestic to the metaphysical plane, but with no faith at all in divine sanction. While praising *The Pretenders,* the secular and guiltlessly indignant Brandes, whose clear call to cultural authority Ibsen envied, enthusiastically spotted the metaphysical design of Ibsen's criticism of morality. He is awed by the Bishop's words to Skule, God's stepchild on earth: "The right is his, for he is the fortunate one. Tis even the summit of fortune to have the right. But by what right has Hakon the right and not you?" What a dimension opens here, raves Brandes, that dimension of depth from which morality is seen, like the homeland by an exile, from a distance:

> What depths must there not be in the mind of the poet who can conceive of a thing like that! At a single turn of the wrist, in a flash so rapid that the eye can scarcely follow it, Morality is thrown at the feet of Nature, the ethical dissolved in the metaphysical. "With what right did he obtain the right?" This question is an attempt to get behind Morality, to attack it in the rear, kill it from behind.[56]

In Brandes's view, Morality wins out, putting forth a double effort to overcome the attack by using the enemy's most dangerous word,

55. Kierkegaard, *Journals and Papers,* I, 97–98.
56. Brandes, *Henrik Ibsen,* 15.

right. This resistance, he notes, is the most telling difference between the world and time of Oehlenschläger's *Aladdin,* in which fortune and justice, life and morality, are rather simply reconciled, and Ibsen's more complicated age and genre.

Rousseau's transference of conscience from universal standards of judgment to private sentiment, his personal appropriation of virtue, had stimulated Diderot to question the scope and power of his moral authority.[57] The question, gathering around itself more and more anxiety through the nineteenth century, is intimately related to the problem, also raised to anxiety by Rousseau, of being at one and the same time exceptional and representative. The weightlessness and absurdity that threaten the modern hero who must be his own judge motivate Allmers to elision of the divine name. Relating to Rita his dream of a sound and happy Eyolf, he exclaims:

> Oh, how I thanked and blessed—*(checks himself.)*—Hm—
> *Rita (her eyes on him).* Whom?
> *Allmers (evasively).* Whom?
> *Rita.* Yes, that you thanked and blessed.
> *Allmers (deprecatingly).* I said I was only dreaming—
> *Rita.* One you don't believe in yourself?
> (*I,* LE, II, 910)

This confrontation, brought on by the dialectical stimulation of dreaming by judging, measures the distance of those who advance into waters deeper than the secure shallows of retribution, Providence, where they try to avoid the suffering that comes from joining creation and responsibility. At the threshold to a parody of this advancement, Solness must move past the secure worry that "The young . . . they're retribution" (*I,* MB, I, 811), even though his fall seems to prove it.

In *The League of Youth*—whose original subtitle, "The Almighty God and Co.," reflected the recourse of political to religious rhetoric—Aslaksen, complaining of his misfortunes, blames Daniel Hejre's bankruptcy, Providence, the Chamberlain, and the force of circumstances before he gets to himself. Ibsen sees his temptations here, but even more in the makeup of the lawyer Stensgaard who, "his mind, his character, his will, his talents, all pulling different ways" (*W.I,* LY, V, 126), seems to carry the uncertainty of political

---

57. Jean-Jacques Rousseau, *Emile; or, On Education,* trans. and ed. Allan Bloom (New York, 1979), 290.

conviction that makes him, especially in his successive courtships, a Holbergian allegory of fickleness.[58] He gave to Aslaksen the plaint against the bankrupt Hejre, modeled from Ibsen's father, along with parasitic attributes of self-pity and resentment. But, like Mortensgaard, Stensgaard is judged a man of future political success because "he's lucky enough not to be hampered by scruples or convictions or social position." Whereas Lundestad, by his own analysis, and the Chamberlain are "liberals for [their] own sakes," Stensgaard is more dangerous since he has the knack of being "liberal for other people's sake, too," the characteristic humane cover for personal ambition or evasion (*W. I*, LY, V, 129). This is not the joyous active leader longingly projected by Rosmer, but one who can act for others by avoiding the whole question of guilt. Aslaksen, the master displacer, educated in "the school of experience," in his next appearance in *An Enemy of the People,* thinks he can "not do any real damage to society" by supporting local authority (*I*, EP, III, 329), while Stockmann, the robust doctor of modern conscience (in this he is like the Ibsen of the cause of Scandinavianism), sees nothing *but* damage to society in the distinction between local and general interest.

Political action so often serves as a purifying conduit for guilty indignation that it can be deemed an extension of dreaming. Without the obstacle of self-judgment, it keeps us pinned to the small world, our backs to the great one. Like Flaubert, Ibsen felt that art could not directly and positively proclaim (and be heard), in the second half of the nineteenth century, the alliance of justice and beauty: "My opinion is that at the present time it is of no use to wield one's weapons *for* art; one must simply turn them *against* what is hostile to art."[59] He could not be a Bjørnson whose political activism stimulated his art, though he envied him. Here was a man of exceptional creative will who had, even without Ibsen's distancing, managed to be responsibly representative to his homeland and to humanity at large. Bjørnson believed those who identified him with Stensgaard enough to be seriously upset. But we might better see in Stensgaard a parody of Ibsen's own frustrating inability to invest his creative passions in social action. Ibsen could never be politically naïve enough, like Stockmann, nor so innocent, as to be a healer in his homeland above party and cabal. Nor could Ibsen hold the

58. Meyer, *Ibsen,* 313.
59. Henrik Ibsen to Lorentz Dietrichson, December 19, 1879, in *Correspondence,* 324.

Enlightenment's confidence in the common "judgment of every thinking man" (*I*, EP, III, 327). But by reversing his own exile from distance to re-entry, Ibsen puts us on notice that Stockmann's fate would have been his own if he had stayed at home instead of attacking the enemies of justice and beauty from a position privileged enough to demand that self-judgment accompany the judgment of others.

Both Stockmann and Ibsen, in their "restless, unruly, combative nature" (*I*, EP, II, 317), are dangerous animals, men of ideas, who burst into "print on all kinds of . . . subjects" (*I*, EP, I, 286–87; II, 317). The capability of the scientist to attack stupidity and deceit by analysis and appeal to the laws of evolution is the advantage both Flaubert and Ibsen wished for, the advantage of fighting for an unambivalent cause with an unambivalent weapon. But it is important to note that Stockmann boasts to his children about his new school, "You won't learn a blessed fact" (*I*, EP, V, 385), for facts can be suppressed and manipulated by hypocritical humane principles. If, with facts, Stockmann was, in the words of his wife, "in the right" but without power, would he be more effective as a genealogist of motives and a carrier of spirit? Could the artist join critical power to creative dreaming only by distance? Then would he engage and enjoin his exile? The split between dreaming and judging, creation and criticism, continues that between will and morality Ibsen experienced as a child. Only self-judgment could activate dreaming to a position of power free of the taint of mandarin escapism. Only the parody of missionary passion could make of the exceptional man's exile the representative man's medicine to his sick society.

When Lady Inger complains that "fate made me a woman, but burdened me with a man's work" (*O. 1*, LI, I, 284), she captures the feeling of Ibsen, who often put himself into the bodies of frustrated women hungering for power, concerning his guilty ambition. The identification with a woman helped him to explore the relationship between creativity, inhibition, and public action. In a conversation with Ernst Motz about *The Master Builder*, Ibsen spoke of Solness's elevation out of paralysis through the symbolic imagination and the need to pay for it with his body.[60] This secular version of Christian

---

60. Meyer, *Ibsen*, 727.

sacrifice is thoroughly parodied by the absence of worthy disciples and the irresponsible projection of a fantastic individualism. From that distancing, Ibsen's art comes into power. Rousseau brought prophetic criticism and healing together in his idealizing fiction; Ibsen did it through his parody. To take responsibility for his dreaming was to attack the aestheticism that, like Kierkegaard's crowd, was untruth. Politics' favorite authority for displacement of self-judgment, Providence, could support only the League of Youth (*W.I*, LY, V, 143). The individual, Kierkegaard's most reverent category, needed a knight of parody. In a letter of 1865, Ibsen speaks of how greatly exile helped him to drive out his native aestheticism, "as great a curse to poetry as theology is to religion."[61] For all his revolutionary contributions to the stage, Ibsen was a continual foe of the formalism that would see in art, not an agent of the Great World that did not need it, but an ultimate value.

The problems of authority and integrity in representation from a distance are persistently examined in Kierkegaard's literature. There, the poet-existence, like that of the preacher, abstracted from life itself and at peace in the Bible's fairy tales, is crucified: "To what extent should a person dare present the ideal of the Christian although he himself is so far from it? A poet-existence which is not at all related in striving to the ideal, but merely presents it, is one thing; it is something else actually to present the ideal which he himself is far from being."[62] The irony that keeps the wound open between being and writing, "word and action, will and task, life and teaching" assures also, in the plays, a gap between aesthetic morality and spiritual morality.[63] In every play the recourse to consoling phrases is immediately mocked, even by those whose own lives are propped by rationalizations. Borkman's resentment against

---

61. Henrik Ibsen to Bjørnstjerne Bjørnson, September 12, 1865, in *Correspondence*, 86. Compare Strindberg's comments on the Théâtre Libre: "a theatre where . . . one can get to see everything . . . what has so far been hidden behind theological and aesthetic veils" ("On Modern Drama and Modern Theatre," trans. Børge Gedsø Madsen, in Cole [ed.], *Playwrights on Playwriting*, 21). And compare the severe comment of Janko Lavrin (*Ibsen and His Creation*, 126): "Ibsen's creation of Art [could] never become creation of Life, but remained to the end only a stern criticism of Life."

62. Kierkegaard, *Journals and Papers*, I, 373.

63. Ibsen, Speech to the Norwegian Students, September 10, 1874, *Speeches and New Letters*, 50.

his wife is behind his put-down of Foldal's dream of a true and waiting woman: "Oh, cut that poetical rot!" (*I*, JGB, II, 978). When
the crushed Foldal asks, "You call my most sacred faith poetical
rot?" we recognize Ibsen's most cherished maneuver, the parodying
of his own ideals, and the parodying, further, of a moralizing patronization of them. The aesthetic projection of salvation comes
out of the dreaming that is lazy about self-judgment. Borkman,
himself a failed man of action, is given the authority to show up the
cheat of the poet-existence, immediately qualified by the delusion
of power and patronization: "It's the cause of your never having got-
ten anywhere in life. If you could only rinse your mind of all that, I
could still help you get on your feet—and to move ahead." Even
more surprising is to find the rebuke against the poet-existence in
the mouth of Torvald Helmer at the moment of his greatest moral
cowardice and Nora's greatest determination:

No more playacting.
(*I*, DH, III, 187)

Oh, quit posing. Your father had a mess of those speeches too.
(*I*, DH, III, 188)

Such double parody keeps Ibsen's judgment from the monolithic
and self-righteous prosecution that makes a tyrant of Torvald, and
from the dangers of Rousseau's dreams of an innocent language. By
making poetry judge itself, Ibsen frees it to a higher task of working
for the Great World. Freighted with full consciousness of its deceits, it can carry morality to myth and psychology to spirit. Because ascent must end in an absurd death, the impossibility of the
creative will's enslavement by Christian morality is even more fully
registered than it could be by the protest of a tragic heroism. Parody
allows Ibsen to extend the conflict between will and morality to its
farthest reaches, to render the tragic desperation of the struggle and
its comic excess. He uses Borkman's relentless "rage for power" (*I*,
JGB, II, 987) and turns its energies, in his hero's despite, to the art
that uses its aesthetic privileges for a world Borkman cannot enter.
It must be able to endure the distance between language and desire
opened up by irony, without sacrificing extension:

Borkman. All the sources of power in this country I wanted at my command. The earth, the mountains, the forests, the sea—I wanted to

subjugate all the riches they held, and carve out a kingdom for my-self, and use it to further the well-being of so many thousands of others.

Ella (lost in memory). I know. All those many evenings that we talked about your plans—

Borkman. Yes. I could talk with you, Ella.

Ella. I used to joke about your projects and ask if you wanted to wake all the slumbering spirits of gold.

Borkman (nods). I remember the phrase. *(Slowly.)* All the slumbering spirits of gold.

Ella. But you didn't take it for a joke. You said: "Yes, yes, Ella; that's exactly what I want."

(I, JGB, II, 986)

But Borkman can share, for a moment, the double vision of Scho-penhauer, even if he cannot profit from it:

Foldal. Oh, it's a terrible tragedy—

Borkman (nodding to him). I guess, almost as terrible as yours, when I stop to think about it.

Foldal (innocently). Yes, at least as terrible.

Borkman (with a quiet laugh). But from another perspective, it's really a kind of comedy, too.

(I, JGB, II, 976)

Many a theoretician of modern art has noted the inevitability in our age of an ironic curtailment of pure form, especially tragedy. In the wake of Hegel's aesthetic theories, of his analysis of the Roman-tics, Kierkegaard stands behind the by now much rehearsed recog-nition that "the modern predominance of comedy and irony" is the natural consequence of an age "built upon isolation and disjunc-tion," having "lost substantial categories of family, state, race."[64] The individual, without recourse to a higher authority, is reduced to an undramatic guilt and pain, paralyzed by remorse. The old dia-lectical relationship of the tragic hero flanked by a vigorous ethical and metaphysical universe, between guilt and innocence, individ-uality and fate, pain and sorrow, is lost to us and our art. Kierke-gaard can use this devolution to his advantage, for the knight of faith, as a stark spiritual individual, participates in the teleological

64. Kierkegaard, *Either/Or: A Fragment of Life,* trans. David F. Swenson and Lillian Mar-vin Swenson, with Howard A. Johnson (2 vols: Garden City, N.Y., 1959), I, 147.

suspension of the ethical. Nietzsche managed the loss by refusing to join the aestheticians who diluted Hegelian history into a nostalgic version of German Hellenism and by demanding a hard investigation of the relations between ethics and tragedy. Drawing on the vision of Schopenhauer and Wagner, he delegated to the high aesthetic sphere an indifference to morality that likens it, in paradoxical power, to Kierkegaard's religious sphere. With Ibsen, they both turned away from the temptation to use art as a palliative for life's terrible division and disappointments and knew that their overly powerful wills, however guilty, were the source of their creation and had to be represented in any transformation. None of them could really believe Schopenhauer's solace of art's power to liberate the will, nor could any of them revere tragedy "because its greatest function was to dispose one to resignation."[65]

Though tragedy was in Nietzsche's early view a beguiling compensation for the destructive evanescence of historical moments, revealing behind "the entire world of phenomena" the "sublime aesthetic joy in the heart of the original Oneness," it never denied the will's part in hoisting us to that height from which we could affirm the pain of existence without dying of it. Nietzsche's heroic diction of "joyful" and "powerful" overcoming opens for us a world, however fitfully and fictionally experienced, that asserts itself as value and courts the need he later mocked for the waiting world behind the world.[66] What interests us here as readers and watchers of Ibsen is the way in which a kind of Great World, far less immanent than Hegel's *Geist*, seems to detach itself in this ascent from the deaths and pains of the bodies that stimulate it. Its manifestation serves as a direct rebuke to the Christian world which sets itself against the fullness of life, makes desire guilty and spirit morally smug. To move morally beyond good and evil and aesthetically beyond pity and terror, Nietzsche's Dionysian tragedy, like the literature of Kierkegaard, had to make use of the suffering the will causes and meets. This keeps the "eternal wound of being" from premature healing by theology, aesthetics, and moral or rational explanations

65. Nietzsche, *Twilight of the Idols*, 82.
66. Nietzsche, *Birth of Tragedy*, 133, 24; M. S. Silk and J. P. Stern, *Nietzsche on Tragedy*, 294; Daniel Haakonsen, *Henrik Ibsen: Mennesket og kunstneren* (Oslo, 1981), 168; Nietzsche, *Birth of Tragedy*, 50, 142–43.

from the idea of a benevolent deity serving "the Socratic zest for knowledge."[67]

The older Nietzsche, mindful of the metaphysical seduction inherent in the early theory of tragedy, insists even more strongly on the price paid for saying yes to life "even in its strangest and sternest problems," for supporting the "will to life" that rejoices "in its own inexhaustibility through the *sacrifice* of its highest types." Ibsen more often wards off inherited or artificial solutions by subjecting to parody the missionary purity of the so-called highest types whose destruction, by the impotence of their sacrifice, provokes the great dimension we are never strong enough to enter. Arne Garborg early spotted the relationship between Ibsen's parody and poetry, but deemed his doubting soul as "not fully developed, not free," cowardly in the face of its mission. It is important to recognize how far Ibsen was exiled, as well, from resignation, adjustment, and acclimatization, or from the lowering of ideal expectations Relling advises.[68]

When Nietzsche says—even against those who view tragedy from only the moral perspective—that "this world can be justified only as an aesthetic phenomenon," he, like Ibsen, draws the poet from the Gyntish existence, the sterile remorse of Rubek, or the theological imperatives of Manders.[69] But Ibsen's Great World, for all its mythic scope and timelessness, aches with the psychological and historical origins of his exile, from which we see it in its evolutionary spiraling future like a planetary homeland going its way without us.[70] The distance that served as a creative ascent to the tragic philosopher and dramatist is registered in Ibsen and his scene as depth and often parodied as height. Detached from ethical

67. Nietzsche, *Birth of Tragedy*, 108. See also comment of Keith M. May in *Ibsen and Shaw*, 209: "Ibsen alone in modern times has something of the pre-Christian and pre-Socratic spirit. We misconstrue him and do so symptomatically or *morbidly* if we see him as a writer of social drama with a reformist message. Society in Ibsen is governed by nature. . . . It is we not Ibsen who assume that identifiable contemporary causes produce the passions of the characters rather than functioning just as occasions of those passions."

68. Nietzsche, *Ecce Homo*, 80 (recapitulating an argument of *The Birth of Tragedy* and *Twilight of the Idols*); Janko Lavrin, *Ibsen and His Creation*, 122; Meyer, *Ibsen*, 401. Rolf Fjelde's assumption that the late plays stretch uncomfortably toward life-denial is open to the charge that the Great World is never so well nurtured as by a silly ascent that ends by freeing it from the small world and from its agent, art ("The Dimensions of Ibsen's Dramatic World," in Haakonsen [ed.], *Second International Ibsen Seminar*, 176).

69. Nietzsche, *Birth of Tragedy*, 142–43.

70. Compare the words of Bolette (*I*, LS, III, 635).

choice and psychological guilt, distance becomes the favorite dimension of the Gyntian aesthete who needs a wide geography to escape from the terrors of depth. The psychological and artistic advantages of the dialectical relationship between distance and depth, so fully exploited in his greatest plays, cast suspicion on the common assumption that in *When We Dead Awaken*, Ibsen was lamenting his departure from his poetic and epic beginnings. He could have divided, like Flaubert, his punished from his liberated aesthetics, but he knew his power derived from their parodic joining.

The formalistic vengeance of severing life from art against the Christian severing of life from morality was not a choice that interested Ibsen.[71] Madame Bovary had well illustrated how the romance of Christian virtue stimulated low aesthetic sentimentality. The exile responsible to both self-realization and social criticism might have kept Ibsen free of the impure rebuke Manders, whose morality distances us from desires, dead ideals from living truths, launches against Osvald's exile: "It would really be tragic if distance and devotion to anything like art should dull his natural feelings" (*I, G, I,* 213). This is surely behind Ibsen's defense against accusations of coldness for his refusal to visit home: "Do not think that I lack the warmth of heart which is the first requisite where a true and vigorous spiritual life is to thrive." Manders's words, purified from his context, could have provoked the frequent identification of child killing with the killing of life by art, a merger mistakenly perceived as the emphatic reproach in *When We Dead Awaken.* Nietzsche fiercely separated artists from Christians who are "starvelings of life, who necessarily have to take things to themselves, impoverish them, make them *leaner.*" Like Nietzsche's philosophy, Ibsen's art hounded his body to death to affirm that his exile was not free to divide it from spirit, spirit from soul, a divorce that would famish both terms.[72]

71. Nietzsche (*Ecce Homo,* 134) uses the formula "Dionysus against the Crucified" to indicate how opposed to the creative will was Christianity.

72. Henrik Ibsen to Hedvig Stousland, September 16, 1869, in *Correspondence,* 178; M. C. Bradbrook, *Ibsen the Norwegian: A Revaluation* (London, 1966), 10; Arne Duve, *Symbolikken i Henrik Ibsens skuespill* (Oslo, 1945), 341; Nietzsche, *Twilight of the Idols,* 72; Nietzsche, preface to *The Gay Science,* 35; Nietzsche, *Thus Spoke Zarathustra,* 42. See also Ernst Cassirer, *An Essay on Man: An Introduction to a Philosophy of Human Culture* (New Haven, Conn., 1966), 143.

Exile chiefly, wrote Ibsen to Bjørnson, helped him to overcome the aestheticism he identified as both a natural folly of youth and the heritage of culture. Even Christ, seen through the hollowed hand, a view of the aesthete of primary emotion, could appear "an interesting phenomenon in the world's history." For high aestheticism, it is essential that "a poet by nature belongs to the farsighted." He sees home most clearly "from afar and during [his] absence."[73] But from his earliest plays—in one, for example, *St. John's Night*, written on a professional trip to the theaters of Copenhagen and Dresden, which he disclaimed but which clearly reflects his culture's infatuation with nationalism and the recovery of aesthetic resources—Ibsen sets in dialectical relationship the art that protects the small world and the art that would break through it. Poulsen is never more "aesthetic" than when he pretends to be creatively rescuing his country's past for the sake of both philosophical value and nature: "For my part, I regard goblins and fairies and the like as symbolic concepts which in the past wise men used to express ideas for which they did not have the correct abstract terminology. And nature is so interesting in consequence . . . so philosophically significant" (*O. 1*, SJN, I, 218). We do not need to wait to be educated by Ibsen's rough and rude importation, in his mature art, of folktale, ballad, and legend, circulating in the cities from the 1830s on, nor for their traumatic entry into an atmosphere that refuses the relaxed Heibergian blending of genre and discourse, to spot Poulsen's pretense of philosophical depth as a foppish pose.[74] With no power to transform, that character has to give up his love of a wood nymph when he is aesthetically put off by her tail. In a scene that reverses this rejection, the troll world, provisionally rising above national type, gains vengeance on Peer Gynt's aesthetic greed.

The flight from self-realization which is such a large purpose of Peer Gynt's poet-existence is here tagged as the discovery of "my original Self," "my primitive Self" (*O. 1*, SJN, I, 231). And when

73. Henrik Ibsen to Bjørnstjerne Bjørnson, September 12, 1865, in *Correspondence*, 86. Ibsen suggests that Bjørnson was never tempted by aestheticism: "You have never gone about looking at things through your hollowed hand" (107). Ibsen, Speech to the Norwegian Students, September 10, 1874, in *Speeches and New Letters*, 51.

74. See discussion of national heritage in Trygve Knudsen, "Phases of Style and Language in the Works of Henrik Ibsen," *Scandinavica*, II (1963), 3.

Poulsen asserts that anyone incapable of viewing life with a poetic eye is only half alive, we have to retort that anyone seeing life with only his kind of poetic eye is fully dead (O. *1*, SJN, III, 247). The distancing by fancy from the self, under the guise of recovering one's home and homeland, is an abuse exposed in all Ibsen's major plays where the rhetoric of self-realization abounds as a symptom of a displaced and distanced self. Hjalmar, who has never developed from the child so "clever at disclaiming other people's poems and ideas" (*I*, WD, V, 475), is farthest from himself when he recites, to cover up his thoughtlessness to Hedvig, "It's still our home. And I'll say this: it's good to be here" (*I*, WD, II, 420). And Torvald is, as well, when he periodically exclaims: "Ah, how snug and cozy it is here."

The artist who, even as a child, feared the waste of his powers in engagement, strangely links the memory of height and the imagination of punishment to the town square of Skien, specifically, to the view from the church tower into the barred windows of the town hall cells.[75] The privilege of seeing others from a distance, which courts the sin of aesthetic self-protection and fear of conflict, is recognized in all its ambiguity in Ibsen's poem of 1859, "On the Heights." A young man seeks solitude, like Allmers, and finds a stranger in the mountains. He looks down on his mother's home, which is burning, and borrows the aesthetic detachment of his friend who looks upon the terrible scene through his hollowed hand. In the same manner, he looks coolly upon a girl he had abandoned and knows he is now free of life's clutter and collisions:

> I am steeled, I am done with the lowland life.
> Up here on the heights are freedom and God.
> Men do but grope in the valley.[76]

The image of looking down upon the abandoned home is a favorite one of Ibsen in the earlier poems and plays before *Pillars of Society*. In *Olaf Liljekrans*, the hero reminds Alfhild that life may "shine like the stars of heaven/But only when seen from a distance" (O. *1*, OL, II, 509), and Brand looks down from the heights on his old home, remembering his lonely childhood:

75. Meyer, *Ibsen*, 29.
76. Translation by Michael Meyer, *Ibsen*, 185.

A heavy weight lies on me, the burden
Of being tied to another human being
Whose spirit pointed earthwards.

Now, as I approach my home, I find
Myself a stranger.
(M, B, I, 33)

In *Peer Gynt*, distance, the abandoned home, and the aesthetic view are clustered together in Act IV as Peer looks at the Sphinx through his cupped hand. Exile perilously courts a moral, psychological, and affective aestheticism, but without this temptation, the chosen fate would have little value for Ibsen.

By tying low aestheticism parodically around the neck of the modern call to being, like a stone, Ibsen keeps his art an investigator of origins, not its victim. The exile from home and the ascent into mountains make an intensely personal topography, but they play off the biblical and Romantic trajectories in which prophetic powers need distance. Dreamscapes of flying, climbing, and seafaring that Faust gives to Peer Gynt; the crossing of Alps and gazing into abysses; the Wordsworthian scene of what Abrams calls "the power-politics of vision" between the mind of man and Nature; the satanic temptation to possess all the glories of the world—all these are recognizable in Ibsen's texts.[77] But while the Romantic poets, like Nietzsche and D. H. Lawrence after them, successfully competed with biblical design in the quest for a new vision, Ibsen did not want to compete, drawing, instead, upon the deformation of biblical word and power by years of priestly abuse and bourgeois leveling in which religion had been damaged by sterile theologians, and art by aesthetic and rhetorical manipulations of morality. Ibsen might have asked, with Nietzsche and Lawrence, how spirit and morality, passion and purpose, ever became so split asunder, but he could never fashion a Zarathustra, overcoming his disillusioning descents from the mountain as a new Moses, a new Christ. The parodic chastening of Ibsen's climbers made them a "bridge," instead of a "goal," Nietzsche's imperative transformation in the task of

77. M. H. Abrams, *Natural Supernaturalism*, 448–62. See also F. D. Luke, "Nietzsche and the Imagery of Height," *Publications of the English Goethe Society*, XXVIII (1958–59), 94. Relevant commentary can be found in Durbach, *Ibsen the Romantic*, passim, and Northrop Frye, *A Study of English Romanticism* (New York, 1968), 33ff.

self-overcoming, but a bridge that only by its collapse leads us to the place where come to life "many gods . . . blissfully self-contradicting, communing again and belonging again to one another."[78]

While Zarathustra may be "ashamed that he still has to be a poet," we know that his parables serve reality. How are we to credit art's power to serve reality when it surfaces as an immature and romantic wish for another? "Vine-leaves in his hair" is murdered when it tries to open a future, humiliates wish into satire, as it is humiliated by parody. We surely feel the power of Herman Bang's claim that Hedda's home is elsewhere, but her distance, vitiated by the aesthetics of liberation, cannot find a true marriage with depth: "It's liberating to know that there can still actually be a free and courageous action in this world. Something that shimmers with spontaneous beauty" (*I*, HG, IV, 772).[79] The judgment that should give power over herself instead becomes the aesthetic evasion of having power over another. It is frozen, like Rubek's regret, in satire. Severed from responsibility, it can only seek to divide what the muse had joined, and the burning of the future is a fatal aesthetic betrayal of spirit, a symptom of the detachment of her judgment from self-judgment. The past communion of Løvborg and Hedda was really based upon confession rather than creation, on shared secrets of his licentious life, rather than mystery. When Hedda goads Løvborg into the test of self-control, it is still an aesthetic ethical stance she is after, the appearance:

> Hedda (*with a laugh*). Poor me, then I have no power over you at all?
> Løvborg. Not in that area.
> Hedda. But seriously, I think you ought to, all the same. For your own sake.
> Mrs. Elvsted. But Hedda—!
> Løvborg. Why do you think so?
> Hedda. Or, to be exact, for others' sakes.
> Løvborg. Oh?
> Hedda. Otherwise, people might get the idea that you're not very bold at heart. That you're not really sure of yourself at all.
> (*I*, HG, II, 742)

---

78. Lawrence, *Phoenix II*, 418; Nietzsche, *Thus Spoke Zarathustra*, 215.

79. Nietzsche, *Thus Spoke Zarathustra*, 215; Herman Bang, "Hedda Gabler," *Tilskueren*, IX, (1892), 827–38.

And as soon as she exults over the aesthetic picture of his self-control, she double-crosses the motive: "For once in my life, I want to have power over a human being" (*I*, HG, II, 745). Self-judgment, responsibility, and exile are hopelessly severed, but the destruction they submit to and stimulate by their frustration frees the Great World from those who would use it as a refuge for resentment and for beauty unburdened by the difficult dialectics of creation.

Because Hedda only dreams of spiritual freedom before her death, without working for it, her suicide can be but a parody of the tragic climax. Her body registers the unbearable sterility of her culture, but her consciousness is too afraid to investigate its origins. Thea and Tesman, the scribes of another's imagination, can free us only into a "progressive" future, but we need to find it by tracking desire back to its beginnings. Hedda's death may be to them a scandal, but not a stumbling block. The stage is sated with solutions, but Hedda's aestheticism has all the energy of a problem, even if she has to use her personal fate as an answer, and she generates a future beyond Tesman's ken.

Through Hedda and Løvborg, Ibsen's creation acknowledges the impure source of his best gifts and liberates them to their work. When Kierkegaard speaks of the torment of Moses in exile, a prophet who, we might assume, is sure of his call, he is surprised to find his own: "What a maiming it must be for an individual to be used in that way. . . . Moses is willing, he strikes the rock, but doubtingly, and as punishment—we imagine it, as punishment he does not get to enter the promised land."[80] What a maiming, we might echo, Ibsen subjects his characters to, and how fruitfully the punishment nurtures creation, forever short of the Promised Land. Hedda serves the Great World because Ibsen practices his torment in her; in Thea and Tesman, he finds only fixed patterns of his life's urges and compromises. We ought not think of Ibsen's self-investment in Tesman and Løvborg as of the same quality. If, as Arne Duve contends, Tesman represents the bourgeois life Ibsen settled for and Løvborg the idealized self he had betrayed, we must remember that Tesman is a cartoon of comfort because he harbors a minor attribute, but Løvborg, like Hedda, is punished because he carries the problems of art and spirit. We can easily assume that Ibsen ac-

80. Kierkegaard, *Journals and Papers*, VI, 3.

cepts the necessity of daemonic life-lies as the sum and substance of wisdom if we feel that he is in the shrewdly resigned body of Relling and the driving body of Gregers for the same purpose.[81] Julian's dream of the Third Empire beyond the mutual torture of pagan sensuality and Christian asceticism cannot allow *him* to profit from its historical distancing. The wounded eagles, wild ducks, and even birds of prey that flutter into the plays never represent the rich freedom of the Romantic bird soaring into the element.

A common critical opinion identifies these maimed missionaries with the life, in all its joy, art had been forced to sacrifice and waste.[82] Though Ibsen's well-documented sexual inhibitions flirted in his old age with charming youth, as if it were all too late, this kind of antithetical patterning of life against art is only a low aesthetic design. Its job is to bring to the surface the supreme value Ibsen attributes to the dialectical relationship between the parody of morality that represses desire and that of the mission that idealizes it.[83] The parody earns its power by its refusal to claim purity of party or purpose and by working only on potentially active agents. The celebrated and frequent cry in the plays for *livsglede*—the joy of happy, spontaneous, sensuous living—is *not* parodied, though it might be perverted in a Captain Alving or Løvborg, for it is a fixed standard and cannot really conduct us to the full world of richly constellated spheres. This is a sign that it is not, after all, Ibsen's highest value, but we can think of *livsglede* as an imperative preparation, like social liberties, for a higher struggle. Self-realization, brutally parodied, has infinite possibilities of expansion and direc-

81. Arne Duve, *Symbolikken i Henrik Ibsens skuespill*, 16. See also D. Russell Davis, "The Death of the Artist's Father," 140. In *The Real Drama of Henrik Ibsen* (Oslo, 1977), Duve's emphasis on superstitious numerology in the plays as ritualistic exorcism of past guilts is interesting and persuasive, but slights Ibsen's scorn of wallowing in retribution and exculpation. The complex dialectical use of the higher types considerably disturbs the notion of André Gide ("Evolution du théâtre," *Oeuvres complètes* [14 vols.; Paris, 1932–39], IV, 215–16) that Ibsen's Christian bourgeois heroes are condemned to wear "le triste manteau de nos moeurs." And it disturbs, as well, the contention of Austin E. Quigley ("Ibsen: A *Doll's House*," *The Modern Stage and Other Worlds* [New York, 1985], 92–114) that Nora's final scene sins against Ibsen's concern for an immanent solution to a sick culture, a solution like that of Mrs. Linde.

82. See, for example, Arne Duve, *Symbolikken i Henrik Ibsens skuespill*, 348: "John Gabriel selv er Ibsens misbrukte liv som har fatt sin straff." ("John Gabriel himself is Ibsen's misused life which has received its punishment").

83. This is one of the reasons we feel the strong subjective pressure in cool objective forms. See Maurice Valency, *The Flower and the Castle*, 123.

tion, but not *livsglede*. Mrs. Alving goes past her recognition of thwarted *livsglede* to a higher, more tormented medium, but it is obvious that she had to go through the recognition of its suppression. Life and art must be bound by guilt and lived through dialectically; *livsglede* is thrown out as an antithetical reproach to Manders's morality.

Nietzsche defined his philosophy as exile from the homeland that had "excommunicated by morality" everything that now seems "strange and questionable in existence." By choosing to live "in ice and high mountains," the philosopher has "learned to view the origin of moralizing and idealizing very differently from what might be desirable."[84] Such a simultaneous scrutiny of himself and society led Ibsen, in exile, to distance himself from the forms and styles cherished by a homeland enormously vulnerable to aesthetic idealizing. The complete abandonment of poetry for prose was provoked by many historical determinants between his trip to Copenhagen in the early 1850s, while still under contract to the Bergen theater, which exposed him to the theories of Herman Hettner on bourgeois drama, and the great message of Brandes, carried by his celebrated Inaugural Lecture of 1871. Hettner recognized the necessity and inevitability of the double demotion of the most honored and honest drama from regal and historical to bourgeois and social. As a representative of the new tragedy of idea, which could use ordinary people to register disaster brought on by social conflict, he singles out Friedrich Hebbel whose play *Maria Magdalena* (1843) had so gripped Ibsen that he confessed to a lasting and permanent impression. In his preface to the play, Hebbel had contended that "the theatre must never tire of repeating the eternal truth that an immoderately self-centered existence does not just accidentally produce guilt but necessarily and essentially entails it." This guilt, it is important to note, is detached from the Christian order of sin and spreads from the assertion of the will in a world of insecure authority, whether it emanates from "laudable or wicked aspiration."[85] The derivation of guilt from a disequilibrium larger than

84. Nietzsche, *Ecce Homo*, 34.
85. Friedrich Hebbel, "A Word About Theatre," trans. Joel Agee, in Herzfeld-Sander (ed.), *Essays on German Theater*, 79–80. See also comment of F. W. Kaufmann, "Ibsen's Conception of the Truth," in Rolf Fjelde (ed.), *Ibsen*, 26: "Every choice involves the rejection of other possibilities . . . so that guilt is inescapable."

what could be accounted for by simple ethics, planted by Hegel and Schelling, would feed the phenomenological aestheticians and philosophers of the future, but what counts for us is to imagine how closely this reading of the modern motive corresponded to Ibsen's desire to project a scene too great to be defined only in terms of the moral transgression the domestic confinement seemed to demand. In this sense, Ibsen's plays, like Racine's *Phèdre*, open mythical depths beneath inhibition.

Though we have no trouble attaching the paralysis of sick conscience in Ibsen's major characters to ethical violations, we also are fully aware of the inadequacy of ethics to measure responsibly the ambitious drive of the will past bourgeois morality. Neither Hettner nor Hebbel would dissolve the drama of psychological conflict in a world order or destiny. A metaphysically stranded psychic intensity, a guilty disequilibrium of the striving will, a moral restriction of life by social convention, carried by a prose that registers both the passion of impulse and the absurdity of life, would surely interest Ibsen, seeking a way out of the trap of nationalism and aestheticism. These were recognized by Brandes, whose internationalism and fervor for social problems virtually authored the liberal breakthrough, the Scandinavian *gjennembrud*, as the twin obstacles to Denmark's growth in art and attitude. Brandes's interests and bias had impressed Ibsen before the Inaugural Lecture, but this call to reform clearly reflected his own fears and hopes. He wrote to Brandes in 1872 of the volume the lecture appeared in: "No more dangerous book could fall into the hands of a pregnant poet . . . all development hitherto has been nothing more than a stumbling from one error into another. But the struggle is good, wholesome, and invigorating; to me your revolt is a great, shattering and emancipating outbreak of genius." Brandes targets Oehlenschläger's Aladdin as the hero of an aestheticism that must yield to a more complex moral and psychological character and scene, and his Nordic heroes he terms "too abstract and ideal to mirror . . . the age in which they were created." The aesthetic tradition of *Märchenlustspiel* and folk ballads promoted by Heiberg and sanctioned by Hettner stood behind a few of Ibsen's early plays that mixed fantasy and everyday reality, as the nationalistic sagas stood behind *The Vikings at Helgeland*. If we see the beginnings here of his great characters of the future, we are sympathetic to Bjørnson's complaint that the ballad and saga had burdened, rather than liberated, Ibsen's art with the language of dead poetry.[86]

Ibsen, himself, was impressed with the "living and colloquial language" of Bjørnson's plays A Bankrupt and The Editor, both printed in 1875. He was interested as well that their contemporary prose discussed contemporary problems. Brandes greeted the plays as the kind that would feed the long overdue breakthrough of Scandinavia to European culture at large, already knee-deep in realism and naturalism practiced by the novelist who, as Emile Zola contended, "no longer separates . . . characters from the air he breathes." Blasting away at the lethargy of Danish literature, Brandes proclaimed in his lecture: "What keeps a literature alive in our days is that it submits problems to debate. Thus, for example, George Sand debates the problem of the relations between the sexes, Byron and Feuerbach religion, John Stuart Mill and Proudhon property, Turgenev, Spielhagen and Emile Augier social conditions." What makes a literature dead is the low aestheticism that uses art for escape: "It deals not with life but with dreams. Like idealism and fear of reality in all literature, this trait is due to the fact that our poetry developed as a kind of solace for the very real troubles of a politically sick and corrupt period, as a kind of spiritual victory to compensate for the material defeat."[87] The call to a serious contemporary literature quite consciously puts the nice and cozy homeland on the defensive.[88] The greatest European writers "often lived like nomads and gypsies far from an orderly bourgeois existence"; Scandinavian writers have been influenced by "clergymen . . . or students of theology."[89] Like Ibsen, Strindberg, and Nietzsche, Brandes links low aesthetics and theology as killers of art and spirit.

While Brandes historically charts the value of poetry to the Romantics when it is leveled against society's philistinism, he contemporaneously reminds us of how much of existence has been hidden

86. Georg Brandes, "Inaugural Lecture," in Eric Bentley (ed.), Theory of the Modern Stage, 381; Henrik Ibsen to Georg Brandes, April 4, 1872, in Correspondence, 233–34; Harold O. Dyrenforth, "George Brandes: 1842–1927," Educational Theatre Journal, XV (1963), 143–44; Brandes, "Inaugural Lecture," 392; Meyer, Ibsen, 116, 168.
87. Emile Zola, "Naturalism on the Stage," trans. Samuel Draper, in Toby Cole (ed.), Playwrights on Playwriting, 10; Brandes, "Inaugural Lecture," 389.
88. Taking advantage of Brandes's lead, Holger Drachmann scandalized the middle class by mocking its smug and provincial comfort in his poem of 1872, "Ude og hjemme."
89. Brandes, "Inaugural Lecture," 394.

behind its diction when he asserts: "Wish is poetry; society, as it exists, is prose." The secularism of Brandes's idealism, which aimed at a revolution in social attitudes and structures, balked at the fanatic idealism of Brand which seemed to him an inevitable result of an unhealthy "enthusiasm for asceticism and positive religion." If the moral principles of Ibsen's hero were realized, it would cause "half of mankind to starve to death for the sake of an ideal." Like many commentators after him, Brandes responds to Ibsen's critical temper, but remains confused by its troubling ambivalences: "Does *Brand* stand for revolution or reaction? I cannot tell, there is so much of both in it." It is precisely this ambivalence that will continue to trap Ibsen's missionary spirit and give to his plays and his purpose the depth and integrity that so powerfully mark them. And we can see clearly the very particular use Ibsen made of Brandes's call to exile against nationalism and aestheticism, his call for a literature of social and political problems. Brandes's priority places the question of political freedom before that of a more subjective freedom of the will. It is precisely the old guard of Denmark's idealist traditions who will whine: "Why on earth do you want political freedom when the true freedom is the inner freedom of the will?"[90] Behind this ascription, we recognize Ibsen's links with the high spiritual idealism fathered by Kierkegaard. In the negative dialectical design that tempts so many readers into an identity between social and spiritual freedoms, Ibsen supports Brandes's preferred subject matter, but also obstructs it. The parodic tension between political and spiritual freedom that is so gripping in the plays from *A Doll House* to *Rosmersholm* owes its presence to Brandes's recommendation, but by no means follows it.

Kierkegaard's version of Brandes's formula, that Christianity is prose, not poetry, hence to be identified with the most authentic reality, is the kind of transvaluation that Ibsen provokes in order, while honoring Brandes's fierce antagonism to aestheticism and the poetry of idealism, to save the great Freedom from absorption by the small. Though what comes after understanding has a higher rank, for Kierkegaard, than what comes with it, his witty distinction between poetry and faith might sound like one Brandes could support: "Poesy is the illusion which precedes the understanding;

90. Brandes, *Main Currents*, II, 28; Brandes, "Inaugural Lecture," 395, 396, 398.

religiosity, the illusion which comes after the understanding." But Kierkegaard suggests, in fact, a more complex relationship between wish and society than that of Brandes, in his discussion of Oehlen-schläger's *Aladdin*. Fully aware of the perils for the life of spiritual choice of fairy tales in which fortune and misfortune make suffering accidental, Kierkegaard is, nevertheless, willing to endorse their intensity of wishing: "The reason why *Aladdin* is so invigorating is that this place expresses a genial and childlike audacity in the most extravagant desires. How many are there in our age who truly dare to wish, dare to desire, dare to address Nature with anything more than a polite child's please, please, or else with the rage of a lost soul."[91] Far more impure than Aladdin, Hilda still charms us by this quality and signals the unwillingness of Ibsen to reconcile the ideal with the daily even though he would, like Kierkegaard, insist on punishing it by making it live in bourgeois houses. And when Hilda's wish meets that of Solness, the communion of will and love, a provisional illusion of transference, can attempt the impossible: "Don't you believe with me, Hilda, that there are certain special, chosen people who have a gift and power and capacity to *wish* something, *desire* something, *will* something—so insistently and so—so inevitably—that at last it *has* to be theirs" (I, MB, II, 830).

In relation to the aesthetic wish, the ethical, as Brandes would agree, is defined as "the power to demand actuality." While there is a gap between the wish and demand, there is also a dialectical connection over it, so that they continue to stimulate each other to a richer sense of what we have, what we have lost, and what we might gain. If in the aesthetic fairy world of fortune and misfortune suffering is always accidental, in the ethical world of social problems there is some redress. But by choosing suffering, as the necessary exile of the will in the family and the world, the artist can extend the hope of changing "our whole conception of society" to a hope of keeping the Great World clear no matter how slow or impossible historical progress. Kierkegaard gives to Ibsen the use of the ethical world and the breach with it. The prose by which faith distances the poesy is the medium by which it manifests our gapped

91. Søren Kierkegaard, *Concluding Unscientific Postscript to the Philosophical Fragments*, trans. David F. Swenson and Walter Lowrie, ed. Walter Lowrie (Princeton, N.J., 1941), 408; Kierkegaard, *Either/Or*, I, 21.

reality. Johannes Climacus, "merely a humoristic experimenting psychologist," volunteers his services: "If then no one else can be found willing to bring together in exposition the absoluteness of the religious and the particularity of life, which togetherness is in existence precisely the ground and significance of the religious suffering, then I propose to myself the task." The alienating powers of irony assure the suffering of reality for Kierkegaard, as parody does for Ibsen.[92]

That is why the impulse of Scandinavia's Neo-Romantics of the 1890s to "put all the Old Guard under one roof," to confine Ibsen to a middle period that is misread as a sellout to Brandes's realism, is so outrageous.[93] Archer persuasively argues that we see a major turning point—away from the Scribean well-made play with its middle-class melodrama of secrets, letters, and quid pro quo of the first acts—in the last act of A Doll House when Nora orders Torvald to sit down. Here is the beginning, claims Archer, of the true Ibsen of his greatest period, ready to emerge as soon as he threw off the masquerade of French technique.[94] But, in fact, the true Ibsen had always lurked behind the contemporary scene and was certainly consciously playing mystery against secret, self-realization against a romance of self-sacrifice, spiritual depth against melodramatic suicide, from the very beginning of the play. The opening of a new moral and aesthetic dimension out of old measurements is, in fact, the major motion and meaning of A Doll House. The retention of the neat structures of the well-made play and clear gestures of melodrama's villainy and self-sacrifice as baffles against the design of desperate descent served to fashion an atmosphere charged with ethical and psychological complexity. The confinement of spirit in recognized rooms forced an enormous swelling of resonance in the tiered communication. Peter Brooks is surely right to link Ibsen with Balzac and James as one who forced theatrical melodrama to work for the deepening of consciousness: "Only Ibsen, who can be

92. Kierkegaard, Journals and Papers, I, 424; Brandes, "Inaugural Lecture," 397; Kierkegaard, Concluding Unscientific Postscript, 431.

93. Brian W. Downs, Modern Norwegian Literature, 1860–1918 (Cambridge, 1966), 10; see also George Steiner, The Death of Tragedy, 291. Steiner contends that Ibsen's middle period is not true tragedy because remedies are suggested.

94. Archer on Ibsen, 132. Meyer, Ibsen, 136–37, insists rightly, I believe, on the dominating influence of Holberg and Shakespeare for these effects.

said to have reinvented in the structure of the well-made play some of the intense ethical concern of melodrama—transmuted in his late plays into the melodrama of consciousness—offered a valid contemporary example." The melodrama of "hypersignificant signs" that opens the plane of representation to a new dimension, is, actually, present from A Doll House on and a testimony to Ibsen's determination to make prose carry both the criticism and spirit dissipated by a self-conscious aestheticism and a priestly moral rhetoric. Ibsen's poetry of realism, already in A Doll House, played a growing anxiety against a late point of attack, the descent into childhood against the childish games on the surface.[95]

Haakonsen makes the necessary contrast: "With Scribe, dialogue may be exciting or piquant on the stage because someone is standing behind a door or a curtain. But Ibsen's dialogue may be exciting because his characters may be hiding behind their words, hiding behind the thoughts or plans they express in their speeches."[96] This drama of dimension on Scribe's stage is the sign that Ibsen knows, like Zarathustra, that he must still be a kind of poet of parables in a society neither spiritually nor aesthetically ready for the Great World. Though Scribe can foil contemporary faults, he is thoroughly at home with them. Kierkegaard describes his lack of moral passion, his spirit of adjustment to the times: "This is approximately Scribe's frame of mind: he does not hate the good; on the contrary, he presumably holds it in high honor, even with a certain abstract enthusiasm, but he does not want anyone to be good. His enviousness does not want such a thing, since he himself does not strive in the good."[97] It is the urge to enlarge the world for will that

95. Peter Brooks, The Melodramatic Imagination: Balzac, Henry James, Melodrama and the Mode of Excess (New Haven, Conn., 1976), 161, 29, 125, 195. Brooks notes the connection, in James, between the renunciation of melodrama and the temperamental attraction to it.

96. A major point in Daniel Haakonsen's book, Henrik Ibsens Realisme (Oslo, 1957) is that Ibsen's realism is no block to deeper levels of exploration. The more profound tragic design of The Wild Duck is dependent upon the social realism of the surface. See also Sandra E. Saari, "Rosenvold and Rosmersholm: Protagonist Implies Interpretation," Contemporary Approaches to Ibsen: The Fourth International Ibsen Seminar, 1978 (Oslo, 1979), 106. See also Joseph Roach, "Ibsen and the Moral Occult," in Telling Right from Wrong: Morality and Literature (St. Louis, 1987), and Jens Arup, "On Hedda Gabler," Orbis litterarum, XII (1957), 18: "So far from providing an entertaining diversion, the farcical and melodramatic touches prevent us from side-tracking the seriousness at stake."

97. Kierkegaard, Journals and Papers, I, 42. For a discussion of the relationship between the well-made play and Ibsen's deformations, see Cary M. Mazur, "Ibsen and the Well-Made Play, in Yvonne Shafer (ed.), Approaches to Teaching Ibsen's A Doll House (New York, 1985), 69–75. See also Irving Deer, "Nora's Uncertainty," in the same volume, 86–90.

is missing in Scribe, and it is this goad in Nora that connects her more, in the sound opinion of Iselin Maria Gabrieli, with Brand than with the social realism of Brandes, Augier, and Dumas *fils*. The same lack of intensity and depth leads Dumas *fils* to an aesthetic didacticism. In the face of the educational deformation of his nervous century, Dumas in no way exhibits signs of a frustrated or indignant will: "I am neither God nor an apostle, neither a philosopher nor a mountebank. I am someone who walks by, who looks, who sees, who feels, who reflects, who hopes, and who says or writes what hits him in the simplest and most immediate form, the most adequate for what he wants to say." We could hardly be further from Ibsen's temperament. Because Dumas *fils*'s energy, claims Henry James, "was not fed from the imagination," not one of his characters "has known the little invisible push, that even when shyly and awkwardly administered, makes the puppet, in spite of the string, walk off by himself and quite 'cut,' if the mood takes him, that distant relation to his creator." The effect is like that of a "guest arriving to dine accompanied by constables." James clearly sees the debt of Ibsen to Dumas *fils*, whose wit and sharp reading of social falsities supported the earnest reforming interests of realism: "The energy that went forth blooming as Dumas has come back grizzled as Ibsen." But who could doubt that James identifies Ibsen, and himself, with the poets when he launches this metaphorical contrast between the vaguer masters and the splendidly specific Dumas:

> His terrible knowledge suggested a kind of uniform—gilt buttons, a feathered hat and a little official book; it was almost like an irruption of the police. The most general masters are the poets, with all the things they blessedly don't hold for so very certain and all the things they blessedly and preferably invent.[98]

Yet many a master has missed this constant attribute of Ibsen's realism. Gide, eager to use his art to reclaim the generosity of pagan heroism in society's despite, complains of Ibsen's confining of the creative will in the dollhouses of Norway: "The playwright condemns his heroes when he puts on their shoulders the melancholy cloak of our manners and morals." By this punishment, he would

98. Iselin Maria Gabrieli, *Rilettura di Ibsen* (Naples, 1977), 58; Alexandre Dumas *fils*, preface to "Le Fils naturel," *Théâtre complet d'Alexandre Dumas fils* (8 vols.; Paris, 1890–98), III, 10 (my translation); James, *The Scenic Art*, 275, 277, 278.

seem to cooperate with Christianity's leveling of character. Whatever his debt to Hugo's grotesque mixtures of tone and class, mood
and sign, Ibsen could hardly think of the theater as an imitation of
God's creation of full color and desire in an age whose greatest writers associated Christianity with the long suppression of sensuality
and spontaneity, the double nature of man, with the banishment of
the Great World. How could a Christianity that had, by Ibsen's
day, sentimentalized and deformed life and art, lead poetry to truth?
Ibsen's psychological, physical, spiritual, aesthetic exiles—so closely
tied to home and homeland and so ardently straining towards the
Great World—could never find their way to the ancient and mythological past Flaubert and Gide used as an escape from their own
realism, nor to the Christian world of Claudel. Yeats, like Gide,
feels in Ibsen's atmosphere a masochism of deliberate confinement,
but he unwittingly pays homage to a larger world waiting to be lived
in:

> At the first performance of Ghosts, I could not escape from an illusion
> unaccountable to me at the time. All the characters seemed to be less
> than life-size; the stage, though it was but the little Royalty stage,
> seemed larger than I had ever seen it. Little whimpering puppets moved
> here and there in the middle of the great abyss. Why did they not speak
> out with louder voices or move with freer gestures? What was it that
> weighed upon their souls perpetually? Certainly they were all in prison,
> and yet there was no prison. In India there are villages so obedient that
> all the jailer has to do is to draw a circle upon the ground with his staff,
> and to tell his thief to stand there so many hours, but what law had
> these people broken that they had to wander round the narrow circle all
> their lives.

That Yeats associates this scene with Ibsen's cruel realism and his
resistance to poetry is clear when he adds: "May not such art,
terrible, satirical, inhuman, be the medicine of great cities, where
nobody is ever alone with his own strength?" The threshold of the
Great World vigorously opened by the unbearable conjunction of
confinement and full consciousness cannot compensate Yeats for an
art that fails to feature "the soul rejoicing in itself; the faith in mas-
terful spirits and energy of the soul."[99]

99. André Gide, "L'Evolution du théâtre," 215–16 (my translation); Victor Hugo, preface to Cromwell; W. B. Yeats, "Language, Character, and Construction," in Cole (ed.),
Playwrights on Playwriting, 40.

Like Kierkegaard, Ibsen knew that in an age ruled by the tyrannical sentimentality of aesthetic morality, the necessary art was
"the art of taking away": "When a man has his mouth so full of food
that he is prevented from eating, and is likely to starve in consequence, does giving him food consist in stuffing still more of it in his
mouth, or does it consist in taking some of it away, so that he can
begin to eat?" That is parody's job, but it is also the job of the temper urged on Ibsen by Brandes, to whom he boasts that he had already, in *The League of Youth*, taken away monologues and asides.
Brandes, who knew that during his Italian years (1878–1885) Ibsen
had learned "to economize in all ways, with his money, his working
material, time and person," might have wanted to advise him, like
the friends of Flaubert, to put his lyricism on dry bread and "to en-
dow art with the pitiless method, with the exactness of the physical
sciences."[100] If Socrates's science, the art of taking away in Nietzsche's view, had destroyed myth, "displaced poetry from its native
soil," rendering it "homeless," it might, in the hands of the homeopathic artist, be just the medicine needed for the provinces and
cities. Doubtlessly, the new prose that protests against true poetry's
exile is in a risky business. Because of the lost world it avenges, it is
the mask of "profound spirit." Unamuno congratulates himself on
not having viewed Ibsen on stage, for he would have been put off by
the vulgarity of scenes like the stocking seduction that also made
James uncomfortable. But James knew that while one of Ibsen's
"rude and indelicate" hands kneaded "the soul of man like a paste,"
the other was busy drawing spiritual and psychological depth out of
a rough and realistic surface: "His recurrent ugliness of surface, as it
were, is a sort of proof of his fidelity to the real, in a spare, strenu-
ous, democratic community; just as the same peculiarity is one of
the sources of his charmless fascination . . . he squeezes the attention till he almost hurts it, yet with never a conciliatory stroke."[101]

100. Kierkegaard, *Concluding Unscientific Postscript*, 245; Meyer, *Ibsen*, 311; Haakonsen,
Henrik Ibsen: Mennesket og kunstneren, 138. This was the advice of Maxime du Camp and
Louis Bouilhet, who urged Flaubert to turn to his bourgeois subject; see Francis Steegmuller,
Flaubert and Madame Bovary (Boston, 1970), Part III. See also Gustave Flaubert to Mademoi-
selle Leroyer de Chantepie, March 18, 1857, in *Selected Letters*, 195.

101. Nietzsche, *Birth of Tragedy*, 104–105; *Beyond Good and Evil*, 51; Miguel de Unamuno, *Mi religión y otros ensayos breves* (Buenos Aires, 1942), 58; James, *The Scenic Art*, 252,
248.

The desire to have his characters speak the language that is sufficient unto their day, avoiding the declamation that would, in Kierkegaard's words, be "insufficient, because it is so abstract in comparison with existing, in the sense which this has in reality," would seem once more antagonistic to spiritual possibilities. Yet, like Kierkegaard, Ibsen takes away in order to fatten, and the hypocritical Sunday orator, who gives us "Sunday glimpses into eternity," is as deformed by idealizing theology as the homeland poet by the low aesthetics of provincial and pastoral celebration. The preacher must learn that it is "precisely with the living-room he has to do," the dramatist that he must present "a human being as he is in daily life." This spatial and linguistic confinement and deprivation on the stage of parodied idealism puts the needed dialectical pressure on the small world to yield a portion to depth. The enormous intensity of Ibsen's spare atmospheres has frequently been noted. James and Joyce found it spellbinding. And Brandes speaks of the way Ibsen can get away with absurd premises and gaps by airtight construction and concentration against the competing prisons of morality: "In order to keep the reader in the atmosphere of the drama, Ibsen has to expend prodigious care in the sealing up of all its doors and windows, so that not a breath of every-day common sense may penetrate into it. Were this to happen, the spell would be broken." He risked, thereby, foolishness—the mark, to Chekhov, not only of saints but of "emancipated thinker[s]." [102] Here is a rich Kierkegaardian dialectic between the Sunday and daily demand that invigorates what Yeats felt as an absurd captivity. The absolute is always in danger of becoming fantastic, aesthetically and theologically, if it does not throb in constrained and relative contexts. Ibsen responds to literalists of Brand's religion: "The demand 'All or nothing', is made in all domains of life—in love, in art, etc." Since this call to the absolute is the best part of Ibsen, his art must suffer the degradation of his guilt and inadequacy, do its work in bourgeois living rooms. For art to carry the difficult love, once joined to power in the Bible where it was free of aesthetic and theological distortion, it must endure the terrible tension between relative contexts and absolute impulses, both aggravated and protested by par-

102. Kierkegaard, *Concluding Unscientific Postscript*, 415–16; Brandes, *Henrik Ibsen*, 112; Anton Chekhov, "Advice to Playwrights," in Cole (ed.), *Playwrights on Playwriting*, 23.

ody. Ibsen, by this means, advances on that Third Empire which does not have to use art to generate "a new category . . . a new vital force of which we who live not can have no clear conception." There, poetry, philosophy, and religion will be liberated into life and free of that sick idealism that burdens them in an overly moral world. [103]

In a section of *The Will to Power* entitled "Toward a Critique of the Big Words," Nietzsche attributes to aesthetic morality the inevitable fate of higher feelings to become, themselves, a *source* of "misfortune and . . . loss of value." [104] When philistine priests of the provinces measure spirit by a diction and expectation of progress, our vocabulary of value is benighted and protective. Ibsen continually went back to the rhythms of the Bible's prose to recover a power immune to the aesthetics and theology of modern guilt. [105] When they appear in the plays, they must show up the political and psychological contexts that distort them and remind us of the inadequacy of our poetry to express spiritual depth and breadth. Here then, once more, is a reason to take away in order to feed. Suppose we emphasized in our art, which prides itself on being adequate to the imagining of the elves, fairies, trolls, and mermaids of national legends and stories, a diction that is "deliberately inadequate" especially when it strives for beauty and spirit, so that the poverty of our vocabulary of value, and its gradual breakdown, might reflect the sickness of our glib culture, the passion of our lonely need, the presence of a world we are not yet ready to enter. [106] Like the Words-

103. Henrik Ibsen to Peter Hansen, October 28, 1870, in *Correspondence*, 199; Speech at the Banquet in Stockholm, in *Speeches and New Letters*, 56–57. See also Johnston, *The Ibsen Cycle*, 74.

104. Nietzsche, *Will to Power*, 50.

105. In a letter to Bjørnstjerne Bjørnson, September 12, 1865 (*Correspondence*, 86), Ibsen writes from Ariccia in Italy: "It is delightfully peaceful here; we have no acquaintances; I read nothing but the Bible—it has vigour and power."

106. In *The New Spirit* (New York, 1930), 129–30, Havelock Ellis speaks of Bjørnson's enthusiasm for Norwegian color and life in fancy and fact and his belief that the ideas of the people are, consequently, "unmeasured." Johnston, *The Ibsen Cycle*, refers to the Hegelian standard of "inadequate" in speaking of the education of civilization towards consciousness, but Bradbrook, *Ibsen the Norwegian*, is more to the point when she notes that Ibsen heralds Beckett and Pinter by using a deliberately inadequate speech (152). Eric Bentley (*The Life of the Drama* [New York, 1965], 96) notes, "Ibsen should be credited with the invention of an anti-poetry. He made a fine art of the understatement, the evasion, the unfinished sentence. In a sense, his writing undercuts poetry—and reduces it to triviality." Northam, *Ibsen*, 181, suggests that society's prose has chased Hedda's poetry into depth.

worthian turning from a moral diction of the eighteenth century to a studied vagueness groping for a deeper response to ambivalent feelings, Ibsen's choice of an allusive, impressionistic, and fragmented speech, though never free from parodic shadowing, sounded a depth beneath the smooth surface of control. [107] It reminds us that his characters are possessed either by a dead language that uses them or by one impulsively and ardently moving toward a larger life.

Despite the defensive scorn of Hamsun and Strindberg, Ibsen clearly anticipated the interest of the naturalistic theater in ridding the stage of declamation for a spoken language and of the symbolist theater in finding impressionistic gesture and silence. If Ibsen could only ironically agree with Zola that "there is more poetry in the little apartment of a bourgeois than in all the empty, worm-eaten palaces of history," his parody could certainly exploit the assumption. The atmosphere of *The Master Builder* might surely have drawn from a general interest in the unconscious suffusing the symbolic pastorals of Norwegian fiction and the manifestos of 1890:

> Among more and more people who live a strenuous intellectual life and who are sensitive of temperament, strange kinds of psychological activities often arise. These may be quite inexplicable sensory states: a dumbfounded, causeless rapture, a breath of psychic pain, a perception of having been spoken to from afar, from the air, from the sea . . . a sudden, unnatural revelation of hidden kingdoms.

Ibsen's drama accommodates the languages of these atmospheres, and *The Wild Duck* and *Rosmersholm*, particularly, anticipate what those who deemed him old-fashioned promoted. Maeterlinck was perhaps within his rights to use *The Master Builder* as the most splendid example of the symbolist theater. The taking away of unproblematic confidants had stranded Gregers and Hjalmar, Borkman and Foldal, in parodic misunderstanding and had, in Lukács's view, introduced a "new element into the dialogue": "What is said becomes ever more peripheral to what is not expressible. The melody in dialogue is ever more submerged in the accompaniment, the openly spoken in the allusion, in silence, in effects achieved by pauses,

---

107. See Georg Lukács, "The Sociology of Modern Drama," 156.

change of tempo, etc." Maeterlinck greatly admired the subtext of Ibsen's play which is spun out under the conversation:

> Side by side with the necessary dialogue will you almost always find another dialogue that seems superfluous; but examine it carefully, and it will be borne home to you that this is the only one that the soul can listen to profoundly, for here alone is it the soul that is being addressed. . . . One may even affirm that a poem draws the nearer to beauty and loftier truth in the measure that it eliminates words that merely explain the action, and substitutes for them others that reveal, not the so-called "soul-state," but I know now what intangible and unceasing striving of the soul toward its own beauty and truth.[108]

The poet, as Maeterlinck calls the dramatic author, gives us a language in which inner and outer dialogue are fused. But the symbolist gives us, too, the kind of static theater that has such difficulties on the stage and that marks so much impressionist drama. It tends to a new version of the aestheticism Ibsen despised. The re-mythologizing and visionary Yeats may have linked Ibsen with Maeterlinck in their rich compensation for a missing multitude, symbolic emanation, but in fact, Ibsen's subjection of all symbolic emanation to parody whenever it rises in bourgeois houses, his mode of giving it value, is what dramatizes both the atmosphere and language to an intense dialectic between represented anxiety and authorial indignation. The wild duck is cursed as a symbolic Christ by Gina, loved by Hedvig for her deep sea life and longing, and is altogether immune to the small world that continually bothers her. The rude entrances and exits of character and levels of diction measure the breach of understanding that is Ibsen's favorite device for disturbing poetry into prose, for spoiling reconciliations and mediations, what Kierkegaard called the "fantastic language of fantastic beings." His counterpointing is a deliberate "crucifixion of the understanding." It registers the aesthetic, moral, and psychological disjunction between Rubek's words, "The world knows nothing; understands nothing" (*I*, WWDA, I, 1035), and the last line spoken

108. Emile Zola, "Naturalism in the Theatre," in Bentley (ed.), *The Theory of the Modern Stage*, 365; quoted in Harald Beyer, "The Neo-Romantic Reaction," *A History of Norwegian Literature*, trans. Einar Haugen (New York, 1956), 251; Georg Lukács, "The Sociology of Modern Drama," 156; Maurice Maeterlinck, "The Tragic in Daily Life," in Cole (ed.), *Playwrights on Playwriting*, 33.

by the father in Hebbel's *Maria Magdalena* that Ibsen so admired: "I no longer understand the world." [109]

When Ibsen formally distanced himself from his own poetry and poetic ambitions in drama for the sake of his multi-leveled prose, Brandes wondered whether or not "some time during the battle of life, a lyrical Pegasus" was killed under him, and many readers have read into his last plays an aching remorse over the decision to aban-don epic poetic form. But I think it more likely that the disjunctive rhythms of his prose, as he grew more and more secure in relation to the perils of aestheticism, theology, and nationalism, became such a supple instrument of criticism and evocation that they absorbed the symbolic and formal values of his poetry, which might have died from his brutal parodic assaults. In international fiction, of course, the general diffusion of plot by subtle perspectives was at least as striking a tendency as in the drama. Maeterlinck might have decided this: "I have come to believe that an old man sitting in his armchair, simply waiting by his lamp, listening unconsciously to all the eternal laws which reign around his house . . . is living in reality a deeper, more human and more universal life than the lover who strangles his mistress, the captain who wins a victory, or the 'husband who avenges his honor.'" [110]

But the novel takes the position up with a vengeance. In his preface to A *Portrait of a Lady*, James argues for the new kind of adventure, Isabel's great meditative vigil:

> Reduced to its essence, it is but the vigil of searching criticism; but it throws the action further forward than twenty "incidents" might have done. It was designed to have all the vivacity of incident and all the economy of picture. She sits up, by her dying fire, far into the night, under the spell of recognitions on which she finds the last sharpness suddenly wait. It is a representation simply of her motionlessly *seeing*,

109. William Butler Yeats, "Language, Character, and Construction," in Cole (ed.), *Playwrights on Playwriting*, 43; Kierkegaard, *Concluding Unscientific Postscript*, 110, 496; Meyer, *Ibsen*, 117.

110. Meyer, *Ibsen*, 331; Brustein, *The Theatre of Revolt*, 65; Marvin Carlson, *Theories of the Theatre: A Historical and Critical Survey, from the Greeks to the Present* (Ithaca, N.Y., 1984), 296. See also Maurice Valency, *The Flower and the Castle* (385): "Maeterlinck dis-places reality and ends up conventional. Ibsen's mystery rises out of the real. It is the poetry of life itself." In *Script into Performance: A Structuralist View of Play Production* (Austin, Texas, 1977), 153–72, Richard Hornby discusses the relationship between Ibsen's realism and sym-bolism in this context. See also *Archer on Ibsen*, 136: "His analysis has all the thrill of adven-ture, all the fascination of permanence."

and an attempt withal to make the mere still lucidity of her act as "interesting" as the surprise of a caravan or the identification of a pirate.

The modern novel, as Bakhtin has anatomized it, is the usurping genre that gains its power from its vigil of searching self-criticism. His theory of the "novelization of genres" in modern literature accommodates the Ibsen form and strategy of dialogue between criticism and poetry, parody and "a new world still in the making." Most evident in his texture is the counterpointing heteroglossia of tiered and plagiarized communication Bakhtin sees as a sign of subversion of the glib and closed formulas of a tyrannical and philistine society. As much as Lawrence and Joyce, the bourgeois Ibsen was destroying bourgeois form, genre, and style.[111]

It is quite surprising, then, to have to list as one of the most common complaints against the Ibsen texture that it suffers from a poverty of diction and crudeness of expressive language. It was not merely in translation that Ibsen seemed a message man because his language did not lure contemplation. The art of taking away positively lured misunderstanding. Even Strindberg, an exuberant parodist of *A Doll House*, had to admit that the misreading of Ibsen proved "the dangers of writing literature." Yeats felt impelled to ask: "Ibsen has sincerity and logic beyond any writer of our time . . . but is he not a good deal less than the greats of all times because he lacks beautiful and vivid language?" Joined to the scorn of his vulgar scene and surface, this lament had wide support. M. C. Bradbrook is right to protest the glib ignorance of loss in translation that mutes the powerful tension between the harsh economy of his Nordic diction and the psychological subtlety and depth of his texture: "Instead of the scented, coloured opulence of the multifoliate rose, it has the austere unchanging tenacity of the mountain pine. Instead of the play of metaphor, it offers riddling understatement, or ironic implication."[112]

Though it would be impossible to think of Ibsen's style, in any

111. James, preface to *Portrait of a Lady*, 14; M. M. Bakhtin, *The Dialogic Imagination: Four Essays*, trans. Caryl Emerson and Michael Holquist, ed. Michael Holquist (Austin, 1981), 39, 5, 7. In his *Theory of the Modern Drama*, trans. Michael Hays (Minneapolis, 1987), 16–18, Peter Szondi claims the novelization forced Ibsen to murder characters by forcing them to speak, publicly, thoughts that belonged in a novel.

112. Strindberg, *Getting Married*, 48; W. B. Yeats, "Language, Character, and Construction," in Cole (ed.), *Playwrights on Playwriting*, 38; Bradbrook, *Ibsen the Norwegian: A Revaluation*, 88.

period, as baroque, the development from aesthetic variety and nationalistic scope to the increasing economy and concentration of his art has a design similar to that of Borges:

> So that I began by being very complex, I wallowed in newfangled words or archaic words, and I wrote in a very complicated way. Now I do my best to be simple, since I know that things are complex. So that even if my sentences are simple, the meaning is never simple, since the world is not a simple thing, but a very complex thing. I think I began by being baroque, by being a seventeenth century writer by attempting to be Shakespeare. We all do that, I suppose. But now, I fall back on being my self. I try to record with dictionary words.[113]

By his parody, Ibsen burns through that bourgeois language of "point of view" Yeats scorned, to the classless and universal level the poet aimed for.

More than one critic has suggested that the grand ambition of *Emperor and Galilean*—a play Ibsen insisted was a crucial undertaking, but that critics deem at best an "enormous flawed adventure into the philosophy of history"—raised his argument permanently to its full spiritual height.[114] But when he forced the demand for spiritual expansion into the small bourgeois living quarters of his contemporary world, he gained a dialectical and dramatic dimension, resonant with collisions and assaults, that orphaned the silly beauty of the refrains of desire. He found a form and a diction that could represent and counterexile. We think of the stranded bits of adolescent and proverbial poetry unable to expand into mature language without a world in which to exercise: "the depths of the sea" ("havsens bunn"), "the forest will have its revenge" ("Skogen hevner"), "with vine-leaves in his hair" ("Med vinlov i håret"), "your gold and green forest" ("med ditt gull og med dine grønne skoge"), "the slumbering spirits of the gold" ("Alle gullets slumrende ånder"). And, though their simplicity shows up rehearsed rationalizations, we are amazed that Arthur Symons could think they

---

113. "Borges Discusses Emily Dickinson," in Carlos Cortinez (ed.), *Borges the Poet* (Fayetteville, Ark., 1986), 17.

114. See, for example, Rolf Fjelde, introduction to Fjelde (ed.), *Ibsen*, 8. See also Johnston, *The Ibsen Cycle*, 50–51; Johnson contends that, with a widening vision fed by Hegel, Ibsen saw the "well-made play" as a "dollhouse."

were, in their contexts, Ibsen's idea of beauty.[115] There is the poetry, as well, of failed dreams that overcomes the humiliation it attracts and releases the Great World by its homelessness.

The misuse of power and the unpardonable sin of killing love in a human heart considerably maim the imagination with bad faith, but do not annihilate its value for our journey:

> Borkman. I only remember that when I was alone then, struggling in silence with all the vast projects that would be set in motion, it seemed to me almost as if I were a voyager in the air. I walked the sleepness nights, inflating a huge balloon that would sail out over a shadowy, perilous ocean.
> (I, JGB, II, 984)

Nor does Rita's grounding of Allmers in earthbound remorse block the lyric of power of Allmers's claim of attachment to the Great World, an interiorization of Eyolf's death: "We've some part of the sea and the stars in us too, Rita" (I, LE, III, 929). The poetry of depth is even more spare than that of extension and returns us to the wonder of the child's world with "no demands, and no dreams" (I, R, III, 555). Parodic context and lyric abbreviation keep these evocations segregated from the automatic politics of aesthetic morality, the sentimental rhetoric of the nice cozy home. The insistent incremental climbs of desire and justification stopped suddenly by guilt, the hammering bullets of demonstrative pronouns, the longing aborted by expletive, give short but all the more powerful shrift to a poetry struggling towards authenticity. Solness is unchained from a dead past and its paralyzed language of guilt and duty by the augmentation of his wish to will from Act I (I, MB, I, 806) that anticipates Hilda's declaration of genesis in Act III (I, MB, III, 850) and gives us Rousseau's language of the heart:

> Hilde. Ja, men selv om nu så var—?
> Solness. Det er så! Det er så! Jeg vet det.
> Hilde. Nå, men De er da i alle fall ikke skyld i det.

115. Arthur Symons, "A Theory of the Stage," in Bentley (ed.), The Theory of the Modern Stage, 341. Eric Bentley has expressed amazement as well over this judgment in The Life of the Drama, 96. On the interdependence in Ibsen of realism and symbolism, see James L. Calderwood, "The Master Builder: Failure of Symbolic Success," Modern Drama, XXVII (1984), 616–36.

Solness (fester øynene på henne og nikker langsomt). Ja, se, *det* er det store, forferdelige spørsmål, det. *Det* er tvilen som nager meg—både natt og dag.
Hilde. Dette her!
(*N,* BS [BM], II, 463)

Solness (fortrolig). Tror ikke De også det, Hilde, at der finnes enkelte utkårne, utvalgte mennesker som har fått nåde og makt og evne til å *ønske* noe, begjaere noe, *ville* noe—sa iherdig og så—så ubønnhørlig—at de *må* få det til slutt.
(*N,* BS, II, 465) [116]

The plain refrains of common language made into evocation by their attachment to will and desire, the "aldri i denne verden" of Nora and Rebecca, hold the Great World waiting against the "lunt og hyggelig" doublets of Scandinavian philistinism. Ibsen likes to counter these comfortable doublets with his own alliterative and ominous double-entendres. The Rat Wife senses there is something in Allmers's house that "nager og gnager,—og kribler og krabler" (*N,* LE, I, 490) The retribution of Hedda is nailed down by thumping alliteration: "Nu brenner,—nu brenner jeg barnet" (*N,* HG, III, 425). [117] One of the most gripping and moving verbal dramas of Ibsen's prose is the dialectical contest of the deep spondaic beat of judgment and blame against the quiet monotone of self-judgment

116. *I,* MB, II, 827:

Hilda. Yes, but even if this were so—?
Solness. It *is* so! It *is!* I know.
Hilda. Well, but in any case it's not *your* fault.
Solness (fixing his eyes on her and nodding slowly). Ah, you see—that's the enormous ugly riddle—the doubt that gnaws at me day and night.

I, MB, II, 830:
Solness (confidently). Don't you believe with me, Hilda, that there are certain special chosen people who have a gift and power and capacity to *wish* something, *desire* something, *will* something—so insistently and so—so inevitably—that at last it *has* to be theirs?

117. *I,* LE, I, 878:

Rat Wife. If your graces notice anything here that nibbles and gnaws—and creeps and crawls—

I, HG, III, 762:
Hedda. Now I'm burning—I'm burning the child.

and resignation. The sentence of retribution as Allmers intones "Dom over deg og meg" (*N, LE,* II, 506) transforms itself through the rest of the play until it spreads out into the last words of acceptance:

> *Allmers.* Oppad,—imot tindene. Mot stjernene. Og imot den store stillhet.
> *Rita.* Takk!
> (*N, LE,* III, 518)

All the bitter judgment launched against and by Borkman comes to rest in the stark stance of competitors, dead in life, over a dead body of the man they fought over: "Vi to skygger—over den døde mann" (*N,* JGB, IV, 563).[118] No common phrase is more raised to multiple use and melodramatic significance by desire and by its par-ody than the simple "vi to" which struggles to close off the world in every play.

Igna-Stina Ewbank notes that while Ibsen's language must feel lived in and through, it must, at the same time, constantly be mod-ulated by its use as self-protection. As Wordsworth works through the intense impression of the visible world and its gradual annihila-tion to reach the shores of spirit, to "see into the heart of things," Ibsen stimulates a flurry of rhetoric and rationalization as his mate-rial for annihilation in order to reach the border of the unspeakable: "Solen, Solen." Andrew Kennedy is persuasive when he notes that "such a conjunction, of psychological complexity and linguistic

---

118. *I,* LE, II, 910:
Allmers: Yes. A judgment on you and me.

I, LE, IV, 935–56:
Allmers (his eyes fixed on her). Upward.
Rita (nodding in agreement). Yes, yes—upward.
Allmers. Upward—toward the mountain peaks. Toward the stars. And toward that great silence.
Rita (extending her hand to his). Thank you.

I, JGB, IV, 563:
Ella. We two shadows—over the dead man.
See the important recognition of Inga-Stina Ewbank in "Ibsen on the English Stage: 'The Proof of the Pudding is in the Eating,'" in Durbach (ed.), *Ibsen and the Theatre,* 36–37, that the hammering vertical and inward drive of Ibsen's language by which he achieves depth is alien to the moral life in English literature "which tends to be lived horizontally."

transparency, was hardly possible before Ibsen." Ultimately, we all sense a version of the Borges paradox in the Ibsen play, that the simpler the language and the starker the rhythms, the more complex the life behind them. Inga-Stina Ewbank describes the Wordsworthian power that works its way through and around the single word by playing on an image of M. C. Bradbrook, in relation to Shakespeare: "The informing power that radiates through *Rosmersholm* down to the single word, seems to me to be a sense of life as mysterious and ultimately unknowable."[119]

The Norwegian landscape lends Allmers the double perspective of his author, though it is never free from the holographic projection of self-pity and rationalization:

> *Allmers (gazing out over the water).* How cruel it looks today, the fjord—lying so heavy and full of sleep—blue-gray—with flakes of gold—reflecting the rainclouds.
> *Asta (imploringly).* Oh, Alfred, don't sit staring out at the fjord!
> *Allmers (not hearing her).* On the surface, yes. But in the depths—*there*—the undertow pulls—
> (*I*, LE, II, 896)

This kind of scene, in "unholy alliance" with intrigue drama and fourth-wall realism, elicits, in the words of Joan Templeton, "the brilliant bastard form with which [Ibsen] invented modern tragedy."[120] Brian Johnston is sensitive to the combination of archetype and parody as he feels the presence of all dramatic forms on Ibsen's stage, the "ghosts of older theaters." Behind *A Doll House*, *Ghosts*, and *Enemy of the People*, Greek designs; behind *The Wild Duck*,

119. Inga-Stina Ewbank, "Ibsen and 'The Far More Difficult Art of Prose,'" in Haakonsen (ed.), *Second International Ibsen Seminar*, 73–75; Andrew K. Kennedy, "The Confessional Duologue in Ibsen," in Haakonsen (ed.), *Fourth International Ibsen Seminar*, 36, 41. Kennedy notes that "even the tentative, indirect language of self-revelation is placed in a robust structure" (36). Inga-Stina Ewbank, "Ibsen and 'The Far More Difficult Art of Prose,'" 76.

120. Joan Templeton, "Of This Time, of *This* Place," 65. See Philip E. Larson, "French Farce Conventions and the Mythic Story Pattern in *Hedda Gabler*: A Performance Criticism," in Daniel Haakonsen (ed.), *Contemporary Approaches to Ibsen: Proceedings of the Fifth International Ibsen Seminar, 1983* (Oslo, 1985), 202–23. In *Contradictory Characters: An Interpretation of the Modern Theatre* (New York, 1973), 29, Albert Bermel speaks of the way Ibsen "jeopardizes" his drama by undercutting it with his "sly comedy." And in "'The Play-within-the Play' in Ibsen's Drama," in Haakonsen (ed.), *Second International Ibsen Seminar*, 101–17, Daniel Haakonsen notes that the camouflage of many plays within each play gradually insinuates tragedy into the bourgeois scene.

Shakespearean; behind *Rosmersholm*, Enlightenment concerns; behind *Lady from the Sea*, Romantic textures; behind *Hedda Gabler*, Scribean economy. The moral passion for permanent ideals should be chastened by this lesson in the evolution of aesthetic styles.[121] If Hugo's motley of incestuous doubling of corpse, son, and lover colors the melodrama of *Lady Inger, in* anticipates as well the decadent grotesque of sphinx and vampire in Hedda, Hilda, and Irene. But the Romantic diplomacy that mediated grotesque collisions into "l'harmonie des contraires" is violated by the necessity to represent the demands of tyrannically charming breadwinners averse to ugliness, and then to parody them by showing the fatalities of their fiction. If, as D. H. Lawrence believed, all good art submits itself to its own criticism, it also carries within it the submerged history of its genre.[122] It carries as well its own history, for Ibsen comes to his full power only when his earlier represented Viking energy and immediacy are dialectically and explosively squeezed by the bourgeois world. This pressure and thickness are absent in Bjørnson's bourgeois dramas. Ibsen's greater dimension doubles the education that exposes our perversions by an education to what we have lost. In this way, too, Ibsen made his exiling prose out of the twinship of his critical and poetic urges.

The mixture of comedy and tragedy perpetrated by Ibsen's parody, equally adept at exposing untrue marriages as at depicting and defeating the longing for the true one, persecutes what it inherits to empower the Great World's Freedom on the stage and to distance the habit that Nietzsche hates, the "translation of reality into a morality." As much as Kierkegaard tortures fairy tales to serve spirit, Ibsen taunts the promise of generic harmony or the harmony of contraries. The doubling of a comedy of aesthetic disturbance, carried by Ekdal Sr., Engstrand, Brendel, with the tragedy that erupts in a nice and cozy home, exiles uncritical idealism. Though, in Kierkegaard's view, tragedy and comedy have this in common, that both are based on contradiction, they differ in two crucial ways: "The tragic is the suffering contradiction, the comical, the painless contradiction," and the comic knows the way out, though it exits

---

121. See Johnston, *The Ibsen Cycle*, 64. He claims in the preface that Ibsen's realism is the "cunning tactics of a militant Romantic who is subversively smuggling the explosive Romantic powers into the pragmatic bourgeois world that had turned its back upon them" (ii).
122. Lawrence, *Phoenix*, 476.

into another chimera, whereas despair does not know the way out and can appeal to tragedy to heal contradiction only by death or by a higher consciousness of pain. No consciousness is large enough or privileged enough in Ibsen to overcome contradiction by its climax of spiritual anxiety, though Nora, Mrs. Alving, Ellida, Rita, and Allmers may seem to be ready. The Great World carries its tensions guiltlessly and richly. Since, however, it refuses access to Ibsen's suffering, potentially tragic figures, trapping them in parodic contexts, the way out, cast so often in scenes of hyperbolic and painful destruction, is delusive.[123]

Shaw astutely notes the comic attributes of the tragic design that lead the hero or heroine into a higher chimera:

> His heroes dying without hope or honor, his dead, forgotten, superseded men walking and talking with the ghosts of the past, are all heroes of comedy: their existence and their downfall are not soul-purifying convulsions of pity and horror, but reproaches, challenges, criticisms addressed to society and to the spectator as a voting constituent of society. They are miserable and yet not hopeless; for they are mostly criticisms of false intellectual positions which, being intellectual, are remediable by better thinking.[124]

The characteristic Shavian emphasis on intelligent remedies ignores the gap between the small and the great worlds and misconstrues the struggle towards the highest freedom as intellectual. But his comment recognizes the refusal of tragic climax and catharsis to those who carry the illness and guilt of their society, project its typical rationalizations, and rebel by impossible demonic ascents. The mixed form of Ibsen holds together the necessity for social, moral, and political reform of a specific society with the faith that we cannot possibly heal it, though our lone journey towards the Great World we are not ready to enter has something to do with its recovery.

It is Nietzsche who best extends our understanding of why Ibsen cannot be turned to the intellectual solution, even though he him-

123. Nietzsche, *Will to Power*, 364; Helge Rønning, "Individualism and the Liberal Dilemma," in Haakonsen (ed.), *Third International Ibsen Seminar*, 115; Thomas F. Van Laan, "Generic Complexity in Ibsen's *An Enemy of the People, Comparative Drama*, XX (1986), 95–111; Kierkegaard, *Concluding Unscientific Postscript*, 459, 464.

124. G. B. Shaw, "Tolstoy: Tragedian or Comedian?" in *Major Critical Essays*, in *Collected Works* (New York, 1932), XXIX, 276–77.

self thought the playwright was tempted by this siren. We have been courted by the most impressive tragic poets of purpose, moralities, religion, preserving the species and promoting the interests of God, Nietzsche reminds us. They have been the raisonneurs, confidants, and valets of the bourgeois stage, assigning to faith in life the highest reasons of religion and ethics culminating in the "thou shalt" of Christian humanism. In actuality, this is an age not wise enough to become conscious of its own comic postures and pretensions, not yet able to laugh at the fact that purpose hides the real agents of life's preservation: "instinct, drive, folly, lack of reasons." Ibsen is a dialectical poet, like Nietzsche, who exposes these "great teachers of a purpose," by "laughter, reason, and nature," so that reality can be returned to its full medium.[125] It is comic or parodic distancing that investigates the projective designs by which our purposes dominate each other, and that, for the Nietzsche of *The Gay Science*, blocks the great metaphysical delusion of a world behind this world. Were it not, then, for the impure origins of the Great World generated by the failures of so many of Ibsen's characters to find either a personally or socially persuasive purpose or realization, we might well end in the interesting dilemma described by Thomas Whitaker, who claims that "*Rosmersholm* focuses on the paradox that Ibsen's 'realism,' as a stylistic perspective and as our habitual mode of constituting the world means no genuine engagement with the real but a flight from it—a quest for absence."[126]

We surely see no social benefit from a double suicide. Nevertheless, escape from the politics of power and purpose in this world and in that of Hedda Gabler, when engineered by the comic and painful parody of classic tragic forms, of bourgeois dilemmas, Romantic missions, and the romance of Christian self-sacrifice, achieves a

125. Nietzsche, *The Gay Science*, 74, 75. See also the important comments of Arnold Hauser on the development of antibourgeois sentiment and character in the drama of bourgeois artists: "The attacks on the middle class became a basic characteristic of the bourgeois drama, and the rebel against the bourgeois morality and way of life, the scoffer at bourgeois convention and philistine narrow-mindedness, becomes one of its stock figures. It would shed an extraordinarily revealing light on the gradual alienation of modern literature from the middle classes to examine the metamorphoses this figure underwent from the 'Storm and Stress' right up to Ibsen and Shaw" ("The Origins of Domestic Drama," trans. with the collaboration of the author by Stanley Goodman in Bentley [ed.], *The Theory of the Modern Stage*, 419).

126. Thomas R. Whitaker, "Killing Ourselves," *Fields of Play in Modern Drama* (Princeton, N.J., 1977), 37.

positive dimension and depth that keeps the mystery and freedom of the larger medium intact. To the degree that higher types have cooperated in banishing by low and high purpose and guilt the "love that belongs to life on earth—this lovely, miraculous earthly life—this life full of mysteries" (*I*, WWDA, III, 1090), to that degree are they drawn by all the forces of the sea. The homeopathic service of Ibsen's art—to raise in our imaginations an evolutionary site on which the divisions between the known and the unknown, comedy and tragedy, passion and responsibility, will and duty, engage in an unselfconscious drama of natural dialectical collision— because it recognizes its impure source, can modulate our stiff structures towards the guiltless roll of creation.[127] To earn the right to punish the most dangerous of bourgeois myths, aesthetic and ethical purity, Ibsen's artists and his art must subject themselves to the shipwreck he often identified with civilization. Lyngstrand rises from the sea like the sailor-husband in his projected sculpture, haunting the bedroom of his unfaithful wife, like Ellida's sailor himself, as a sign of the fact that "the whole history of the world" is "one great shipwreck" which the individual, alone, might survive.[128] Or the artist must live in the body of Borkman so that art's Celtic animism and Orphic powers can be perverted by dreams of the unfettered will's mystery over man and nature:

> *Borkman.* That wind works on me like the breath of life. It comes to me like a greeting from captive spirits. I can sense them, the buried millions. I feel the veins of metal, reaching their curving, branching, beckoning arms out to me. I saw them before me like living shadows—the night I stood in the bank vault with a lantern in my hand . . . I love you, you riches straining to be born—with all your shining aura of power and glory!
> (*I*, JGB, III, 1021)

No play of Ibsen more richly explores the privileges and limitations, pains and powers of art in the face of life's expansive desires than *Lady from the Sea*. Though the mermaid was a favorite figure of Scandinavian ballad and legend, she was also used by those interested in the theory of evolution as a poetic resource for the recovery not only of our authentic past, but of the mythical wealth of forms

---

127. Chamberlain, *Ibsen: The Open Vision*, 135; Johnston, *The Ibsen Cycle*, 63, who speaks of the rich "fusion of the dialectic and of archetypal recollection."
128. Henrik Ibsen to Georg Brandes, September 24, 1871, in *Correspondence*, 218.

lost to the imagination.[129] No one knew better than Ibsen how science could, through art, serve spirit, because no one knew better how closely bound were the tasks of a necessary social criticism and a necessary personal self-realization. The mermaid was a frequent intermediate evolutionary form of fictive projection in the nineteenth century, and, because she loves the human in fairy tales, her disturbed amphibiousness is an ideal image of our ontological and psychological homelessness. Gasping on the strand between two worlds, she could be patronized, made foolishly derivative and aesthetic, without even the dignity of her traditional seductions and sacrifices, when cast upon the canvas of a Ballestad who is prematurely adjusted and acclimatized before suffering the struggle of spiritual becoming. But when she lends her doubled condition to a story half dreamed through, half observed, of the dripping ghost of the dead sailor standing over his unfaithful wife—the amazing subject of a sick artist's projected sculpture and a sick woman's actual brooding—she has the power of high art to transform reality, if not to save it. In front of the reformed Wangel, Ellida muses: "In freedom—responsible to myself! Responsible? How—this transforms everything!" (I, LS, V, 685). In its place of exile, art makes the marriage between freedom and responsibility out of a murderously erotic will, transgressing the father's law, and has to remake it over and over again. The astonishment of Lyngstrand at the intensity of the sailor's will he witnessed is the measure of how thoroughly civilization has muted it, how imperiously it needs to return to lost love, and how difficult is art's job of making it responsible:

> Lyngstrand. And he said that with such a power of will, I thought he'd be the man to do it, too.
> (I, LS, I, 613)

Art must make a room for that fierce wish Kierkegaard enlisted in the work of faith. Unlike Ballestad's borrowed and dead picture, Lyngstrand's conception is vibrantly saturated with the artist's spirit

---

129. See Gillian Beer, *Darwin's Plots: Evolutionary Narrative in Darwin, George Eliot, and Nineteenth Century Fiction* (London, 1985), 104–105. See also Richard Chase, *The American Novel and Its Tradition* (Garden City, N.Y., 1957), 186n, who reminds us that for American naturalists (and this is even true of Zola) naturalism might have begun "as a special emphasis within the limits of realism" but "it culminates in a form of poetry." See also Johnston, *The Ibsen Cycle*, 123, who, from the Hegelian angle, notes that the "prospect" scene of Act II, with its view over distant mountain peaks and fjords, suggests that the commonsensical and restricted reality of the return will not be a decision that Spirit can long be happy with.

and imagination; it is not merely observed, but lived through ("gjennomlevede"). Perhaps this process is the artist's counterpart to Brandes's social and political breakthrough ("gjennombrudd"), for it is recommended with the fervor of a manifesto. In an often quoted letter to his mother-in-law, Ibsen explains: "The essential thing is to protect one's essential self, to keep it pure and free of all intrusive elements, and to draw a clear distinction between what one has merely experienced and what one has spiritually *lived through*, for only the latter is proper matter for creative writing."[130]

The task of living through is, like the saving of the self from life's shipwreck, that of the single individual, as free as possible from social contamination and compromise, yet, paradoxically, in the service of society. The process is described in a conversation between Ellida and Lyngstrand—both of whom have, in some sense, come out of the sea—and Arnholm. Ellida asks if the sculptor will recreate imagined mythical and heroic figures of the past, mermen and mermaids, Vikings, and Lyngstrand replies that his subject will be based on something of his own experience:

> *Lyngstrand.* And she would be dreaming, too. I really believe I can develop it so you can actually see that she's dreaming.
>
> *Ellida.* What an astonishing conception! (*Shuts her eyes.*) Yes, I can see it as clear as crystal.
> *Arnholm.* But how on earth, Mr.—Mr.—! You said it was something you'd experienced yourself.
> *Lyngstrand.* That's right. I did experience all this—at least up to a point.
> *Arnholm.* You witnessed a dead man that—
> *Lyngstrand.* Well now, I didn't mean experience strictly speaking. Not actuality. But something very much like it—
> (I, LS, I, 611)

Already in *A Doll House*, Ibsen had shown us that lived-through art is quite the opposite of the willed aesthetic compositions. This is forgotten even by writers as great as Schiller. Brandes testifies to this response: "Henrik Ibsen once drew my attention to this in speaking of 'Die Jungfrau von Orleans'; he maintained that there is no 'experience' in that play, that it is not the result of powerful per-

---

130. Henrik Ibsen to Magdalene Thoresen, June 5, 1870, in *Correspondence*, 192. I use the translation of Meyer, *Ibsen*, 332.

sonal impressions, but is a composition.[131] Ellida, too, is an artist of evolution as she describes her regressive past in a guiltless time we find for a moment in every play:

> *Ellida.* We never talked of his past.
> *Wangel.* What did you talk of?
> *Ellida.* Mainly about the sea.
> *Wangel.* Ah—! About the sea.
> *Ellida.* About the storms and the calms. The dark nights at sea. And the sea in the sparkling sunlight, that too. But mostly we talked of whales and dolphins, and of the seals that would lie out on the skerries in the warm noon sun. And then we spoke of the gulls and the eagles and every kind of seabird you can imagine. You know—it's strange, but when we talked in such a way, then it seemed to me that all these creatures belonged to him.
> (I, LS, II, 626)

Nietzsche had marveled at the "restless and inquisitive spirit of science" dedicating itself to the destruction of myth and to the displacement of "poetry from its native soil," rendering it homeless.[132] Capitalistic greed, clearing the forests, and Christianity's morality had orphaned nature's wild beasts and forced them into lofts where an old man, like the mermaid, wanders between two worlds. Ibsen was certainly not alone in sensing, in the theory of evolution, a resource that could serve spirit instead of killing it. In spite of his view that Darwinism came out of a tired Malthusian society, fearful of profusion, that it misgauged the importance of a cultural genealogy that had assured the survival of the meekest, and mistakenly assumed an ordered progress leaving little room for the choices of the spiritual aristocrats, Nietzsche profited greatly from evolutionary designs that could expose the artificial theological distortions of nature. The Romantic Hegelian faith in the development of consciousness broke through the chastening irony and parody of both Ibsen and Nietzsche, to a difficult faith in the Third Empire, and there enjoined, as in so many writers and thinkers for the next four decades, evolutionary patterns:

> For I believe that the teaching of natural science about evolution has validity also as regard the mental factors of life. I believe that the time will soon come when political and social conceptions will cease to exist

131. Brandes, *Main Currents*, II, 37.
132. Nietzsche, *The Birth of Tragedy*, 104–105.

in their present forms, and that from their coalescence there will come a unity, which, for the present, will contain the conditions for the happiness of mankind. I believe that poetry, philosophy and religion will be merged in a new category and become a new vital force, of which we who live now can have no clear conception. It has been said of me on different occasions that I am a pessimist. And so I am in so far as I do not believe in the everlastingness of human ideals. But I am also an optimist in so far as I firmly believe in the capacity for procreation and development of ideals. Especially, to be more definite, am I of the opinion that the ideals of our time, while disintegrating, are tending towards what in my play "Emperor and Galilean" I indicated by the name of the third kingdom.[133]

If they threatened the orphaned will with fatalism and passivity, Darwin's designs helped writers, too, to authenticate philosophy and art as double agents of reality, turned to the exposure of maladaptation signaled by overly moral defenses and the demonic disequilibrium of a compensatory idealism already targeted by Hegel. Science's sanctioned powers of distancing moral defenses could well save the artist in exile from theologies of purpose and aesthetic evasion. They could recover guiltless aggressive instincts and release a rich bestiary of passion for art to plunder, keeping the Great World cleared of anthropomorphic appropriation. Humbling special creation, evolution had to leave the origins of species mysterious; it did not kill, but confirmed the unfathomable reality of earth Ibsen's Irene knows we have curtailed.

Though Borghejm boldly stands up to the "laws of change" in the name of progress rather than rationalization, it is finally Allmers, prepared by a lifetime of neurotic repression, and the passionate Rita, who opens us to its genuine poetry, which is out of our scientific and moral reach. In a beautiful scene of *Little Eyolf,* when Asta sees Allmers's passage to marriage as a painful capitulation to "the law of change," Borghejm rejects the resignation implicit in Allmers's phrase: "Pah—that must be a stupid law! I don't believe one particle of it" (*I*, LE, III, 921). The law of change grows out of its protective phrasing by the end of the play and, though it is kept from the transcendental power of Kierkegaard's repetition, it is attached to the ever vulnerable psychological transformation of the two who

133. Ibsen, Speech at the Banquet in Stockholm, September 24, 1887, *Speeches and New Letters,* 56–57.

must endure Ibsen's full parodying of the rhetoric before they can feel they have lived it through (*I*, LE, III, 913; IV, 928–29). The image is now experienced as it is by Ellida. Wangel, the scientist, confesses to his wife: "I begin to understand you—little by little. You think and feel in images—and in visions. Your longing and craving for the sea—your attraction toward him, toward this stranger— these were the signs of an awakened, growing rage for freedom in you. Nothing else." (*I*, LS, V, 686).

Art's evolutionary metaphors and rhythms guarantee the anxious openness to the unknown that will keep marriage from closing out self-realization. Ellida's qualification of Ballested's final remarks, which divide our sea from our land self, is the crucial difference between the evolution of low aesthetic compliance and the problems of high art's perpetual struggle towards Freedom:

> *Ballested.* Except for the difference—that the mermaid dies of it. But people, human beings—they can acclam-acclimatize themselves. Yes, yes—that's the thing, Mrs. Wangel. They can ac-cli-matize themselves.
> *Ellida.* Yes, they can, Mr. Ballested—once they're free.
> *Wangel.* And responsible, Ellida.
> (*I*, LS, V, 688)

Ibsen has, perhaps, so successfully taught us to feel the unending struggle of self-realization caught between the family and the darkening seasons that we are ready to assent to Brandes's witty remark on the unconvincing ending of *Lady from the Sea*: "There are few things less capable of calming a woman who is longing for a free, adventurous life with all its mysteries than the offer of such moral advantages as free choice with responsibility."[134] It is certain that "acclimatization" suffers as much parody as "the call of the ideal" in *The Wild Duck*, so that it cannot serve as a strategy of retreat from the great task urged by our maladaptation. Ballested has never spiritually lived through the seasons, and this opens up the gulf of misunderstanding between statements similar on the surface. Ellida's poetry has existential scope and substance and will take us beyond the happy ending: "Oh no, that isn't true. The joy—it's much like our joy in these long, light summer days and nights. It has the hint of dark times to come. And that hint is what throws a shadow over

134. Brandes, *Henrik Ibsen*, 103.

our human joy—like the drifting clouds with their shadows over the fjord" (*I*, LS, III, 639). Ballested's observation smacks of the memorized pathos of the aesthetic purveyor of resignation: "How sad to think. We've been summer's happy children now for weeks and months. It's hard to reconcile oneself with the dark days coming. Yes, I mean, it is at first. Because, you know, people here learn to accli-, acclimatize themselves" (*I*, LS, V, 671). And, we might add, to avoid the struggle towards Freedom. Even though Lyngstrand is one of those maimed artists whose weakness keep us represented rather than excluded, his projected sculpture, showing up Ballested's plan for a painting, generates not only Ellida's drama but the misunderstanding necessary for depth. The play is full of semicomic deceits and misconceptions: the girls' secret birthday for their mother, the mistaken assumption of Arnholm as to his beckoning, Lyngstrand's mistaken notion about his health. A conversation between Arnholm and Dr. Wangel suggests Ibsen's intentions:

> *Arnholm.* How can you explain the power this stranger has over her?
> *Wangel.* Well—there may be aspects of the problem that just don't admit explanation.
> *Arnholm.* You mean something that *can't* be explained, inherently— and permanently?
> *Wangel.* Something that can't, anyway—by what we know now.
> (*I*, LS, IV, 658)

That the scientist is not as comfortable as he seems here surfaces in Wangel's fierce rejection of Ellida's obsession (like Rita's later) with her dead child's eyes: "I don't believe one word of it! It's pure imagination on her part—and nothing else." Arnholm's biblical phrase "signs against signs" keeps the connections open between fact and fiction, science and poetry, and gives to art's dialectical binding the highest language, one that responds to evolution of the known and the unknown alike.

Ellida neither disappears into the unknown, nor beaches herself in a dead marriage. Marriage thrust out upon the scene of a mysterious and indifferent universe in *Lady from the Sea* and *Little Eyolf* guarantees that the nice and cozy house will not protect it. Acclimatization on the other side of Freedom is quite different from the transplantation Wangel speaks of and that forces art to work itself into exile: "Haven't you ever noticed that the people who live out close by the sea are almost like a race to themselves? It's as though they lived the sea's own life. There's the surge of the waves—the ebb and the flow—in their thoughts and feelings both" (*I*, LS, IV, 656). These rhythms of depth, Ibsen's own trademark, turned to the great task of binding social and personal responsibility, allow his art to speak to more than a race apart. Ibsen cripples Lyngstrand with bad health, the romance of the waiting muse, and misunderstanding of his future precisely in order to make the creative struggle of Art for Freedom a possibility and imperative for us all. This art's resistance to generic complacency and bourgeois belief in scientific progress is a lyrical version of Strindberg's airy boast: "Like everything else in creation I'm subject to the laws of evolution, and it's through our relapses that we advance."[135] The relapse is forced even on a future seeker like Bolette, who has to dream of the Great World's time and space while resigning herself to a fixed marriage: "Imagine—to be free—and to come out—into the unknown. And not to worry about the future" (*I*, LS, V, 679).

Ibsen could never assume the stance that had proved so successful and moving for Hardy, who gains a "melancholy satisfaction of life" by "dying, so to speak before one is out of the flesh." If symbols were to liberate Ibsen from the small world, he had to make them suffer, like the legendary mermaid who paradoxically submits to the transiency of mortal life, to win an immortal soul, aesthetic and parodic impurity before they could be primordial carriers for all of us.[136] And the mermaid could be maimed in the tongue, the tail, the finger, the ear as a sign of absolute commitment and its fate in a relative world.[137] She cannot permanently seduce or save, nor take

135. Strindberg, *Getting Married*, 29.
136. Thomas Hardy, *Portable Hardy*, ed. Julian Moynahan (Harmondsworth, Middlesex, 1977); Duve, *Symbolikken i Henrik Ibsens skuespill*, 25. See Hans Christian Andersen's "Little Mermaid" and Ibsen's 1851 piece, "Professor Welhaven on Paluden-Müller's Mythological Poems," on the uses of mythology, quoted in the larger version of Meyer's *Ibsen* (Garden City, N.Y., 1971), 70.
137. See Maurice Gravier, "Le Drame d'Ibsen et la ballade magique," in Haakonsen (ed.), *Second International Ibsen Seminar*, 152; also Brendel's recommendation in *I*, R, IV, 579–80. See also the anatomy of the biocentric tradition interestingly traced by Margot Norris, *Beasts of the Modern Imagination: Darwin, Nietzsche, Kafka, Ernst, and Lawrence* (Baltimore, 1985).

"refuge completely in another." Otherwise, the mutation of our medium, our maladaptation, could never earn the transformation that draws on both development and death.[138]

138. Johnston, *The Ibsen Cycle*, 248. In the fourth act of *Emperor and Galilean*, Julian rebukes his pagan followers for cowardice in comparison to Christians willing to sacrifice hands and ears.

THREE

The Small World

Ibsen's determination was, from a distance, to bring to light the terrible paradox that both home and homeland, protected by the dead language of Methuselah morality (*I*, EP, IV, 356), were in exile from life. Rousseau before him had stamped the universal paradigm of counterexile, but he had set against the violations of the language and sincerity in Paris, the recovery of natural and unconstrained conduct and conversation at Les Charmettes, at home with Mamma. Rousseau was condemned to shuttle between city and country because he opposed the immorality of the first to the morality of the second, for loss and recovery were both in the world. Ibsen could confront the empty morality of the home and homeland only with the unmaterialized fullness of the Great World. The living urgency of his "pulverizing" prose (*I*, EP, III, 324), counterpointing in his confined atmospheres, whether inside or out of the poisoned house, low and high aesthetic diction, theological slogans and spiritual hunger, the logic of cause and effect and the poetry of sign against sign, opened up in living rooms of nice and cozy homes the fearful fissures through which we see the depth and value of an unabbreviated medium.[1] It restored

1. R. M. Adams, "Ibsen on the Contrary," in Anthony Caputi (ed.), *Modern Drama* (New York, 1966), 351, captures well the power and simplicity of Ibsen's "perfectly lucid double vision, hidden behind the polished facade of an amazingly supple and indirect dialogue. There is nothing more to it, really, than placing a blank short perspective next to an

151

the distance that, for both Kierkegaard and Nietzsche, protects us against the infringement of dead universals, and counters estrangement with strangeness.[2] Self-parody made parody a responsible alienation. By mocking the Moses in him, Ibsen justified his mission of harrowing us into a counterexile against the exile we call home.

Metaphor and myth, even at the fighting level of Stockmann's animal and pollution imagery, disturb the domestication of the living truth. What is more, the language of projection and self-justification is decoded by a relentlessly revealing and direct diction of indignation and confession. Stockmann's words, that "need no specialist to understand," are not fig leaves for our nakedness, and they estrange us from our disguises. How far we are from the vivid integration of feeling, reason, and ethics in the Enlightenment's *Encyclopedia* to which Rousseau contributed and which Stockmann honors by refusing to separate fact from principle: "Indigence is not a vice; it's worse. We receive a man of vice; we flee from the *indigent*. He is seen only with his open hand extended. There are no *indigents* among the savages."[3] The language could, sometimes with trying and patient effort, finally, as in the novels of Jane Austen, correspond to housed morality in deed and principle. Such correspondence was so out of the question by Flaubert's day that his dictionary and novels felt compelled to take revenge on received ideas by refusing to rescue the stupidity of a dead language and a sentimental morality.

The entire action, in Ibsen, of revenge, participation, and provocation of a new dimension, a "new living reality," quite opposed to that "perfect unity of will" Kroll identifies with home (*I, R, I,* 506; II, 545), is so spatially confined that every slogan and rationalization is put on the rack. The gradual loss of the eighteenth-century dialectic between a public life in which the assumption of roles expressed social identities and the home in which natural character and sympathies were at play has been described by Richard Sennett

---

infinitely lengthened one, and making a counterpoint of the two. . . . Ibsen's is an art of seeing into something and through it, not of raising hackles on the audience by promoting an intense reaction for or against it."

2. See Theodor Adorno, *Minima Moralia,* 94.

3. Alain Pons (ed.), *Encyclopédie; ou, Dictionnaire raisonné des sciences, des arts et des métiers, 1751–1772: Les articles les plus signifiants de Diderot et al.* (Paris, 1964), 371 (my translation).

and others.[4] The house of Stockmann, distinguishing itself from surrounding nineteenth-century homes which rehearse theatrical roles and language, hide feelings, facts, and character, is orphaned and endangered by a bureaucratic public world. The doctor's generous table welcomes visitors freely and is suspected by the majority as a vengeful seduction to political purpose (I, EP, IV, 363). The air and light that come through the open doors and windows make the interior utterly at odds with the stultifying dollhouses we are used to in Ibsen. Petra might note the similarity of public and private spheres: "At home we have to keep quiet and in school we have to stand there and lie to the children" (I, EP, I, 296). But the children in the Stockmann family have their sparkling say and pagan spunk.

What a difference between Mayor Stockmann's remonstrance to Petra, "Ah, so we've learned to voice opinions," so reminiscent of Torvald's, and Stockmann's bantering put-down of Katherine, free of both bureaucratic blame and autocratic tyranny: "Go home and take care of your home and let me take care of society" (I, EP, II, 320; II, 341). For there really is still, in Stockmann's mind, a healthy difference between those realms which he maintains, finally, by counterexiling his own home against the majority, his own school against the sniggering secrets of an institution indistinguishable from the lying liberal press. Stockmann's energetic "revolution against the lie that only the majority owns the truth," trumpeted in sledgehammer exclamations that demolish the specialists (I, EP, IV, 356), contrasts markedly not only with Billing's slogan "We're on the verge of a revolution!" but with the silly conspiracy of Kroll's children whose petty political games reflect the maneuvers of the liberal press of Mortensgaard (I, EP, III, 324, 326; IV, 356). Kroll's shock that public life has infiltrated the home is highly ironic in view of the recognition by Ibsen and others that "human relations in the public world were 'deformed' according to the same rules that determined human relations in the family." Hjalmar's great relief in entering his refuge after an uncomfortable party at Werle Sr.'s, at which he feels socially displaced and denies his father, is again heavy with irony. Who would imagine that the bureaucratic anonymity of the court officials in the play's first scene

---

4. Richard Sennett, *The Fall of Public Man: On the Social Psychology of Capitalism* (New York, 1978), 179ff.

had anything in common with Hjalmar's magic den, yet the home insists on consensus to support the "breadwinner's" missionary fiction.[5] The realism of Hedvig and Gina is not out to undo Hjalmar's rhetorical protection, for the majority cannot be misunderstood. Because the father's fiction of authority depends wholly on the cooperation of his cast, the home is a bureaucratic theater, and it is no wonder that personality is pressed into ritualistic service.

It is typical of Ibsen to give to Gregers an insight that is based on the wrong assumptions and used for the wrong purposes. He underrates Gina and overrates Hjalmar to punish his father and justify the mission that will keep him safe from his own complexes: "and there he sits right now, he with his great, guiltless, childlike mind plunged in deception—living under the same roof with that creature, not knowing what he calls his home is built on a lie" (I, WD, II, 409). Hjalmar's deceit is of another sort, deriving from his own lack of responsibility and weak character that make him vulnerable to Gregers's game of ritualizing domestic personalities into roles. Sennett analyzes the way in which the private world came to reflect the disequilibrium and anonymity of the public world, a favorite device of Dickens:

> The family was supposed to be a place in which people could express their personalities; but if they inflated details of family interaction into psychic symbols, they would, against desire, against their will, be experiencing the instability of social relations all over again. . . . If family members treated their relations with each other as hieroglyphics to be understood by wresting a meaning from details of unstable appearances, then the enemy had come within the place of hiding. Personality would produce again the very disorientation which people were seeking to flee.[6]

The orphaned realism of Hedvig and Gina in such an atmosphere, and their ennabling roles as butter bearers to the "breadwinner," considerably qualify the validity of Relling's smug recognition— which, to be sure, has some measure of truth: "Oh, life would be

---

5. *Ibid.*, 179. Ibsen might well have been influenced, too, by the same double representation in novels like *Martin Chuzzlewit* and *Bleak House* of allegorical anonymity in public and private worlds and names (of children, government officials, and institutions).

6. Sennett, *The Fall of Public Man*, 179. See also Leo Lowenthal, "Motifs in the Realistic Plays of Ibsen," in Fjelde (ed.), *Ibsen*, 144.

good in spite of all, if we only could have some peace from those damned shysters who come badgering us poor people with their 'summons to the ideal'" (*I*, WD, V, 490). The majority had moved inside the house that was to serve as refuge from the crowd's untruth. Mayor Stockmann's definition of society fits the family that both he and Gregers, from their celibate pulpits, define as truly married. Of his brother's freethinking, the mayor notes: "In a well-ordered society, that's nearly as inexcusable. The individual has to learn to subordinate himself to the whole—as, I should say, to those authorities charged with the common good" (*I*, EP, I, 291). Typically, later in the play, Ibsen lets one of his manipulative minds counter this assumption with a question he himself could stand behind: "But how about self-government as part of a citizen's education—don't you care about that?" (*I*, EP, III, 329).

Between *An Enemy of the People* and *Rosmersholm*, the so-called liberal breakthrough that impeached the king's conservative ministers and put Sverdrup's cabinet in power had both erupted and failed to realize its promises. There was no radical break with the past, despite changes in governmental forms, since common interests continued to be the interests of particular groups and the Krolls had merely yielded to the Mortensgaards. The clergy's decrease in power did not shut off its necessary biblical sanction of civil authorities. That is why Mortensgaard can still say, "What the party needs is Christian elements" (*I*, EP, II, 536). In a conversation with Kroll, Rosmer, for all his squeamishness in the face of public life, confesses that the liberal breakthrough had given more "independence to the ideas of individuals" (*I*, R, I, 507) who had concerned themselves with the woman's question, the marriage question, democratic reforms in church and state, and utilitarian capitalism. But, in fact, the paradoxical tension between individualism and liberalism, the so-called liberal dilemma, seriously refuses that confidence. Stockmann had anticipated the marital squabbles between freethinking and liberalism, as he seems to have heard Kroll make the alliance between free love and free thought:

> *Stockmann.* The worst of it is that everyone the country over is a slave to party. But *that's* not the reason—it's probably no better in the free United States; I'm sure they have a plague of solid majorities and liberal public opinions and all the other bedevilments. They might kill

you, but they don't go in for slow torture; they don't lock a free soul in the jaws of a vice, the way they do here at home.
(*I*, EP, V, 368)[7]

The countersociety of the radical artistocrat that Stockmann proposes as a solution to the preservation of true individualism may be naive, but the energy of its motivating indignation is a measure of Ibsen's sense that liberalism, as much as philistine bourgeois morality, had set itself against life. Where is the broad-mindedness both Stockmann and Brandes identify with true morality? In *The Will to Power*, Nietzsche opposes socialism, the "*tyranny* of the least and the dumbest," to the natural "morality of development," and all Ibsen's subterranean allies, jealous for the inequalities of spiritual aristocracy, identify it with a "will to negate life."[8] Lawrence complained that modern democracy is the greatest enemy of true individuality and that bullying liberal bureaucracies are the negative form of power. For Dostoyevsky, the most dangerous attribute of social utopian systems was the elimination of the freedom and individuality guaranteed by the necessary suffering of active love.

The Viking past, which comes into this play and others to counter the biological, cultural, moral, and spiritual etiolation of modern civilization's evolution into specialized anonymity, combats the linking of free thought to party. In the breakthrough year of 1884, when Sverdrup became prime minister, Ibsen wrote: "I admit . . . that in politics, too, I am a pagan; I do not believe in the emancipatory power of political measures; nor have I much confidence in the altruism and goodwill of those in power." For a time,

---

7. See Helge Rønning, "Individualism and the Liberal Dilemma," in Haakonsen (ed.), *Third International Ibsen Seminar*, 119, 121, especially the discussion of Hans Skjervheim's *Det liberale dilemma og andre essays* (Oslo, 1968). In reviewing the literature on Scandinavian individualism, Rønning paraphrases the emphasis of Gunnar Ahlström in *Det moderne genombrottet i Nordens litteratur* (Stockholm, 1947). An *Enemy of the People* belongs in the 1880s literature that exposed the contradictions between true liberalism and its degradation in the practice of political liberals, as inevitable a disappointment as it is reprehensible: "While Schiller and his contemporaries revolted against a feudal society on the basis of an ideology of an emerging bourgeoisie, . . . individualism was closely associated with the concept of the bourgeois utopia. In An *Enemy of the People* the same individualism is directed against a society that has emerged by ideologically maintaining, but not realizing such an idealistic individualism" ("Individualism and the Liberal Dilemma," 117). Marxist critics are eager to separate Ibsen's diatribes against the majority from Ibsen's feelings for the working class. This attitude is discussed in Horst Bien, *Henrik Ibsens Realismus*, 246.

8. Nietzsche, *Will to Power*, 77.

the political naïveté of Stockmann allows him to view as anti-thetical the independent liberal press and the "bureaucrats" who "clamp down on a plain, honest man!" (*I*, EP, II, 322–23). But when authority is the mere hat or cane of his brother, and the press serves it, the individual has no public world against which to define the self. Identity is incestuous. Solness, chained to a dead family and, like the Hunger Artist, unable to find the food he needs in the public world, and afraid to forage, asks a startling question of Hilda: "How did you ever become what you are?" (*I*, MB, III, 856). The double transference is sealed by her answer: "How have you made me into what I am?" Hjalmar is well aware that his sense of reality depends upon the belief of a child locked up in his house: "I was blissfully happy . . . Not so much from the invention itself, but be-cause Hedvig believed in it—believed in it with all the power and force of a child's mind" (*I*, WD, V, 484). This communion is the doubling Freud, with Otto Rank, associates with primitive and pri-mary narcissism, by which the ego is enhanced and preserved from death. No wonder Ibsen hounds it to destruction. In a later world and stage, the double becomes the symptom of an inadequate ego. Missing the public term so necessary for personal definition, Kierkegaard could use God for the task of becoming what we al-ready are. But in Ibsen's world, the bureaucratizing and leveling of old hierarchies made the ghostly public life feel like a missing half. This split is a historically anxious one that considerably sickens the old dream of ontological androgyny.[9]

The church is a spectral omnipresent warden, Irene's nun, and the State is represented by the Manders who boasts to Mrs. Alving, herself split between being and becoming, "struggling with ghosts" inside and out, "I am the same as I always was" (*I*, G, II, 239).[10] If Nietzsche indicted us for draining the life out of both the world of appearance and of referential value, Ibsen, like so many other writ-ers of the second half of the nineteenth century, concerned himself with the mutual ghosting of the private and public spheres. When the supporting fiction fails within the house, as it inevitably does, where in the public world can we find compensatory life? Here is

9. Henrik Ibsen to Bjørnstjerne Bjørnson, March 28, 1884, in *Correspondence,* 379; Freud, *"The Uncanny,"* in *Collected Papers,* IV, 387–88; Gay, *The Tender Passion,* 331.

10. Arild Haaland, *Seks Studier i Ibsen,* 36, justly maintains that Manders's claim to vic-tory over temptation is a weakness of affect like that of his society.

the biblical whited sepulcher of hypocrisy and, if Rørlund had typically displaced that epithet onto the great threatening societies of the capitals—which, devoid of "moral foundation" are "gilded, glittering facades" (*I*, PS, I, 17)—Ibsen boomerangs his ascription and lends it to Dr. Stockmann for his war against the provincial establishment (*I*, EP, I, 298). But Rørlund's blind belief that great cities are phantasmagoric bureaucracies of anonymity was ironically backed by the major novelists and poets of the century. The Paris of Balzac and Baudelaire; the London of Dickens; the St. Petersburg whose spectral origins, with the Romantic and Gogolian doubles, grotesque and pathetic, Dostoyevsky turned to a target of spiritual indictment, are all populated by the walking dead, by parasites, projections, demons that signal the collapse of private and public character, the thinning of reality to phantasmagoria, the repression of desire and will. No wonder Hardy's Jude laments, "I am fearful of life, spectre-seeing always."[11] The underground man, deformed by an education that studiously denied the necessity of suffering, has only an abstract St. Petersburg of so-called active, normal, stupid new men against which to shape a self. The public world is so engineered out of value by environmental fantasists of happiness that it can neither receive nor respond to those who would acknowledge the necessary tension between the moral, philosophical, affective, and spiritual impulses of body and mind. The self demonically grows into a frenzy of hyperconsciousness, tossed between dreams of vengeance and masochistic mousy impotence. The hysterically unbalanced titanic rise and fall of Solness and Borkman are intimately related to the ghosting of authentic civic and spiritual authority.

Ambitious creators must be blasted fathers. And it is not a strong, healthy, ethical public that destroys them; it is the terrible isolation of the need to judge oneself when the unbalanced ego projects a high mission against the refusal of society to furnish a worthy one. The fascination with suicide in the 1890s, reflected particularly in art and literature, is attributed by Durkheim to a society that fails in its task of stimulating character by reasonable resistance which Rousseau saw as the first experience of good education. If society is too rigidly repressive and controlling with

11. Thomas Hardy, *Jude the Obscure*, ed. Norman Page (New York, 1978), 121. Compare the atmospheres of Conrad's novels, especially *Lord Jim*, suffused with the presence of the ghosts of failed ideals.

Torvald's everlasting morality of church and law, or softened by what Hedda calls the everlasting presence of fond aunts and specialist husbands, it does not listen to the frustrated will.[12] The everlasting insignias of office and the prosecuting demands of its moral imperatives, whether in the mouth of Torvald, Manders, or Ivan Karamazov, pretend to a fantastic permanence and perfection that abbreviate reality, imprison spontaneity, and haunt us with ghosts, redundant selves, of suppressed instincts, history, relations, evolution.

Ivan Karamazov's devil, ironically, yearns for the gravity of earthly realism, but he himself is a projection of man's absurd yearning to be real and free at the same time from suffering and injustice. Because he refuses responsibility for brothers and active love towards neighbors, Ivan is as abstract as St. Petersburg, as the devil divorced from God. The double that frightens abstract egoists serves as a symptom of displacement, of narcissism, and, poignantly, as the only available modern antidote for loneliness. When Solness seems to call out, in Hilda, his repressed past, for the sake of overcoming his terror of the future, he laments: "I've been so alone here—and felt so utterly helpless watching it all" (*I*, MB, I, 811). When Dostoyevsky's Golyadkin accuses his supplanting double of immorality for his refusal to keep his own place, he is as mistaken as Ivan's devil about his categories. The trapped determinism of cause and effect conditions the silly confusion of origins and ends, for Ivan's fantastic life is the source of the devil's envy of reality and Golyadkin's divided self is a cause of his displacement. For the same reason, what seems accidental doubling of Rosmer's sexual guilt and Mortensgaard's exposure, of his idealism and that of Brendel, is, in fact, symptomatic. A society that mouths everlasting truths and idealizes its bureaucratic institutions and monuments, whether they are called Circumlocution Offices, Chancery, or Crystal Palaces, loses both hierarchical and dialectical tension and extension and fosters in its fantastic worshipers a vulnerability to haunting by dead eyes and white horses.[13]

Shaw had continually warned against the compensatory idealization of public organizations which makes democracies more dangerous than theocracies and absolute monarchies—when, like God,

---

12. Emile Durkheim, *Le Suicide* (Paris, 1897), 224, 288.
13. These institutions and monuments are, of course, mocked by Dickens and Dostoyevsky.

they are invented and then obeyed, they are redundant and protective of our hopes and fears, rather than critical of them. Nietzsche protests the obscuring of origins in this idealization: "The hypocritical show with which all civil institutions are whitewashed, as if they were products of morality—e.g. marriage; work; one's profession; the fatherland; the family; order; law." These are our wardens against the clash with reality, the ghost bureaucracies in which the playfully critical appropriation of hats, canes, chairs is judged an act of immorality committed by the only moral man in the community because his identity cannot be usurped. As Golyadkin's servant puts it, "Nice people don't live falsely and don't have doubles"[14]

Mrs. Alving suggests a truth everywhere illustrated in modern literature, that without a living relationship to the public and private past, there can be no future, and in a society devoid of living social and spiritual authority, ghosts remain ever unappeased: "It's all kinds of old dead doctrines, and opinions and beliefs, that sort of thing. They aren't alive in us; but they hang on all the same, and we can't get rid of them" (I, G, II, 238). Our ghosts make no great public claims, for we have lost our Hamlets, our shadowing Christ, our hierarchies. They hang endlessly in the air as rationalizations, projections, transferences trapped in a world that can neither overcome them by epic action nor send them to hell.[15] Joyce's great novel is filled with the epic envy of easy concourse between the living and the dead, and necromancy is not the least of Bloom's anachronistic virtues. The modern specter mutters the refrain of Mummy in Strindberg's Ghost Sonata: "God, if we could die! If we could only die!" We are all, like Irene, "our own shadows" (I, WWDA, II, 1068). Through all the major plays of Ibsen, the ghosts, trolls, demons of our lost selves are not just the products of a guilty conscience, but also of an evasion of reality. Nora's anxiety about her doll-secret is a part of a larger anxiety over leading a doll-life. And there really is very little difference between the two kinds

---

14. Shaw, The Quintessence of Ibsenism, 106; Nietzsche, Will to Power, 175; Fyodor Dostoyevsky, The Double, trans. George Bird (Bloomington, Ind., 1958), 157.

15. Brian Johnston, The Ibsen Cycle, 11, notes that the second part of Hegel's Phenomenology is filled with ghosts from the pained past, like the damned souls in Inferno, to illustrate the errors and inadequacies of partial vision. The final view of Hegel keeps the ghosts in their places and the cunning of history wears them out, but the intent is true, as well, of less consoling texts, like James's short stories, Joyce's Ulysses, Hardy's poems.

of ghosts Rubek describes to Irene: "You have a shadow that tortures you. And I have the weight of my conscience" (*I, WWDA,*
II, 1069). Since the Great World's cast of characters has been banished from both the internal and external stage, its only means of
expression is through this haunting. What is a symptom of an abbreviated sphere, soul, and psyche is also a presence that testifies to
the refusal of a larger world. Where both internal and external reality have been deformed and denied, their primordial and mythical
representatives will press their secrets into greater mysteries, most
often in the house that is vulnerable to the invasion of a force Freud
calls "unheimlich," uncanny, a term that binds together home and
concealment. The most worn out of all stage conventions, the
ghost, rebounds from its exile to the wings by tenaciously transgressing thresholds as an indispensable sign of ontological, social,
and psychological guilt. Instead of being a call to action, it is a sign
of blockage, but by making itself available in metaphor and myth, it
reminds us of our task to open the corridor between past and
present, duty and desire, flesh and spirit, language and feeling. The
ghost is an unappeased transition as much as it signals an unat-
tended sickness.[16]

In one of the most powerful scenes of *Rosmersholm,* Rosmer, tormented by the suspicion that he might have committed psychic
murder of his wife Beata, engages Rebecca in an active opposition
to the ghost's emanation from the dark silence. The recovery of a
steady state of innocence is devoutly desired, but Rosmer is wise
enough to know he will never be able to transcend his past completely. Perhaps, he almost hysterically hopes out loud, he can
"overpower the dead" with a "new, living reality," rooted in marriage with Rebecca (*I, R,* II, 544–46). In this scene of rising will,

16. Freud, *"The Uncanny,"* 192; Strindberg, *The Ghost Sonata,* Scene 2, in *A Dream Play
and Four Chamber Plays,* 212. See Rolf Fjelde, "The Dimensions of Ibsen's Dramatic World,"
in Haakonsen (ed.), *Second International Ibsen Seminar,* 176: "Nothing illustrates Ibsen's fore-
closure of the supernatural so well as his brilliant metamorphosis of that innocent theatrical
figure, the stage ghost." George Steiner, speaking of the disappearance of the rich mythical
world of reference, notes in *The Death of Tragedy,* 293, that Ibsen turned the disadvantage of
a world order of belief and imagination into an aesthetic advantage by internalizing the
ghosts of the Greek and Elizabethan tragedies: "They arise in the unstable soul. . . . The
ghosts that haunt his characters are not the palpable herald of damnation whom we find in
Hamlet and Macbeth. They are forces of disruption that have broken loose from the care of
the spirit."

climaxing with the common Ibsen vow "I won't go through life with a corpse on my back" and Rebecca's refusal of what she so longed for, the playwright demonstrates the transitional potency of the unappeased specter, of a past that tenaciously punishes the present, not because it has been insufficiently buried, but because it was insufficiently lived. The shadowy third is no longer Christ; the language of spiritual resolution is self-propelled. Markedly different in this respect, too, from Nietzsche, Ibsen makes his vocabulary of "overcoming" symptomatic of a will that has not done its work with the fearful ambivalence of motive in marriage and childhood. The apparent boldness of will is intimately related to its surrender in retreats into childlike love, for both tactics avoid the inevitable conflicts of guilty sexuality. The sickness of the relationship in the present most often results from a ritualistic idealizing of the dead out of their complex reality. Mrs. Alving's penultimate insight into the frustration of the captain's life, like Rosmer's acceptance of ambivalence, had to work its way up through monument, hieroglyph, and symbol. The beginning of wisdom and appeasement is Rebecca's question: "But tell me this first: is it you who go with me, or I who go with you?" (I, R, IV, 58). The surrender to the ambivalence of motive recalls the early exchange between Mrs. Helseth and Rebecca:

> Rebecca. At Rosmersholm they cling to their dead.
> Mrs. Helseth. To my mind, miss, it's the dead that cling to Rosmersholm.
> Rebecca. The dead?
> Mrs. Helseth. Yes, it's, so to say, as if they couldn't quite tear themselves free from the ones that stay on.
> (I, R, I, 498)

At the end of the play, Rebecca and Rosmer combine what here is separated in a living dialectic that shames the bourgeois habits of cause and effect, even though it is an impotent death that must prepare the new reality.

Henry James, whose fiction was certainly touched by this play, raises in "The Altar of the Dead" the connection between the ritualized idealization of a fixed past and the need to protect oneself from difficult engagements with the present. As James puts the temptation, the religion of the dead is an "immense escape from the

actual" into "a simplified intensified essence."[17] The shocking recognition is that the power given to the dead by worship is a form of
patronization that signals a repressed resentment. Mrs. Borkman's
most vengeful and suppressive assault (more conscious than Mrs.
Alving's) is her promise to Borkman to raise a "living" monument
of revised reputation in order to kill the past: "It will be as if a living
fence, a woven hedge of trees and bushes was planted thick, thick
around your buried life. All the dark of the past will be screened
away; and all remembrance of John Gabriel Borkman will vanish
into oblivion" (I, JGB, III, 999).

Punishing the past of others as a displacement of responsibility
for self-judgment is also a tactic of Hjalmar, who scorns Gina for
not casting "a critical eye" on her past which is to blame for his
unhappiness (I, WD, IV, 457). It is easy to spot in the patronizers
of another's past the inadequate judges of personal guilt and responsibility, but we have the same evasion in Rosmer who, in his sterile
nobility, longs for peace from the persistent conflicts of sex and
will. Instead of overpowering the past by "a new living reality," as
much a product of idealization as fixation on the dead, we would
have to bring the past to its full life in relation to the present. At
this point, Rosmer could realize the truth of Ella's words to Borkman: "It's a double murder you're guilty of! Murder of your own
soul, and of mine" (I, JGB, II, 986). The wronged wife of an
evaded past who had asked for both sexuality and tradition is met in
the present by a renunciation of politics, religion, and sex. Rosmer
might feel different from those who use religion as an escape from
sexuality, but, in the given context of a past whose living demands
were not confronted, the surrender of all action does not recover
innocence and is, in fact, as much an evasion of necessary impurity
as a more obvious displacement.[18] Hierarchy, dialectic, evolution
are leveled by negative as by positive conflations. Rosmer's final renunciation is of the value of a life of repression. But if the final
scene, in which the recognition of all the complex suffering of
Beata leads to the sacrifice of marriage in this life, fails to serve the

17. Henry James, "The Altar of the Dead," In *The Cage and Other Tales*, ed. Morton
Dauwen Zabel (New York, 1958), 98.
18. See Peter Gay, *The Bourgeois Experience: Victoria to Freud*, Vol. II, *The Tender Passion*
(New York, 1986), 287.

public as a fruitful climax and never achieves the old transcendental dignity of *liebestod*, it is a choice that is at least free from both
retribution and condescension, beyond the understanding of the
Mrs. Helseths. If no character in Ibsen can take the final step in the
spiraling transvaluation of loss, still, it makes a difference whether
they renounce as escape or as a sign of ultimate responsibility, just
short of creation.

In an analysis of the relationship between anxiety and sexual
guilt that anticipates so much of future psychoanalytic thought,
Schopenhauer underlines the tension between the will to reproduc-
tion and the defeat of death:

> If the will to live exhibited itself merely as an impulse to self-preserva-
> tion, this would only be an assertion of the individual phenomenon
> for the span of time of its natural duration. The cares and troubles of
> such a life would not be great, and consequently existence would be
> easy and serene. Since, on the contrary, the will wills life absolutely
> and for all time, it exhibits itself also as sexual impulse, which has in
> view an endless series of generations. This impulse does away with that
> carelessness, serenity, and innocence which would accompany a merely
> individual existence, for it brings unrest and melancholy into the
> consciousness.[19]

Suppression of the instinct brings only more anxiety. But Ibsen
plays yet another chord in depicting it, for he pits the will to self-
preservation in his sick society *against* the desire for a generation
haunted by the task of redemption and displaced self-realization.
The belief in permanent standards and eternal truths tortures—as
Foucault reads Nietzsche—the bodies of the children, which must
be blasted as the sign of a guilty sexual parental past. Rosmer's arrest
of the generational future of Rosmersholm is intimately related to
his surprise at Rebecca's emergence from his bedroom, the psychic
counterpart of Corneille's old scene of transgressed decorum. The
anxiety associated with sexual conflict is evaded by a paralyzed state
of self-preservation, but suicide is the ransom. The conservation of
the present might mean the repression of the past, or it might be
bought by escape into a myth of the past, as in *Little Eyolf*, in which

19. Schopenhauer, "The World as Will and Idea," in *The Will to Live*, 111. On the medical interest in sexuality in the years of Ibsen's major period, see Frank J. Sulloway, *Freud,
Biologist of the Mind: Beyond the Psychoanalytic Legend* (New York, 1979), 238–76.

the law of change is, for most of the play, used as a sexual excuse that promises a sense of permanence. By perverting generation, the parents in Ibsen's plays paradoxically hope for self-perpetuation without guilt. That is why Ibsen is fond of haunting self-preservation with illegitimacy and lust, or of linking the symbolic or psychic murder of children with the mortality of art. D. H. Lawrence, in his essay on Hardy, had pleaded for the sensual and spiritual wasting of the self into life and out of the stillborn state of self-preservation, and the failure to do that is behind the suicide in Ibsen's plays, behind Mrs. Alving's sudden release from inhibition as she sanctions incest for the sake of releasing the self into "livsglede." Desperation shifts her motive far from the cool utilitarian recognition of the Enlightenment that this might, in some cultures, be a solution immune to sin and salvation, and makes it a kind of deliberate counterdoubling to the ominous signs of inherited traits evident in the features and gestures of father and son. Allmers's escape with Asta, into childhood, is disturbed violently by the recognition of a possible sexuality, for that doubling is a symptom, not a choice.[20]

In all his discussions in and out of art of the deformation of family and society by false sexual expectations, Strindberg cries out: "Where did love—good, healthy, sensual love—go?"[21] He is moved to this question by the parasitic vampirism of his characters and his own marriages, their alternate rising and sinking in the struggle for survival, and by the design of the narcissistic redundancy of self-preservation in which children are power pawns. Spencer's interest in the dissolution of a species developed into the high specialization of self-preservation is moralized by Ibsen who tirelessly exposes the unnatural patterns of modern acclimatization as evolutionary maladaptation. In response to Rita's affective insecurity, Allmers patronizes her with the pretense of evolutionary wisdom: "But my dearest Rita—human beings change over the years—and we have to as well—just like everyone else" (I, LE, I, 891). This response neatly hides his desire that his relations with Asta might be one of Borghejm's lovely things in the world that never end (I, LE, I, 884). Rita, who had stimulated Borghejm's

20. Foucault, "Nietzsche, Genealogy, and History," in *Language, Counter-Memory, Practice*, 147; Lawrence, *Phoenix*, 400–401.
21. Strindberg, "The Father," in *Pre-Inferno Plays*, 59.

wish with her secret allusion to the alliance between Asta and her husband as something that has to come to an end, counters with her characteristically possessive demand: "Not me! And I don't want to hear of you changing either. I couldn't bear that, Alfred. I want to keep you all to myself" (*I*, LE, I, 891). How close this is to Torvald's fantasy in preparation for his sexual claim: "Then I pretend that you're my young bride, that we're just coming home from the wedding, that for the first time I'm bringing you into my house—that for the first time I'm alone with you—completely alone with you, your trembling young beauty!" (*I*, DH, III, 183).

A phrase like "laws of change" may submit to evolutionary passage as a character staggers towards integrity and insight, but often such formulas, passed from mouth to mouth, preserve both the species and the psyche from having to register ambivalence, to hear others and listen to oneself. Plagiarism, like possessiveness and patronization, is a clear sign of an uncreated self. It is here, as so often in modern literature, the opposite of Montaigne's great appropriation of the living words of the past since its purpose is not a shared education, but self-justification and preservation. The sense that we are inevitably half of what we should be is so steady an assumption in Strindberg that he thinks of the stealing of words between characters, in the struggle of the fittest, as a major theatrical scene. In his tooth-and-claw families, characters plagiarize to conquer. In Dostoyevsky, too, plagiarism can be a means of aggressive trapping, as in *The Eternal Husband*, or as a Smerdyakov uses it against Ivan Karamazov, or it can excuse the inability to love one other human being, to get outside of oneself, to suffer constructive guilt. Liza scores heavily against the Underground Man when she exclaims, "Why you—speak exactly like a book," and Ivan's creations constantly plagiarize him to keep him from surprise visits, internal and external. He tames the responsibility implicit in Alyosha's kiss by calling it "plagiarism": "You stole it from my poem."[22]

At an abstract level, as Manders instinctively knows, prosecution is safe from self-judgment, and plagiarism protects individ-

22. See also the Holbergian influence in the connection between "the ludicrous and lofty" in Jens Kruuse, "The Function of Humor in the late Plays of Ibsen," in Haakonsen (ed.), *Second International Ibsen Seminar*, 49; Dostoyevsky, *Notes from Underground*, 86; *The Brothers Karamazov*, trans. David Magarshack (2 vols.; Harmondsworth, Middlesex, 1958), I, 309.

uality from having to love each and every child, brother, father, neighbor. Working his way through a flurry of formulas, Dmitri dreams of the single suffering babe and, instead of trying the parents, like his brother, he becomes himself a babe, wondering at existence, at suffering, at the absurdity of the world, without the need to patronize or judge. At this level, questions have to be asked in a manner so free of blame, so immediate and elemental, that they resist imitation: "' Why are they crying?' Mitya persisted stupidly. 'Why are its arms bare? Why don't they wrap it up? . . . Why are people poor? Why's the baby poor?' . . . And he felt that, though he was asking wild and senseless questions he could not help asking them and that, indeed, that was the way they had to be asked."[23] This is Rousseau's language of the heart. Mrs. Alving is on the verge of asking those wild and senseless questions and, indeed, she crosses the patrolled borders, but without the joy of nascent faith. For Ibsen, plagiarism is first of all a protection against unwelcome psychological, social, and moral knowledge, though it is also, as with Engstrand and Manders, a means of manipulation and control. Mrs. Alving—whose reading, paradoxically, has fed her need for the language of life[24]—confronts Manders's rebuke of her independent thinking:

> Mrs. Alving. But what exactly do you object to in these books?
> Manders. Object to? You surely don't think I waste my time exploring that kind of publication?
> Mrs. Alving. In other words, you know nothing of what you're condemning.
> Manders. I've read quite enough about these writings to disapprove of them.
> Mrs. Alving. Yes, but your own opinion—
> Manders. My dear Mrs. Alving, there are many circumstances in life where one has to entrust oneself to others. That's the condition of this world, and it's all for the best. How else could society function.
> (I, G, I, 214)

Like Ivan's patronizing judgments, (in spite of the fact that they testify to an impressive intellectual source), Manders's precepts can be

23. Dostoyevsky, *The Brothers Karamazov*, II, 596.
24. Ibsen uses the stereotypical modern opposition of books to life in various ways. That Hjalmar has not cut the pages of his books indicates his distance from the life that Hilda feels is antithetical to reading.

stolen only for political manipulation, not for life. Neither the one who pretends to reject God nor the one who pretends to accept Him is capable of Christian love.[25]

Although *Pillars of Society* and *An Enemy of the People* are slogan saturated, *The Wild Duck*, by bringing rhetorical stances inside the home, best illustrates how poisoned the family is by the formulaic taming of feelings. It is one thing to be young and charming by publicly "declaiming other people's poems and ideas" at school (*I*, WD, V, 475), but it is quite another to posture rhetorically at home, so that unpleasantness and self-judgment can be kept at the door:

> *Hjalmar.* Please—don't talk any more about sickness and poison. I'm not used to that kind of conversation. In my house nobody talks to me about ugly things.
> (*I*, WD, III, 444)

Like Torvald, Hjalmar stages reality to keep it out of the reach of suffering. He successively shows us his mastery of the self-pitying rhetoric of the abused breadwinner (*I*, WD, II, 418), the sentimental paterfamilias (*I*, WD, II, 420), and of the rhetoric of suffering (*I*, WD, II, 421) of the martyred and deceived father and husband. As he pastes together Werle's deed, he intones: "Far be it from me to take liberties with another's property" (*I*, WD, V, 483). He even practices the rhetoric of depth: "It's useful sometimes to go down deep into the night side of existence" (*I*, WD, IV, 466). We have little trouble believing Relling's recitation of Hjalmar's sentimental grief speeches of the near future, especially after hearing him appropriate the wit of Werle's party for his family performance (*I*, WD, V, 490). But Hjalmar is not isolated by his phrasing. It keeps the members of his family in their assigned roles and attracts the mission of Gregers and the cynicism of Relling—both, themselves, rhetorically imprisoned by their need to ward off self-examination. When Gregers spews forth blame against his father, ostensibly on behalf of his mother, Werle shrugs, "Word for word, as if I were hearing your mother" (*I*, WD, I, 409). And Relling is condemned to the role of patronizing dispenser of life-lies while fulminating against ideals, a stance that betrays his lack of courage.

25. See John Northam, *Ibsen*, 201, 221. Northam reminds us that Ibsen was one of the writers to feel most acutely that modern society, with its burden of Christian terminology carried without belief, was hostile to self-realization.

Tony Tanner connects "unoccupied women" with "unoccupied language" as carriers of blocked desires in the bourgeois home, and certainly Nora could join the women he sees as primary victims of rhetorical shut-out. If Hedda, isolated from the world of action by her economic needs and cowardice, "turns the gun against the word," Nora, just after we have heard Torvald's outrageously patronizing couch speech of forgiveness, abruptly forces her husband to sit down and to listen.[26] That is the difficult task of the last scene, which—for all its superior density to a similar one in Bjørnson's *The Bankrupt*—some critics find too talky. But the serious act of conversation cannot overturn a lifetime of patronizingly endearing epithets and recitations geared to prevent listening at all costs. Like most marriages, Nora's has become a refuge from attentive listening. As much as *Madame Bovary* and most of modern literature, the plays of Ibsen are about not listening. Ibsen's cherished author, Dickens, himself had many times made the dramatic connections between the need of the weak and patronizing self not to listen and the need to fend off the words of others with balloons of aesthetic morality, nowhere better than in his masterpiece of caricature, Pecksniff, who was above all "a moral man, even up to his throat. All is moral to him."[27] Nor is there anything personal about the language used to confine others to their assigned roles and responses in the tableaux of families of parents and children that Gregers ironically mocks. Morality is always for the sake of the other. "There is nothing personal in morality, my love," says Pecksniff to his daughter. Gregers says to Hedvig, "Oh, if only your eyes were really open to what makes life worth living—if only you had the true, joyful, courageous spirit of self sacrifice, *then* you'd see him coming up to you" (*I, WD, V, 478*). This is the "virulent moralistic fever" that Relling spots as a symptom of those who need to look outside themselves for something to admire. It is a source of Rosmer's bad conscience, sickened in a home in which the father had still to play the Major (*I, R, I, 511*).[28]

26. Tony Tanner, *Adultery in the Novel: Contract and Transgression* (Baltimore, 1979), 100.

27. Dickens, *Martin Chuzzlewit*, ed. P. N. Furbank (Harmondsworth, Middlesex, 1968), 65.

28. See the article of Daniel Haakonsen, "The Function of Sacrifice in Ibsen's Realistic Drama," in Haakonsen (ed.), *First International Ibsen Seminar*, 21–34. See also Dickens, *Martin Chuzzlewit*, 65.

Moralism reflects, as well, the way the public world has deformed Christianity—in which, as in Hjalmar and the underground man, "nothing is active but the tongue"—into an enemy of psychological reality.[29] When Molvik declaims, "The child isn't dead; she sleepeth," Relling joins the phrase killers whose authority is sapped by their own phrase making: "Rubbish!" (I, WD, V, 489). Freud knew that modern civilization could not really live by biblical imperatives and that the more it refused to listen and believe, the more persistently the religious rhetoric would come at it. Rousseau had begun the modern complaint against mediating languages that forced Christianity and nature to be enemies. Why do there have to be so many opinions between God and me? he asks. Conscience can hardly be heard over the babble of its counterfeiters, so that it "no longer speaks to us. It no longer responds to us."[30] In a culture of marrowless truths, biblical morality is quarantined in formulas and social morality in party slogans and plagiarism.

> *Stensgaard.* I've noticed lately that you've taken to imitating me; you're even copying my clothes and my style of writing. Stop it.
> *Bastian.* Why? Don't we belong to the same party?
> (W.I, LY, IV, 107)

Not the least of the motives for Ibsen's anarchism must have been the need to hack up this puppet show.[31] Ardently oversensitive to accusations of his own borrowing, especially in early plays like *The Feast at Solhoug,* Ibsen insisted that his words and scenes grow from within. Those who slandered him, he claimed, were men "whose critical thoughts had long been thought and exposed by others; their views had long since been formulated elsewhere. Their whole aesthetic theory was borrowed, their whole critical method was borrowed. . . . Yes, even their attitude of mind was borrowed. Borrowed, the whole lot borrowed." No wonder we see his critics in his plays. Nietzsche speaks of the way in which his sickness served him by forcing him to listen to that deepest self "buried and grown silent under a constant *compulsion to listen* to other selves." Of course,

---

29. This is the phrase of Henry James, speaking of Hjalmar, *The Scenic Art,* 254.

30. Freud, *Civilization and Its Discontents,* 90; Rousseau, *Confessions,* 295; Rousseau, *Emile,* 290.

31. Compare Gustave Flaubert to Louise Colet, September 4, 1852, in *Selected Letters,* 141.

borrowing is like compelled listening to the phrases of others, as Rousseau affirmed in his *Confessions*, so that no one would have to listen to the self.[32]

Once again, the art of communication becomes the art of taking away. The renunciation of rhetorical cooperation in Nora and Mrs. Alving, who were educated to follow and repeat the opinions of others, is already under way in the midst of anxious, last-minute negotiations with the language that hides the truth. Like Nora's early cry from the heart, adrift from her conversation with Mrs. Linde, "How free you must feel," Mrs. Alving's true speech can be heard in the middle of her conversations: "I never really listened to myself" (*I*, G, II, 235). She might condemn her mother and convention, but this recognition leads her language deeper and deeper away from the surface imperatives of aesthetic morality into the mystery and responsibility of self-judgment.[33] It leads her, too, paradoxically, to listen to the Captain's life. Mayor Stockmann sarcastically refers to the overly spontaneous and original manner of speaking of his brother, which becomes more and more isolated in the course of the play, as the majority can neither listen nor convert (*I*, EP, I, 288). The drama of definition, which carries with it a whole society in Jane Austen, sputters and explodes into frustrated bursts of orphaned recognition or, painfully resigned, directly admits that feeling is hopelessly sundered from principle:

> *Helmer.* Haven't you been happy here?
> *Nora.* No, never. I thought so—but I never have.
> *Helmer.* Not—not happy!
> *Nora.* No, only lighthearted.
> (*I*, DH, III, 91)

It is Brand who shoots down common abuses of the word *love*, but Hedda is just as intolerant: "Love! Has any word been so abused and debased" (M, B, III, 58; *I*, HG, I, 737; II, 724). Ibsen's characters are never rewarded like Zarathustra with the power and ecstasy of transvaluation, but they certainly suffer the terrible burden of moral gravity: "Almost in the cradle are we presented with heavy

---

32. Ibsen's comments on the "trial" of *The Feast at Solhoug* in O. 1, 370, 374; Nietzsche, *Ecce Homo*, 93. See also Duve, *The Real Drama of Ibsen*, 169, who notes that the undoing of repression through the whole play to catch up on exposition is, in effect, the action.

33. See Northam, *Ibsen*, 86, for a good discussion of Mrs. Alving's language.

words and values: this dowry calls itself 'Good' and 'Evil'. For its sake we are forgiven for being alive."[34] Considering the fate of those who do finally listen, we wonder why it is such an imperative task in Ibsen's plays, but without this step, the Great World could not be present on the scene and free from the burden of rewarding us like a sentimental Christian God.

Even the great scenes of communion, which give the impression of intense listening and ride on poetic refrains immune to the conversational tags that plague the bourgeois atmospheres and get the last word in Hedda's play, suffer the isolation and disequilibrium provoked by the release of a guilty desire.[35] These are not the true marriages that can live in or transform the world, for they have neither the interest nor creative power to bind the social future to the personal past. Nevertheless, the communions exhibit a higher form of haunting and doubling that generates a dialectical tension between lower and higher plagiarism. Lower types, like Manders, stimulate parodic repetition by the Engstrands, as Gregers calls out Hjalmar; while higher types, trapped in paralyzing guilt and fear, with a raging hunger for innocence and power, lure out doubles that seem entirely antithetical to the summoning body. In this sense, the returning half—Rebecca, Hilda, Ellida's sailor, Irene, even Asta—responding to the crippled will that would join art and sex guiltlessly, from the beginning, is able to lead the body out of its historical and provincial Christian prison into a larger, mythical world, but one that is only a provisional atmosphere, still parasitic on the need to escape the making of true marriage by the mythical blending of the second with the first family.

The summons indicts both society and the self that has not made its way, painfully, through the labyrinthine convolutions of protective language and idealized institutions and roles to an uncertain and evolutionary future. For the murderously disturbing intrusion can charge longing for love and power, up the mountain to death. Conversation between Løvborg and Hedda, Hilda and Solness, Ella and Borkman, Irene and Rubek, pitches itself at such a high degree of intensity that it would seem to be spoken in the missing language of the heart, and psychic intercourse would be an antidote to psy-

34. Nietzsche, *Thus Spoke Zarathustra*, 211.
35. See Gabrieli, *Rilettura di Ibsen*, 120n; Kruuse, "The Funtion of Humor in the Later Plays of Ibsen," in Haakonsen (ed.), *Second International Ibsen Seminar*, 17.

chic murder. But the absolute social isolation of such moments harbors regression and confession rather than the kind of exchange we recognize as full, freighted with useful suffering, like that between Rita and Allmers at the end of their play. Ghostly eruptions of intimate strangers onto the scene, in Ibsen's plays, do not serve to integrate body and mind and the social world, as the psychologists would have it.[36] They break, however, the neurosis that pins strong wills to the petty and small displacements of Aline and raise expression to the dignity and large absurdity of myth. Unearned release from psychological and spiritual pain cannot reach the Great World, which has no need to escape from morality but rather restores it to fullness and balance in a larger atmosphere in which that morality is a citizen, not a master. But when Asta is surprised by Allmers's return, she immediately refers to feeling rather than duty, and this almost magic elision of the torturing demands of married sex and responsibility is a counterprojection that successfully demotes the lower projections of the moralizing world, posing as standpoints:

> *Asta.* Oh, *that's* what I was feeling. *That's* what drew me out here?
> (*I*, LE, I, 868)

More terrible are the materialized callings of Ellida and Solness, for these are less escapes from present terror than embodiments of the fear of young, uncontrolled, and amoral passions:

> *Wangel.* Why, then in all this time, have you not wanted to live with me as my wife?
> *Ellida.* Because of the terror I feel of him, of the stranger.
> (*I*, LS, III, 629)

The poetry of feeling, screened out by the automatic language of slogans and formulas, can convert the bourgeois determinism of cause and effect of family inheritance to the telegony of sentiment, elective affinities (the playfully bitter jab of Mrs. Alving that Osvald had the minister's look around the mouth, the doubling of Asta and Eyolf).[37] Allmers says to Asta: "Yes, I think that living

36. See Richard Schechner, "Unexpected Visitors in Ibsen's Late Plays," in Fjelde (ed.), *Ibsen*, 168; C. G. Jung, "The Psychology of the Child Archetype," in C. G. Jung and C. Kerenyi, *Essays on a Science of Mythology*, trans. R. F. C. Hull (New York, 1949), 121.

37. See Marvin Carlson, "Ibsen, Strindberg, and Telegony," *PMLA*, C (1985), 776, who notes that "in contrast to Zola, Strindberg and Ibsen emphasized the poetic side of the exploration into heredity if necessary, at the expense of the scientific."

together has shaped us both in each other's image. Inwardly, I mean" (*I, LE, II,* 902). The internal world of passionate feelings, arrested by the terrified restrictions of bourgeois acclimatization, is necessarily immature when it erupts. Christian humanism had forbidden practice in the dialectical dramas between past and present, duty and desire, myth and morality—those couples that freely roam the forests of the Great World. The rich feelings of the past, stamped by bourgeois guilt, are forced into mythopoeic hyperbole because they cannot be domesticated as intruders, strangers, someone standing between sanctioned relations.

Those who call out higher halves are as eager to protect the dangerous past from a prosecuting present as the present is eager to protect itself against the past. And by this double estrangement we sense how much societal abbreviation of our medium depended on our cooperation. That is why it is so surprisingly pathetic to see Hilda, even briefly, worried over Aline's feelings. The drive to self-realization cannot afford to be hooked by intimacy. The epithet of "stranger" permeating the plays registers not only a modern fate, but suppressed desire. In one of his most central and expansive statements, James writes in the preface to *Portrait of a Lady:* "Tell me what the author is, and I will tell you of what he has *been* conscious. Thereby I shall express to you at once his boundless freedom and his moral reference."[38] This generous connection works in Ibsen himself only by making it impossible in the plays. The counterghosting of psychic communion and mythic elevation is never given the power to achieve in this world a larger reality out of the Jamesian marriage of realism and romance. Characteristically, the higher aspirations must be parodied and punished not to educate a consciousness, but to save the Great World from the degradation of our enactments.

The Rat Wife knows that an Ibsen house is most likely to be haunted because it so passionately desires to believe that it is undivided. It was in society that Rousseau felt foreign to himself, not unified, hence, not permanent, and had to act a part instead of be; his rejection of the city's theater, which he validates by confessing his love for it, insures his home in successive exiles against deceit. He is spared there, as well, the public division between happiness and virtue, the language of the heart and the language of power.

38. James, preface to *Portrait of a Lady,* 7.

Ibsen's houses are also resistant to the law of change, but use the theatrical arts most often to eliminate growth. Gregers accuses his father of hosting his party to demonstrate to the public that "family life is in order," a veritable "tableau of father with son" (*I, WD,* I, 409). But it is precisely the tableau of a perfect family Gregers projects onto Hjalmar's thriving fictional nest, while his father and Mrs. Sørby build a true marriage offstage. The habitual staging of home as theater gave to actors and actresses a rich and new doubled representation, in which occasional consciousness of theatricality, in Nora and Hedda, for example, disturbs type as much as the counterpointing languages of theater and the heart.[39] And it gives an ominous cast to Bernick's smugly rehearsed motto that "the family is the core of society" (*I,* PS, I, 33). The collapse of tension between public and private spheres gives the impetus to the theatrical freezing of families. Sennett comments on this nineteenth-century urge: "The principle of personality created instability in a domain—the family—people were resolved to fix into a tableau."[40]

One of the most interesting speeches given to Hedda in a draft of the play merges marriage and theater in a brutally realistic assessment: "Then isn't it an honourable thing to profit by one's person? Don't actresses and others turn their advantages into profit? I had no other capital."[41] Clearly, domestic theater in the unreal cities cleverly disguises the transformation of family to the market intercourse Marx identified with empty liberal formulas, as a symptom of modern alienation. Nora's consciousness of the relations between theater and marriage had been so long enacted that she daily converts her secret nobility into moral melodrama. Perhaps, she tells Mrs. Linde, she will reveal her deed some day to Torvald, but only "years from now, when I'm no longer so attractive. Don't laugh. I only mean when Torvald loves me less than now, when he stops enjoying my dancing and dressing up and reciting for him" (*I,* DH, I, 137).[42] When she does the tarantella, we remember, Torvald worries that art is in danger of becoming too natural, his concern

---

39. Gay Gibson Cima, "Discovering Signs: The Emergence of the Critical Actor in Ibsen," *Theatre Journal,* XXXV (1983), 5–22, discusses the revolution in theater brought about by this playing beyond the boundaries of type, a thrilling challenge to actors and actresses.

40. Sennett, *The Fall of Public Man,* 183.

41. *Ibsen's Workshop,* 383.

42. See Roach, "Ibsen and the Moral Occult," who notes the correspondence between stale theater and stale morality.

conditioned, perhaps, by the knowledge that he needs the theater more than Nora as protection against life.[43] For him, Art must repress, not express, the complexities of the human heart. Krogstad is continuous with the final version in a draft, when he explains to Nora why he does not have the luxury of only vengeance as a motive: "I dare say you have read in novels of villains whose only motive is revenge. . . . I am not like the villains in romances; I have four children to support; they require food and clothing." Helmer's speeches often seem imported from the popular stage, like those of Hjalmar, whom Weigand calls a "virtuoso of emotional melodrama," a talent well suited to his economic parasitism. Though Torvald rebukes Nora's suffering words as playacting, he is never aware of the theater of their marriage. Rank supports the marriage as theater, but when he dies, the marriage is no longer watched, and it loses the protective cover spectacle throws over being. The transition from the party's public theater upstairs to the domestic theater of frenzy downstairs, mediated by Rank, is a powerful one as art gives up its appeal in order to die to aesthetic morality, its Christmas props, its macaroons, its dance costume. The stark, decisive verdict on his life, "Certainty," that Rank delivers over Torvald's head to Nora, paradoxically, opens the overly known and rehearsed life to the uncertainty of a future in which ugliness cannot be kept out of the home. We realize that it is not theater that is the villain, but bad theater, the kind that refuses to explore the self.[44]

Vulnerability to dictated roles derives from the sense of insecurity generated by an education in received ideas and borrowed attitudes. The Underground Man had identified the normal, active man of the nineteenth century as characterless by ascribing to him defined character.[45] That man lives well in a reality engineered by social utopians and makers of rational systems—which is, in fact, fantastic—and he himself is characterless because he is acclimatized to a culture that solves contradictions of personality. The Underground Man has the dubious privilege of hyperconscious awareness

43. Durkheim, Le Suicide, 309–10, notes that nineteenth-century men needed the structure of marriage (even when it was theater) more than women because they needed to rein in their natural dissoluteness.
44. Ibsen's Workshop, 143; Weigand, The Modern Ibsen, 136; Roach, "Ibsen and the Moral Occult."
45. Dostoyevsky, Notes from Underground, 5.

of his narcissistic theatricality. His sense of self is entirely parasitic on its resistance to enlightened formulas of progress, and his body becomes an agent of parody. A public life ghosted of spontaneity and value, and a private life of rehearsed formulas of happiness and virtue, apparently brought together, but not as Rousseau dreamed them, stimulate in the intelligent man or woman a sense of separation between convention and reality that haunts the assumption of unified character. Mrs. Alving's recognition that we are, in a world that has suppressed its better half, made up of ghostly fragments is professed as a strategy of realism in Strindberg's preface to *Lady Julie*. Like Ibsen, he links the instability of modern character with that of origins and motive, in reality, a kaleidoscope of social, psychological, and biological determinations. D. H. Lawrence, typically, infuses the adoption of the expressionistic fragmentation of character representation with prophetic power, making of the abandonment of the old stable ego a call to a richer relationship between the known and unknown worlds, the domestic and the foreign. The will, periodically cancelled by the world without will, is nourished by it as it tolerates seasonal alternations and achieves, in its rhythmic undoing, the great power shut out by intellectual systems of self-preservation.

Ibsen, too, raided the reef of motives and mythical longings against the solemn ship of state language and rehearsed character, and in figures like Stensgaard, Hjalmar, and Ballested depicted those who are at home in the small world as "pieces of human beings, torn-off shreds of holiday clothes that have become rags."[46] But when Solness, fascinated by the uninhibited will of Hilda, asks his famous question, "How did you become what you are?" he provokes a perspective that suggests that patchwork is a willing fate of surrendered possibilities. The Viking power and joy of a vigorous mythical past made suffering elemental like the weather. The terror of suffering that drives the higher types of the small world to hysterically self-conscious declarations of the right to happiness and joy, to beauty and innocent power—all suppressed halves of our natural medium—has prevented character from the fullness of accommodated contradiction. Stockmann's character, defined *for* as much as *against* the world, has no need to seek happiness. When

46. Strindberg, preface to *Lady Julie*, in *Pre-Inferno Plays*, 77.

schools that teach "that work is a punishment for our sins" (*I*, EP, I, 295) are not countered by home, duty and "livsglede" become stage enemies, and "happiness" is an obsession. That is why Nora's qualification of the word is so important at the end of the play, and why Hedda and Mrs. Alving are so sarcastic about the use of *love* to describe infatuation and possession.

In an early draft, Ibsen has Rita say: "If only one does not demand happiness—at any price—I do not see why one should not be able to live one's life."[47] She has made cause of consequence. It is melodramatic Hedda who most fiercely drives happiness, joy, beauty, in desperate isolation from its medium, to death. (Tesman muses: "A beautiful death. What an idea" [*I*, HG, IV, 770]). But her hyperconsciousness of the rights to those gifts is shared by all Ibsen's climbers. In a society ruled by laws that repress rather than protect instincts, it is not surprising that Manders can rebuke Mrs. Alving's confession of misery in her marriage with these words: "But this is the very essence of the rebellious spirit, to crave happiness here in this life. What right have we human beings to happiness? No, we must do our duty, Mrs. Alving" (*I*, G, I, 225).

The Great World needs no such word as *rights*, and happiness is not a cause but a consequence of fullness. Reeducated, Mill (with Carlyle) affirmed that happiness was a by-product, not a goal, of life. And Manders is actually sound when he diagnoses the claim for happiness as against our nature, but he is sick because he cannot see that rebellion in the small world is the beginning of life. The insistence of the anti-utilitarian Nietzsche that the demand for happiness and goodness is a sign of a fantastic denial of suffering and protection against self-judgment is appealing to both Brandes and Ibsen. Only the poor in spirit, says the philosopher in an ironic echo of Manders, ask for happiness.[48] Mrs. Borkman joins the club when she counters Ella's desire for Erhart:

> *Ella (slowly)*. I wanted to open a path for Erhart to be happy here on earth.

47. *Ibsen's Workshop*, 509. On Hedda, see John Northam, *Ibsen*, 86, and Eugene Webb, *The Dark Dove: The Sacred and the Secular in Modern Literature* (Seattle, 1975), 53: "She is disgusted by both decay and the cycle of renewal in life, and what she hopes for is a transcendent grandeur that would transfigure the trivial round of ordinary life into something beautiful and incorruptible."
48. Brandes, *Friedrich Nietzsche*, 104; Nietzsche, *Will to Power*, 211.

Mrs. Borkman (scornfully). Pah! People of our standing have better things to do than think about happiness.

(*I*, JGB, I, 949)

When Ibsen makes happiness, in the mouth of Mrs. Borkman, a class issue, he shows us the full spread of his tiered context. Happiness is denied by the poor in spirit for political advantage and to excuse the failure to confront suffering as an opportunity; it is demanded by the richer in spirit who feel the suffering fully but cannot turn it to creation. And happiness is, as a mere by-product, uninteresting and unclaimed by the highest in spirit who can, at least in Nietzsche's empire, camp on the shores of the Great World. We do feel, in Ibsen's plays, that the highest of his seekers, however perverted, finally seem to have forgotton to think of it. The departures of Borghejm and Erhart for a happiness on earth to which they are suited aim for that blessing as a principle, not a by-product. They are humble enough to settle for the dignity and pleasure of enjoying this life:

> *Erhart.* This is happiness to me, Mother. The greatest, loveliest happiness of life. I can't tell you more than that.
> (*I*, JGB, III, 1005)

However unself-conscious the enactment, because it does not embrace original suffering and guilt, only future struggles of living together, it does not ready the Great World. Happiness is demanded by Ibsen's frustrated characters because it is no longer alive in the blood; it is idealized in culture's institutions, primarily marriage, and in humanitarian projects, which demand the sacrifice of the will's power while pretending to fulfill it:

> *Borkman (with pride).* I've loved power—
> *Mrs. Borkman.* Power, yes!
> *Borkman.* The power to create human happiness for vast multitudes around me.
> *Mrs. Borkman.* You once had the power to make *me* happy. Have you used it for that?
> *Borkman (not looking at her).* Someone very often has to go down—in a shipwreck.
> *Mrs. Borkman.* And your own son! Have you used your power, have you lived and labored, to make *him* happy?
> (*I*, JGB, III, 999)

Power is positively tortured by the Christian binding of happiness to sacrifice.

The problem of happiness was intimately related to expectations raised by inadequate or perverted educations. The promise of the reeducation of civilization, a continual hope of Enlightenment and Romantic poets and philosophers, by the second half of the nineteenth century had to wait behind a ferocious exposure of the abuses of the prime institutions of morality. Ibsen's will, intent on turning to parody our best hopes in order to open a greater tolerance for problems and to prevent a closing on polemical and political solutions for spiritual needs, could *technically* be said to have answered Schiller's call:

> Errors in *education* might be combatted in the stage with . . . success. We are still awaiting the play that will deal with this significant subject. Because of its effects, no subject is of more importance to the state than this and yet no institution is so at the mercy of the illusions and caprices of the citizenry as education. The stage alone could pass in review the unfortunate victims of careless education in a series of moving, upsetting pictures. Our fathers might learn to abandon their foolish maxims; our mothers might learn to love more wisely. The best hearted teachers are led astray by false ideas. It is still worse when they pride themselves on a certain method and systematically ruin the tender young plant.[49]

Yet, since Ibsen's work for a national theater led him into exile, his early interest in national concerns to disillusionment and disappointment with the homeland, he trooped his victims of an education that was deliberately, not carelessly, perverting across the stage from a distance great enough to keep the state from appropriating his services.[50] The novels of Dickens, Flaubert, Dostoyevsky, Fontane, were exhibiting the ravaged bodies of those educated, like Mill, by and to rational systems that kept the suffering of reality at bay and by and to sentimental dreams of purity and peace that made active love an impossibility on earth. The woman's question had raised for literature the problems of double standards and unequal expectations. Since A Doll House made such a sensational contribution to the debate, Ibsen was associated with the Indignation literature of the 1880s, fed by French social dramatists and novel-

49. Friedrich Schiller, "The Stage Considered as a Moral Institution," trans. Jane Bannard Greene, in Herzfeld-Sander (ed.), *Essays on German Theater*, 30.
50. See Brandes, *Henrik Ibsen*, 53, in which he terms Ibsen's pessimism one of indignation.

ists, Bjørnson, Camilla Collett, Brandes's translation of Mill and his discussion of Mme. de Stael and George Sand. The difficulties Ibsen had in detaching himself from political purpose have been told many times. Whether, with Brandes, Scandinavian and continental literature advertised equal rights to sexual expression or, like the converted Bjørnson, equal rights to premarital chastity, whether it exposed as the major injustice the institution of marriage or economic and legal exploitation of women, whether it examined the causes of prostitution or censured the condemnation of fallen women, it consistently concerned itself with the leading theme of Mill, the subjection of one party by another: "The legal subordination of one sex to the other—is wrong in itself, and now one of the chief hindrances to human improvement; and . . . it ought to be replaced by a principle of perfect equality, admitting no power or privilege on the one side, nor disability on the other."[51]

The theme is deeply interesting to Ibsen, but primarily on the spiritual level, in that the throttling of the creative will by sexual guilt was to him essentially an imposed subordination that prevented necessary negotiations between desire and duty. Since, like Kierkegaard, Ibsen thought of spiritual emancipation as a democratic imperative but of the struggle itself as individual and unconcerned with equality, he assumed social interest in the confusion of law and nature, paradoxically, to be both a way to higher freedom and a hindrance to human improvement. Ibsen might imply in his notes to A Doll House Mill's question of how much longer one form of society can be content to live according to the morality made for another, and the claim of Engels that within the nineteenth-century family, the wife plays the proletariat to the husband's bourgeois, but we sense a spiritual gap between Nora's diatribes against the law and religion, Torvald's "schooling," on the one hand, and on the other, the pronouncement that "I have to try to educate myself" (I, DH, III, 192).[52] And we sense a similar gap between Mrs.

51. See Maurice Gravier, Le Féminisme et l'amour dans la littérature norvégienne d'Ibsen à Sigrid Undset (Paris, 1968), 76; John Stuart Mill, The Subjection of Women (with Mary Wollstonecraft, The Rights of Women) (London, 1970), 219.

52. See Friedrich Engels, The Origin of the Family, Private Property, and the State: In the Light of the Researches of Lewis H. Morgan (New York, 1972), 137; Mill, The Subjection of Women, 259. Knut Hamsun, in a lecture of October 7, 1891, calls Ibsen an unconscious "child of Norway, of the century, and of John Stuart Mill," in James McFarlane (ed.), Ibsen: A Critical Anthology, 142.

Alving's rebuke against Manders's borrowed opinion and her recognition that she must listen to herself. Even Stockmann's school is not a school concerned with equality, but with aristocracy of spirit, and that is why he attaches it to categories of evolution that can separate nature from law and custom. He wants to detach Mrs. Borkman from her merging of class and spirit.

Of course, a reform of a general cultural education could disturb the stereotyped role sufficiently to make the individual available to spiritual evolution. Angelism, singled out by Brandes and Strindberg as the most dangerous of deforming expectations, frustrates Hedda into her verbal and murderous transgressions, for in supporting the romance of self-sacrifice, it guarantees the powerlessness that invites exploitation. Mill inherited and emphasized the argument that men's selfishness subjected women to the roles of "meekness, submissiveness, and resignation of all individual will" by appointing them determinants of sexual attractiveness. Morality distorts nature as it enslaves it for women: "All the moralities tell them that it is the duty of women, and all the current sentimentalities that it is their nature, to live for others; to make complete abnegation of themselves, and to have no life but in their affections."[53] Hegel had already persuasively demonstrated the perils and paradoxes of the parasitic slave/master relationship, and his analysis bore as much on psychological as on political arrangements. Nora realizes, finally, that Torvald is the greatest victim of his doll morality. When Krogstad gives us a chance to compare his social subjection with Nora's, when Hedda speaks of wanting to have power over another, actually a symptom of "the slave's fear of the outside world," we see how true it is that the will, forced into resignation, seeks power "most over those who are nearest," and this applies as much to internal as to external forces. The prolonged anxiety attacks exhibited by Nora, Mrs. Alving, and Hedda

53. Mill, *The Subjection of Women*, 232, 233. Shaw comments in *The Quintessence of Ibsenism*, 34: "Now of all the idealist abominations that make society pestiferous, I doubt if there be any so mean as that of forcing self-sacrifice on a woman under pretence that she likes it; and, if she ventures to contradict the pretence, declaring her no true woman." And compare Elias Bredsdorff, *Den store Nordisk krig om seksualmoralen: En documentarisk fremstilling af saedelighedsdebatten i nordisk litteratur i 1880'erne* (Oslo, 1973), 35–36, in which he notes that Bjørnson worried about the sentimental roles of dependence ruining women morally and fostering immorality in unfaithful and domineering husbands, seducers. Motherhood then becomes a role (as Torvald sees it), not a relationship. See *Ibsen's Workshop*, 457.

are internalized civil wars between the rising will and introjected conventions.[54]

Ibsen could forcefully use the body of a woman in which to work out the crippled will's subjection, his major affliction, and to work out his sexual guilt, partly because he believed the woman's will, withdrawn from public life, remained undeveloped in his culture. This is quite in contrast to the will of women in the vigorous Viking culture which, in Maurice Gravier's fancy, would have disavowed its contemporary emprisoned ghost languishing in her dollhouse. But, like Henry James, Ibsen would not let culture, economic deprivation, and convention excuse the will's surrender. He devises furious punishments for the fence-sitters—Mrs. Alving, Hedda— particularly when they recognize themselves as spiritual cowards, whose major drive is to control another to compensate for the failure to gain power over the self. Mill sees the interesting relations between the deprivation of liberty in an active and energetic mind and the desire for power as an external one, but in Ibsen, external obstacles are both the cause and red herring of frustration.[55]

Nothing is so touching in Ibsen as the gradual abandonment by Nora of control of Torvald's fate by idealization, then blame. And nothing is so dangerous, though not irrelevant, as the inadequacy of Mrs. Alving's allusion to her mother as the one who sold her into marriage. Ibsen joins the Indignation writers of his time when he has Mrs. Alving retort to Manders's disgust at Engstrand's paid marriage to a fallen woman: "Then what's your opinion of me, who let herself be married to a fallen man?" (I, G, II, 235).

The shift of blame is the sign of expansion, but that self-recognition is at war with other causes: "If Mother could came back and see me now, where all those splendors got me." Surely the mother and Manders are crucial in creating a "profoundly guilty mother" (I, G, I, 227). Ibsen supports this assumption in a note that might have come out of any feminist literature from Mary Wollstonecraft to Mill: "These women of the present day, ill-used as daughters, as sisters, as wives, not educated according to their gifts, prevented from

---

54. Ibsen's notes to *Hedda Gabler*, trans. Evert Sprinchorn, in Cole (ed.), *Playwrights on Playwriting*, 166. On the relationship between subjection, repression, and blackmail, see Alexander Welsh, *George Eliot and Blackmail* (Cambridge, Mass., 1985), 353.

55. Duve, *Symbolikken i Henrik Ibsens skuespill*, 138, Meyer, *Ibsen*, 643; Gravier, *Le Féminisme et l'amour*, 15; Mill, *The Subjection of Women*, 313.

following their inclination, deprived of their inheritance, embittered in temper—it is these who furnish the mothers of the new generation. What is the result?" No one would deny Archer's complementary interpretation: "His idea had been to show in Fru Alving how a badly educated, badly trained woman was certain to be driven, by men of Pastor Manders' way of thought and feeling, into opposite extremes." But even Mrs. Alving cannot really accept the proffered excuses, and the play is paced by the terrible stuttering, but relentless, shift from external to internal responsibility.[56]

Ibsen himself plants the qualifications we need to doubt the testimony of Solness that Aline would have been a good mother, by her infantile recourse to dolls, so that we recognize that the interpretation owes much to Solness's need for self-punishment. We might ask, too, of other victims of a bad education—Hedda, who murders a real and symbolic child; Nora, who leaves her children when she determines not to be "the *willing* slave" Mill designates as man's major desire; and Rita—is it only a bad education that has made them unfit mothers? By separating the possibility of fulfillment from motherhood, Ibsen is clearly indicting his culture for dividing self-realization from the family. The guilty will of the woman that seeks local power is really quite similar to that of the man, the bad father, who seeks power over many people as a substitute for power over the self.[57]

The major concerns of the woman's question are certainly evident in Nora's last words, for she knows that if she leaves her husband she can take nothing with her, neither her children nor anything that is rightfully her own.[58] But she clearly makes the law impotent by *choosing* exile, a triumph of the spirit ready to suffer the slings of uncertainty.

What helps the spirit to pass from role to becoming, however, is precisely the exposure of cultural abuses. Mill had observed that only royalty and women have no choices in their lives, and Strindberg joins the two restricted classes in the body of Queen Christina,

---

56. *Ibsen's Workshop*, 185; *Archer on Ibsen*, 112.

57. Mill, *The Subjection of Women*, 232. See also Binswanger, *Henrik Ibsen*, 73. The doll-wives of Dickens, David Copperfield's mother and his Dora, Bella Wilfer, whom Ibsen certainly knew, were not yet ready to undergo this fierce dialectical tension between public expectation and private responsibility.

58. Mill, *The Subjection of Women*, 248.

who is an actress of her historical role, trying to separate out the child in herself, the beginnings she has lost. When De la Gardie tells her, "You have played with the destinies of men as if you had been playing with dolls," he relates her theatrical role to the arrested development of self-government.[59] This is a relationship Ibsen carries through by connecting bad parents with confinement to role. Dickens had explored the same link in *David Copperfield*, *Bleak House*, and *Our Mutual Friend*, but none of his characters has the fierce spiritual independence to receive, like Nora, Torvald's final patronizing put-down, "You talk like a child," with the calm recognition that, in fact, the child's view of the law and religion might be a good place to start corrective education, a belief ardently shared by the novelist. Like the Nora of the last act, Dickens's Edith Dombey powerfully realizes the connections between the arrested development of theatrical womanhood and a distorted childhood as she delivers a rebuke to her designing mother that touches every life in the novel: "What childhood did you ever leave me?" Ibsen counterpoints in almost all his plays the child*ish* with the child*like*, both clearly changing directions at Nora' departure: "But now I'll begin to learn for myself. I'll try to discover who's right, the world or I" (*I*, DH, III, 193). Her return with Rank to the childhood of the servants' quarters is the beginning of her re-education, and a redoing of her ethical consciousness, too long infantilized by the aesthetics of "the morality of submission," of chivalry, of patronization, and now, changed by the "prose morality of justice."[60] In truth, Ibsen stretches us beyond Mill's morality of justice into the realm of spiritual inequality, a climb that profits from the return to the power origins of laws, but does not stop with their reform.

Brandes's admiration for Mme. de Stael who became herself out of marriage and in exile, and his witty diatribe against the Romantic men of the Schlegel circle, who dragged their women down, taking from them "their highest interests and noblest sympathies," really support the consultation of nature against custom in the task

---

59. Strindberg, *Queen Christina*, I, 32.

60. Charles Dickens, *Dombey and Son* (Harmondsworth, Middlesex, 1970), 472. See Lou Andreas-Salomé, *Henrik Ibsens Frauengestalten nach seinen sechs Familien-Dramen* (Berlin, 1892), on the connection between spirit and the child in us; Mill, *The Subjection of Women*, 259.

of recovering character. This is a task "independently and uncon-ventionally to interpret human life, human relations" for oneself and to base conduct on that interpretation, which will, paradox-ically and in turn, strengthen society and its children. But typical of Brandes's attachment to rational reform is his insistence that, had the outstanding women of Young Germany—Rahel Vornhagen, Bettina von Arnim, Charlotte Stieglitz—really known something, "followed some courses of study, taken up one or other branch of science," their spiritually elevating thought would have been more potent, to the degree that it had been shaped by steady discipline. Ibsen, on the other hand, for all his protests against doll education, is, like Kierkegaard, so radically resistant to all collective enterprise that he leads us to feel that the bad education of his women is pre-cisely what gives them a chance at *some* liberation from the disci-plined tyranny of law and custom, what enables them to pass from childishness to childhood. Art educates not only by exposing defor-mation, but also by evoking from constriction a sense of what is missing, what has been repressed. The bodies of Hedda and Mrs. Alving stimulate this sense as much as that of Ellida.[61]

It is against the divorce of spirit from power that Mrs. Alving struggles when she cries out:

> Always law and order! I often think they're the root of all our miseries on earth.
> Manders. Mrs. Alving, that's a sinful thought.
> Mrs. Alving. Yes, perhaps it is. But I can't stand it any longer, with all these webs of obligations. I can't stand it. I've got to work my way out to freedom.
> (*I, G,* II, 236)

Strindberg's witty essay protesting Nora's rebellion in *A Doll House,* followed by his short story which charmingly revises it, scores points only against a man who supposedly assumed, like the author himself, that the subject of drama, the center of life, was the struggle between men and women, the man and the woman in us. That is what allows him to call Nora a cruel and antisexual idealist, who wants "free-dom from the laws of nature"; and that is what is behind the Doc-

---

61. Brandes, *Main Currents,* II, 98, VI, 278, 303; Nietzsche, "Uses and Disadvantages of History for Life," in *Untimely Meditations,* trans. R. J. Hollingdale (Cambridge, England, 1983), 94–95. See also Strindberg, *Getting Married,* 42.

tor's comment in *The Father:* "And you know, when I heard Mrs. Alving talk about her dead husband, I thought to myself: It's a damn shame the man's dead."[62] Despite Shaw's demotion of Ibsen's spiritual tendencies, he astutely fingered the "fulfillment of the will" as an ideal that pushes past the control of gender and institution. He himself protested enough against the Comtian stereotyping of women as natural social mediators, superior in power of affection, subordinating intellectual tendencies to feeling. Brandes had surmised that Ibsen's female figures were vivid because woman's character is more "closely allied than man's to the mysterious maternal element in nature" which "offers a greater resistance to his disintegrating reflection." But it might be the childlike resistance of her character to that law which represses her power as it establishes the man's. If Ibsen thought the feminine imagination to be not as creative as the masculine and in need of others to work for, seen in its beneficent form in Mrs. Linde and even Aunt Julle, he more often associated it with the child's, as what Jung calls a "retarding ideal" against the progress of male society. In an ostensibly political statement that bears more interestingly on Ibsen's own creative identifications than on Solness's fears, he boldly asserts, "I fear women, youth, inexperience as little as I fear the true artist. What I fear is the worldly wisdom of the old." The woman in society is almost an allegorical doubling of the artist's creative will in the family, and then in his culture. It roars with the desire for release, a desire we might feel Ibsen saw as more potential *because* it had been maimed and hidden, deprived of the public and domestic power that man had exercised as lord of society.[63]

The sick conscience of Allmers, Rosmer, and even Solness, is, as we might expect, felt as feminine before it is goaded by the masculine Viking energies of Rebecca, Hilda, and Rita. To the extent

62. Strindberg, preface to *Getting Married;* Strindberg, "The Father," II, in *Pre-Inferno Plays,* 41. Haaland, *Seks Studier i Ibsen,* 22, thinks that Nora's exit is vengeance against the collapse of a lifetime of idealizing her men. On the pervasiveness of this narcissistic response in the play, see Carol Strongin Tufts, "Recasting *A Doll House:* Narcissism as Character Motivation in Ibsen's Play," *Comparative Drama,* XX (1986), 140–59.

63. Shaw, *The Quintessence of Ibsenism,* 106; Brandes, *Henrik Ibsen,* 30; Jung, "The Psychology of the Child Archetype," in Jung and Kerenyi, *Essays on a Science of Mythology,* 114; Daniel Haakonsen, *Henrik Ibsen,* 164; Ibsen, notes on *Hedda Gabler,* trans. Evert Sprinchorn, in Cole (ed.), *Playwrights on Playwrighting,* 160; Meyer, *Ibsen,* 469; Mill, *The Subjection of Women.*

that the ruling conscience of the mission-hungry leader is refused guiltless power, the struggling will itself, attracted by the revisions of Christian nobility, becomes a higher victim of modern civilization than the weaker sex. The longing of the paralyzed will for erotic and spiritual freedom and innocent communion is a sign that "the complete human being is no longer a product of nature, he is an artificial product like corn, and fruit trees, and the Creole race and thoroughbred horses and dogs, the vine, etc." [64] When a passionate, natural urge is released against this cultivation, it explodes into that hyperbolic expansion and elevation that courts destruction. The plays are filled with the tension between those who have lost contact with the spontaneous and bold psychic and physical world untamed by the Christian civilization that resists development and dissolution, and those who respond to it. When Hedda feels liberated by what she imagines to be Løvborg's beautiful death, she condemns Brack and Tesman to their roles as specialists of both ancient and modern civilization. Brack's motto that "people *say* such things. But they don't *do* them" (I, HG, IV, 772, 775), marks the specialist as a species so far removed from his origins that his body lives within the balloon of mottoes, formulas, and self-protective verbal tics. Nietzsche's interest in tracing the impetus of his philosophizing in his sick body is a deliberate slap at the specialist's concealment of motive. In a letter of 1870, against the philological separatism of the 1850s and 1860s, Nietzsche declares: "I observe how my philosophical, moral, and scholarly endeavors strive towards a simple goal and I may perhaps become the first philologist ever to achieve wholeness." It is no wonder that his heir, Heidegger, seizes upon specialization as the greatest violation of being, as it mistakes shrewdness and cleverness for spirit. In fact, while it pretends to save the past, it cuts it off from both the present and the future, a severance fatal to the sense of wholeness. [65]

The use of hidden fact as a baffle to hidden feeling is, in Ibsen, among other things, a critique of the specialization that can ma-

---

64. *Ibsen's Workshop*, 186.

65. Silk and Stern, *Nietzsche on Tragedy*, 14; Friedrich Nietzsche to Paul Deussen, February 18, 1870, in *Briefwechsel: Kritische Gesamtausgabe*, ed. Giorgio Colli and Mazzino Montinari (3 vols., Berlin, 1977), II[1], 98: "auch merke ich, wie mein philosophisches moralisches und wissenschaftliches Streben einem Ziele zustrebt und dass ich—vielleicht der erste aller Philologer—zu einer Ganzheit werde." Heidegger, *An Introduction to Metaphysics*, 47.

nipulate evidence, like that of the journalists and civic authorities in *An Enemy of the People*, because it has no living relationship to morality, love, and the passion for truth. That is why Stockmann, who seems to be insisting on the truth of facts, will, against Grad-grinds, teach the relationship of feelings to principles and language in his new school. By concentrating on the fact of forgery itself, to Nora a mere necessity, Torvald shows himself a specialist of an everlasting law, cut off from the natural evolution of ideals and feel-ings. Rousseau planted the seed of rebellion against this tendency when he proudly admitted in his *Confessions* that he might mistake fact, but never feeling. Dostoyevsky's hatred for clinical psychol-ogy's abuse of spirit in the name of legal truth, and Flaubert's mock-ery of the project of Bouvard and Pecuchet, fertilize the soil. Ibsen fools even a dramatist as astute as Strindberg—eager, to be sure, to misinterpret him—who overestimates the factual origin of the truth the master wants uncovered. Repressed facts are symptoms of repressed feelings, and this relationship is what is ignored by the specialist. That is why Ibsen loves to make all factual material vul-nerable to ambiguity, whether it be the story of Nora's trip to the south, of Hedvig's illegitimacy, of Rebecca's incest. And when he does almost surely pin down a fact, like the cancellation of biologi-cal relationship of Asta and Allmers, it can never be free from the inflection of ancestral motive, and still functions primarily as cata-lyst to feeling. The use of the past as refuge is assumed by the spe-cialist whose interest depends on its safety in relation to the present. It is, after all, the fear in the present of feelings that keeps facts fixed and dead.[66]

This has grave consequences for the future, for the closing off of a living relationship between past and present also cripples imagina-tive and creative projection into the future, enslaves it to arrested wishes. Tesman can picture a sentimental future on the personal front, like Charles Bovary, but when it comes to the real task of joining the past to the responsibility that fosters and shapes crea-tion, he is lost: "The future! But good Lord, there's nothing we know about that" (*I*, HG, II, 733). It would never have occurred to him that any other way of knowing could imagine history forward

---

66. Rousseau, *Confessions*, 262; Fritz Paul, *Symbol und Mythos: Studien zum Spätwerk Henrik Ibsens* (Munich, 1969), 42.

189

because the specialist's past is sentimental, thoroughly known and worn, the slippers and aunts of his childhood. His way of knowing is akin to that of Christian moralists, a killer of life's mystery. It is his kind that has "altered" what Nietzsche calls the natural "constellation of life and history."[67] Because Hedda is surrounded by specialists and coddlers of specialists, and because she herself is split between dream and convention, she cannot give birth to a future. We allow the lepers of the life-force to marry, says Ibsen, but what do we expect their offspring to be? The crippled and murdered children of Ibsen's world of specialization are victims of the one-sidedness of the moral mind fending off the unknown, and would feel like the "anachronisms, accidents, fatal accidents, unreal, false notes" in their parents' lives that D. H. Lawrence calls Hardy's sensitive, migratory offspring.[68]

The small world, passionately dedicated to a morality that can entirely dominate it, stupidly incites the unknown world to rebellion by radically reducing our medium: "It is the nature of the conscious mind to concentrate on relatively few contents and to raise them to the highest pitch of clarity. A necessary result and condition of this is to exclude other potential contents of consciousness."[69] If Scandinavian culture had a ready reservoir of daemons, trolls, and mermaids in the mountain, seas, and woods, they were not to infiltrate Ibsen's art as aesthetic ornaments. The unknown recruits them as an army against the three-headed hydra called the small world, against its specialization of time, space, and identity, against its education, against its bad parents. The calling out of spirits, a common ritual in symbolist art and a common interest of those fascinated with the unconscious, the lyrical version of the materializing of doubles or missing halves, Strindberg saw as a regular and incurable need of modern character fated to be patchwork. His already ghosted Stranger speaks for all creatures of higher consciousness when he says to the Lady in *To Damascus I:* "I didn't call;

67. Nietzsche, "On the Uses and Disadvantages of History for Life," in *Untimely Meditations,* 77; *Ibsen's Workshop,* 408. See the perceptive comments on the relationship between history and fiction of John O. Bayley, "The Order of Battle at Trafalgar," *Salmagundi,* LXVIII–IX (Fall, 1985–Winter, 1986), 29.

68. *Ibsen's Workshop,* 186; Jung, "The Psychology of the Child Archetype," in Jung and Kerenyi, *Essays on a Science of Mythology,* 112; Lawrence, *Phoenix,* 508.

69. Jung, "The Psychology of the Child Archetype," in Jung and Kerenyi, *Essays on a Science of Mythology,* 113.

I just longed for you."[70] But Ibsen is not comfortable with pathos. His summoned, uncanny, mythical, and mystic creatures are always of use to parody. Their poetry has teeth and will not be domesticated, like Christianity, to aesthetic uses. Carrying, by their awkward presence, the protested loss of Unity of Being and Culture towards which Yeats's images traveled, they disturb and invade. The children who, in the midst of the family, are turned by their parents into strangers, are aggressively lured by the blue sea, the Rat Wife, for mythic use. Since all intruding strangers are summoned by fear as well as longing, by a need for punishment as much as a need for liberation, they throw off a wicked energy, even when they are, like Hedvig and the wild duck, victims. They punish the parental missions of displaced interest by literally playing out their consequences. Their symbolism is not a mere embellishment, but surrenders itself to unbearably real action. Jung describes the pressure that catapults them into their aggressive role: "If, then the childhood state of the *collective* psyche is repressed to the point of total exclusion, the unconscious content overwhelms the conscious intuition and inhibits, falsifies, even destroys its realization."[71]

Specific children, those products of anxious and specialized consciousness, of ghosted lives, might be, in their deaths, sacrificial redeemers. But we remember that Ibsen is intent upon cutting the conventional Christian connection between children and parents so that we cannot make providential sense of the world and cage it in retribution. Instead, the bad parents are dwarfed by the autonomous expansion of the child into primordial atmospheres that are utterly indifferent to the sentimental interpretations of guilty parents. The primordial child, relieved of the cramped quarters of the small world, assumes a position halfway between life and death, helplessness and divine power, and nakedly strides the blast to a future closed by his family.[72] He is utterly uninterested in judgment, but the capacity for wonder and spirit he carries punishes the spe-

70. Strindberg, *To Damascus I*, in *Plays of Confession and Therapy*, 33. See also Michael-sen, *Ibsens "Bygmester Solness" som tidsdiagnose*, 31, 37.

71. Jung, "The Psychology of the Child Archetype," in Jung and Kerenyi, *Essays on a Science of Mythology*, 114.

72. See Cleanth Brooks, "The Naked Babe and the Cloak of Manliness," in *The Well-Wrought Urn: Studies in the Structure of Poetry* (New York, 1947), 21–46. Brooks comments astutely on the ambivalence of the image in *Macbeth*, I, vii. See also Jung, "The Psychology of the Child Archetype," in Jung and Kerenyi, *Essays on a Science of Mythology*, 111, 123.

cialization of the too well-known universe he left behind more successfully than any spite. In this sense, Ibsen's exile, by which he raised his art from personal rebellion to universal vision, made his childhood primordial as well as specific. In their passage between life and death, the primordial children can turn their backs on education to political fact and moral manipulation.

In Lawrence's eagerness to keep children from the wrong kind of schooling, he urges a distance between parents and children that would prevent a Hedvig from experiencing the overwhelming sense of disappointment for failing to satisfy her father's fiction, a Little Eyolf from having to shoulder his father's mission:

> Communication must be remote and impersonal, a correspondence direct between the deep affective centres. And this is the reason why we must kick out all the personal fritter from the elementary schools. Stories must be *tales*, fables. . . . They must never have a personal, self-conscious note, the little-Mary-who-dies-and-goes-to-heaven touch, or the little-Alice-who-saw-a-fairy. This is the most vicious element in our canting infantile education today. 'And you will all see fairies, dears, if you know how to look for them'.[73]

This is the aestheticizing morality of which Petra complained and on which Ibsen turned his back when he exiled his own poetry. The distance Lawrence calls for in school is the critical space Nietzsche insisted upon for the making of independent minds and hearts, liberated from automatically inherited systems and fairy tales of theology and morality. What is worse, claims Lawrence, is that education suppresses the "fairies that are true embryological realities of the human psyche." The child yearning for premoral magic forests and seas and saddled with criminally guilty origins can break free to new ones only by dying, and nothing so humiliates the paralysis of parents as that journey. In a draft of *A Wild Duck*, Gregers's suggestion that Hedvig sacrifice herself is clobbered by Ibsen's irony as it is, too, in the final version, an irony that lends primordial origins as metaphor to Gregers who thinks he can control their use:

> *Gregers.* You must not doubt the power of self-sacrifice; that is just what is ideal in family life, you see—
> *Hedvig.* Oh, but I don't care about anything of that sort; I don't understand it.

73. Lawrence, *Phoenix*, 625–26.

Gregers. But don't you see that this would be a deed that bore the stamp of the uncommon; and for that very reason your father would recognize the kinship between you and him.
Hedvig. Do you think so?
Gregers. Yes, I'm sure of it. And your father would say: she came from the ends of the earth.
Hedvig. Or from the depths of the sea.[74]

Of course, the possessive and weak Hjalmar isn't up to these origins, but they stay in Ibsen's plays as savage correction. So, too, Little Eyolf changes his origins by following the Rat Wife into the sea. They mythical purger of lies punishes better than the moral one because Gregers's mission cannot be elemental and disinterested. The difference between this innocently aggressive recapturing of origins and Allmers's nostalgic retreat into childhood is crucial. Lawrence again makes the distinction:

> The goodness of anything depends on the direction in which it is moving. Childhood, like a bud, striving and growing and struggling towards blossoming full maturity, is surely beautiful. But childhood as a *goal*, for which grown people aim; childishness futile and sentimental, for which men and women lust, and which always retreats when grasped, like the *ignis fatuus* of a poisonous marsh of corruption: this is disgusting.[75]

Hilda is the most fascinating and vigorous primordial force because, poised on the threshold of adulthood, she is unwilling to give up her full power of will and wish. Carrying, literally and symbolically, none of the baggage of the small world, she is given the privilege of taunting Solness into assuming responsibility for her bold intrusion:

Hilda. Tell me, Mr. Solness—are you quite sure you've never called for me? Within yourself, I mean?
Solness (slowly and softly). I almost think I must have.
Hilda. What did you want with me?
Solness. You are youth.
Hilda (smiles). Youth that you're afraid of?
Solness (nodding slowly). And that, deep within me, I'm so much hungering for.
(*I,* MB, II, 833)

---

74. *Ibsen's Workshop,* 249.
75. Lawrence, *Phoenix II,* 396.

This presumption is a deliberate slap at the aesthetic school of mythical diffusion and claims some affinity to the comic doubling of Gogol and Dostoyevsky. She poses as a retarding ideal to the progressive illusions of the small world, but she needs to make literal the vision she is not mature enough to hold as motivating metaphor to moral transformation.[76] She is eager to cancel the Christian split between the aesthetic and the moral, and her rude sympathies and impatient generosities are really working to free beauty from goodness. She cannot bear the despiritualization of nature that has forced the Christian will into complexes of conscience. The eager and egoistic will of the adolescent *anima* is terrified of inhibiting responsibility and wants to free itself both from resentment of the rising Ragnar and sympathy to the suffering wife, the dead duty hanging around the neck of desire. When Solness gets caught up in the game of retribution, Hilda, vulnerable to Aline's case, holds her ears and blurts out, "Don't say those things! You want to kill me? You want to take what's even more than my life?" (*I*, MB, II, 835). Her dependence on her imagination of his greatness of spirit reminds us that even potentially supernatural forces are demoted, in the modern world, to parasitic doubling.

Hilda boldly assumes the privilege of mythical genesis, though the claim in the small world sounds more like a temper tantrum. Myth assumes, "It is said and, therefore, it must be so."[77] When Solness wants Kaja for herself, Hilda, intolerant of any other love interest and in tune with the Master Builder's passion for power, tells the truer motive to Ragnar: "He wanted to keep you."

> *Ragnar.* Did he tell you that?
> *Hilda.* No, but it's true! It *must* be true! (*Wildly.*) I will—
> I *will* have it that way!
> (*I*, MB, III, 850)

It is this aggressive recapturing of genesis in the teeth of history that moves Solness up the ladder of his desire to deed. Skeptical of the

76. Michaelsen, *Ibsens "Bygmester Solness" som tidsdiagnose*, 46; Weigand, *The Modern Ibsen*, 289. Weigand calls attention to the adolescent narcissism of Hilda's hero-worship. See also the claim of Poul Bager, "Uendelighedens tilbageslag," *Kritik*, II (1969), 51, that Solness's "madness" is already on a different plane of thought and language when Hilda knocks.

77. On genesis in myth, see Raffaele Pettazzoni, "The Truth of Myth," in Alan M. Olson (ed.), *Myth, Symbol, and Reality* (Notre Dame, Ind., 1980), 103. See also Ernst Cassirer, *The Philosophy of Symbolic Forms*, II, 105.

full-hearted story of their first meeting, as edited by Hilda, Solness replies:

> These things you've been saying—you must have dreamed them. (*Putting his hand on her arm.*) Now listen—(*Hilda moves her arm impatiently. Solness appears struck by a sudden thought.*) Or else—wait a minute! There's something strange in back of all this, you'll see! (*In a hushed but emphatic voice.*) This all must have been in my thoughts. I must have willed it. Wished it. Desired it. And so—Doesn't that make sense? (*Hilda remains still. Solness speaks impatiently.*) Oh, all right, for God's sake—so I *did* the thing too!
> (*I*, MB, I, 807)

Eager to raise Solness past the history of his relationship with Ragnar to an original creation, Hilda is hard on him when he refuses his daemon's request:

> Hilda (*looking angrily at Solness*). That was really mean of you . . .
> Solness. You don't know my side of it.
> Hilda. All the same. No, you shouldn't be like that.
> Solness. You were only just now saying that no one but me should be allowed to build.
> Hilda. I can say that—but *you* musn't.
> (*I*, MB, II, 828)

Into the gap between a past alive only as anxiety and a frozen present, Ibsen introduces a full-blown double transference between the child and the parent we are that serves to activate the scene of the disease and open the prison door. Solness wants to be recalled to the mythopoeic wish and world of the child he was, before he knew his will was guilty, and Hilda wants to retard her psychological and historical development so that she can continue to make absolute demands on a relative world with impunity. As a child-spirit on the brink of adulthood, however, she must pay the price of dependency oh her host who has, by an old deed, made her what she is—though, in fact, with Solness, we still want to know how she became what she is. The task she chooses is to establish a reign of beauty and greatness in a world that has banned them, what the bound Hedda could only futilely attempt. What she needs is a tactic of counterforgetting to the world's suppression of the past as guilty. By poetically reediting the past so that only the great, embellished moment can be remembered, she transforms the present, starving for a history liberated from guilt. In an age in which, for so long, the conjunction of life and history has been divided by "an inauspicious star," the starved spirit would feed on forgetting. For, as Nietzsche had claimed, true life is impossible without forgetfulness.[78] By changing forgetfulness into forgiveness, Christianity had moralized time and tortured the life forces, charging them with self-justifying missions. Since the culture has failed so miserably to sponsor a place that the hungriest youth can enter without being tamed or maimed or murdered, that could take into its homes the past as a real child, so it would not, as a stranger, have to haunt its bad parent, the present—is not a builder justified in counterforgetting the present and raising a lost moment, free of moral pain, into an all-embracing, living time? Nietzsche claims, in one climax of his dialectical discussion of history, that "he who cannot sink down on the threshold of the moment and forget all the past, who cannot stand balanced, like a goddess of victory without growing dizzy and afraid, will never know what happiness is—worse, will never do anything to make others happy."[79] This is a particularly interesting credo in light of Ibsen's tenacious belief that such ascents must be paid for by death to prevent them from being legitimate solutions to the problem of happiness. But Ibsen is willing to grant provisional power to the desire to forget the sinful inheritance in a world that has failed Feuerbach's dream of godly humanity.

Bereft of an epic history and world, the materializing of myth seems suspect, silly, stranded. But it insists on its old privilege of being a story so true it makes us recognize its helpers and servers, trolls, daemons, Vikings, as "our most constant desires, habits, impulses, prejudices . . . that function exactly like an Olympus full of deities who want to be propitiated, served, feared, and worshipped."[80] If it is no longer possible to have "everyone in the vicinity" of these gods worship their mythical authority, still, Hilda's poem is not willing merely to ornament the world by hanging

78. Nietzsche, "On the Uses and Disadvantages of History for Life," in *Untimely Meditations*, 62. See also Alex Bolckmans, "*Bygmester Solness*: En Tolkning," in Haakonsen (ed.), *Second International Ibsen Seminar*, 124–33, on the relation of the times registered in characters.

79. Nietzsche, "On the Uses and Disadvantages of History for Life," in *Untimely Meditations*, 62.

80. Jung, *Psychological Reflections*, 214.

imaginary "castles in the air." Provincial repression has compelled her story. Psychology has observed the strange phenomenon in the hysterical personality of the needs of others calling out personal needs. The hysterical dreamers take the story of someone else's experience, heard in the daytime, and receive it as their own because they feel that something is missing in their public and private history. The impulse to believe the story as one's own is akin to the transference desire to "see in the other person the self-transcending life process that gives to one's self the larger nourishment it needs."[81]

Played out against an indifferent public, the double transference can easily be seen as a design of double narcissism. It is not at all interested in the integration the therapists of the modern soul desire. And, unlike Conrad's Marlow, the two counterexcluders do not want other listeners to the story of their hunger. The modern problem, as Ibsen saw it, is not to come to terms with reality, but to find a place for our projections worthy of our spirit that would, if it could, stay in history. In this sense, the space and time opened up by Hilda's prodding are received like fresh air. But the question raised by Ibsen is one he was honest enough to solve in the plays, so that the Great World could have the last word. The tyranny of political forgetting and remembering in the philistine provinces can be combatted by poetic editing that frees fact into metaphor.[82] It is, after all, the sense of history as final and fixed that makes it so terrifying to a present that would grow. But Ibsen, like Nietzsche, well knew the dangers of an unmediated compensation for a repressed past, the danger of gaining an original past without the humility demanded by an inherited one.

The relationship between the exposure of a false perspective and the recovery of an authentic standpoint is always a tricky one in Nietzsche's ceaselessly dialectical drama of transvaluation, especially as it rolls through the abuses of the underhistorical on one side, and the overhistorical on the other. Hilda's conversion of history to transference achieves a vantage point from which to look

81. See Erik Carstens, *Fra en Psykoanalytikers arbejdsvaerelse: Korte afhandlinger og artikler* (Copenhagen, 1970), 163–64; Oehlenschläger's Gulnara, in *Aladdin*, relates a similar experience. Ernest Becker, *The Denial of Death* (New York, 1973), 157; Durbach, *Ibsen the Romantic*, 109ff.

82. See Hayden White, *Metahistory: The Historical Imagination in Nineteenth Century Europe* (Baltimore, 1973), 338–45, 350, 355.

down on a murderously cautious culture, but Hilda is an abusing muse, uninterested in leading Solness patiently through the necessary steps to a creative binding of guilt and responsibility, reserved for her author. By not doing this, however, she opens for us the presence of that Great World, so unspecialized and alive that it can afford to be historically unself-conscious. Hilda's re-creation of a sacred origin of transcendental value is a mythical means, though selfishly used, not of romanticizing the past, but of redeeming the present and the future: "The mythic is not the past. It is even more deeply present because the original event, by repetition, is once again 'presently' produced. 'Original' means not so much 'earlier' as permanent. Primordial reality lies close to present reality."[83]

Of course that present is so antipathetic to the mythical imagination that its time is trapped in repetition rather than transformation. The everlasting train, aunts, days of which Hedda complains are compartmentalized time and space, spread to a dreary flatness by its contrast to eternity:

> Brack: Fortunately the wedding trip's over now.
> Hedda. (shaking her head) The trip will go on—and on. I've only come to one stop on the line.
> (I, HG, II, 726)

The time that jealously separates past from present, desire from duty, morality from death, the known from the unknown, has desacralized the world. Rubek continues Hedda's imagery for his picture of Norwegian provincial life:

> Rubek. And then I understood that now we'd crossed the border—we really were home now. Because the train was stopping at every tiny station—even though nothing stirred.
> Maja. Why did it stop when there was no reason to?
> Rubek. Don't know. No one got off, and no one got on. And still the train stood there, waiting silently, it seemed like forever. And at every station I could hear two men walking along the platform—one of them with a lantern in his hand—and they talked with each other—low, muffled, meaningless words in the night.
> (I, WWDA, I, 1034)

83. Eric Dardel, "The Mythic," in Alan Dundes (ed.), *Sacred Narrative: Readings in the Theory of Myth* (Berkeley, 1984), 231. See the interesting reminder of Rank, *Will Therapy*, 42, that repression concerns not historical facts, but resistance to pain of remembering, in the present, feelings and thoughts that are difficult still, not merely in the past. See also comments of Jung, *The Basic Writings*, 29.

In discussing Nietzsche, de Man centers on the paradox of modernity that even his dialectical cleverness could not accommodate: "Modernity invests its trust in the power of the present moment as an origin, but discovers that in severing itself from the past, it has at the same time, severed itself from the present."[84] The liberal breakthrough, which *was* modernity, tried to solve the dilemma by manifestoes of separation from a past that was a bad parent. Borkman's capitalistic arrogance represents a hyperbolic version of this desire and, like the climb of the Master Builder, his must be punished for violating the future. But surely a richer response would judge the climb from an origin not of spiritual or ethical hubris, but of social and political repression of a difficult national and personal past of complex feelings. The punishment of arrogance belongs to ancient tragedy; the punishment of specialization to modern drama. Solness's leap over his ethical present to a childlike expansion would seem to signal a necessary exposure of the leveling of moral choice as much as his fall signals the psychological irresponsibility of the ascent.

Solness might be, himself, guilty of a counterspecialization, of poeticizing the past away from the present into unearned mythopoeic time and space. But to judge the projections and transferences literalized in the climb as neurotic miscalculation instead of mythical release is surely reductive of Ibsen's implications. If we cannot use myth innocently in this world, it does not mean that we must subscribe to a therapy of adjustment, for while the silly enactment of mythical desire gives the palm to the Great World, acclimatization denaturalizes our forest trolls, servers, and helpers. Nothing can be gained by adjustment—a standard altogether foreign to the daemonic world of transference that restores wish to its full intensity. It is the gap between Tesman's specialized sentimentality that ritualizes the past into aunts and slippers, and the thrilling, absurd, outrageously bold vision offered by Hilda (but not, it is important to note, enacted by her) that keeps the Great World from being closed out, and, in fact, attracts those mysterious echoes that give resonance to all life.

Ibsen's intention was to aggravate the split—a disruption that recalls the sudden intrusion of the unconscious charted by Eduard von Hartmann, embraced by psychological theorists and artists

84. Paul de Man, "Literary History and Literary Modernity," in *Blindness and Insight*, 149.

alike. When the split is mediated, Solness is given the warning to be a better patient. Otto Rank reminds us that the neurotic must, above all, "learn to will, discover that he can will without getting guilt feeling on account of willing"; Hilda brings Solness this possibility. But the psychoanalyst's therapy consists of challenging patients to duel with the doctor's will, not in order to lead them to a counterwill, but to force them, by a resistance to their imperative feelings, to a creative solution to the impasse. Hilda has to be a bad therapist in order to take us further than Ibsen's *life*, which responsibly used his guilt in creation. Her irresponsibility is precisely what keeps us from stopping short of the greatest possibility, as of now still brutally cut off from our reach. Her desire is therapeutically immoral because it does not *recognize* the conflicted way it must "play itself out in the reconstructing of the past." Solness certainly understands the way psychology haunts history when he admits the difference between the cracked flue as cause and as symbol of a secret desire. The superfluity of cause, yoked to accident (to convert it to retribution), is the sign of *this* deception: "that the seeker for help suffers only temporarily or apparently from weakness of will, in reality from too strong a will which he must constantly deny, rationalize, project and even occasionally break." Because Solness's sickness cannot be confined by the category "neurosis," Rank's analysis helps us to register the powers and purposes of Ibsen's art. Though therapy acclimatizes us to this world, art forces us to imagine a greater medium that cannot be reached by building castles in the air, or by climbing them, but cannot even be projected by building nice and cozy houses for provincial citizens.[85]

The animation of unspecialized time, space, identity charges the provincial atmosphere with surprising and threatening intensity. Mythical allusions are continuous with hidden passions. When they appear intrusive, we feel how much the language of the heart has been aborted. That is what gives such power to what otherwise has an air of silly arbitrariness. Osvald's final call to the sun, for example, as a mythical power born of bright days in exile, carries the great night of annihilation to its terrible meeting with revelation, the innocent child's outrageous wish to the cruel justice that scorches our fictions. The unbearable pain of the last scene can only prepare better marriages in the Great World, and for future

85. Rank, *Will Therapy*, 9, 36, 20.

generations, but there is, really, no acclimatized future for Mrs. Alving, or for Hilda, confronted and pursued by mythical passion. That they have entirely used up the future, however, gives them the dubious privilege of preserving the Great World in the small world's despite.

Like so many writers of the nineteenth century, Ibsen could have countered the artificial mythologies of bourgeois morality with parasitic satire or a hyperconscious style, secretly transforming ethical indignation into aesthetic justice, or he could have shamed the small world by counterpointing it with ancient richness of integrated cultures.[86] Instead, he chose to make the mythology, which so naturally served the allusive imagination as metaphor in the classical theater, crash aggressively against the bourgeois myth of the modern world; it is carried by Brendel's castrating imagery, the Rat Wife's deathly seduction, Hilda's daemons, estranged children. The alien crew survives both belief and indifference, idealization and symbolic application, utterly refusing absorption by bourgeois time and space, exploitation by bad conscience and false consciousness. The sentimentalizing and aestheticizing of the Scandinavian psychic and national heritage worked, like flawed repression, to provoke those sleeping spirits and daemons Borkman wanted both to liberate and to possess. Despite his allusions to Viking power, Ibsen had neither the faith nor the patience to search, like other nineteenth-century writers, for the origins that could respiritualize personal and public life, whether in the journey of an Esther Summerson or a Daniel Deronda, or in the art and architecture of the Middle Ages. We see the suggested binding—so typical of the nineteenth century and climaxing in the literature of Proust, Joyce, Yeats, Pound, and Eliot—between the recovery of a living public and a personal past, but it fails to rise to either a political or aesthetic promise and persuasion.

Ibsen's famous tendency to anarchism is not only antipolitical,

86. See Arnold Hauser, "The Origins of Domestic Drama," trans. Stanley Goodman in collaboration with the author, in Bentley (ed.), *Theory of the Modern Stage*, 418–19: "It becomes increasingly difficult to ascertain whether the dramatist's 'super-bourgeois' ideology corresponds to a progressive or a reactionary disposition, and whether it is a question of the middle class achieving victory over itself or simply one of desertion." See Barthes, "Myth Today," in *Mythologies*, 69, 142. Atle Kittang, "Realisme som myte-kritik i *Bygmester Solness*," in Harald Noreng (ed.), *En ny Ibsen: ni Ibsen-artikler* (Oslo, 1979), 104, comments that *The Master Builder* is essentially a critique of mythical bourgeois illusions: the myth of superman, of family, of endless freedom, by which we betray life.

but also antihistorical, for it was impossible, after so much repression, to heal the division between what can be known and what cannot be. In this sense, his uncovering of the past, crucial for shaming the small world, is a red herring, for it is not the true history that emerges from the stuttering investigation, but the vast and terrifying space and time we can neither possess nor yet live in. Like evolutionary and psychoanalytic regression, which in its task of stopping bourgeois moral progress bound ontogeny to phylogeny, the specified melodramatic distinctions of the surface travel back to archetypal blurring and ambivalence, exposing our moral categories of definition as fantastic curtailments of the natural feelings of the species. The past Ibsen is after is that of both biology and mythology, the past of instinct, not fact. The permanent establishment of a beginning that Hilda demands by her story of the first climb and embrace assumes the design of imperative and instinctive myth that roots the past "in a place where one has been . . . and that one has to reach urgently in the present and that some one at a crucial point on the way says does not exist."[87] But her hysterical insistence on narrative control indicates that, to the degree that her use of myth is not innocent, it can only serve a world beyond her reach, in which all citizens will be master livers, and art will be relieved of its task of parodic castigation.

The tendency of mythical thinking to merge identities in body, fate, time, space makes it also vulnerable to exploitation as escape from moral responsibility. The escapist blending of Asta and Eyolf needs to be met by that of the Rat Wife and Asta, the fusion of Allmers and Asta by the doubling of the Rat Wife and Rita, both possessive and alluring, frightening and fascinating.[88] The clear distinction between Gregers and Hjalmar is effaced as their weaknesses blend into each other, a degrading communion. The bodies and fates of Krogstad and Nora; Mortensgaard, Brendel, and Rosmer; Rebecca and Beata; Ella and Mrs. Borkman; Hedda and Løvborg— all suffer the dialectical ebb and flow of identity and distinction that so perilously tempts and teases in the passage between myth and morality. Though he could not be called an expressionist, Ibsen

87. This is a definition of Herbert Mason, "Myth as 'Ambush of Reality,'" in Olson (ed.), Myth, Symbol, and Reality, 15.

88. See Errol Durbach, Ibsen the Romantic, 110ff., for a discussion of Ibsen's use of the Romantic design of incest.

risked undoing the stability of character and scene to break down what Jung called the bulwarks of punishment against the "ancient instincts of freedom." The subtle illumination of scene that gradually blurs the moral opposition of light and darkness prepares us for the chastening. James W. McFarland reminds us how Ibsen, in his poems as well as his plays, keeps light and darkness from serving but one master. They are both desired and feared. Osvald seeks the sun, while Hedda closes the curtains; Little Eyolf and Hedvig are in love with the darkness of the sea, while Erhart travels to lands without dark attics. The Dionysian jungle lurks behind the scene of *Hedda Gabler* in the rooms of Madame Diana, and Hilda dreams of raiding parties spiriting her off.[89]

If we feel how unhoused the mythical carriers of instinct are in this world of fixed definition and curtailed connotation, we feel too how they unhouse, in their turn, the time, space, fates of the philistine parlors. Isolated and awkward, they nest uncomfortably between two worlds, like accidental seabirds. If they are corraled by psychologists to name categories of repressed romance, they also, even in this function, naturalize the guilt upon which moral history feeds. Their corridor, which serves as provisional homeland, seems to Brandes the place of a difficult dualism in Ibsen. In a perceptive comment on *Little Eyolf*, he contends that "a kind of dualism has always been perceptible in Ibsen; he pleads the cause of nature, and he castigates nature with mystic morality."[90] He suggests this might be a weakness, but the critical alternation is the necessary tactic of the art that works between biological destiny and spiritual promise while it lives in the small, overly moral world. Aiming his shot at the perversions of nature, we remember Ibsen still cannot invest his fullest value in those who march off capable of *livsglede*. As myth takes us towards the Great World of mystic morality, it enlists as an ally against the pretensions of *theological* mystical morality the biological world imported by evolution and naturalism. The great speech of Borkman, ostensibly to Ella, is resonant with both the

89. James Walter McFarlane, *Ibsen and the Temper of Norwegian Literature* (London, 1960), 66; Cassirer, *An Essay on Man*, 77; Knight, *Henrik Ibsen*, 63; Errol Durbach, "The Apotheosis of Hedda Gabler," *Scandinavian Studies*, XLIII (1971), 143–59; Nietzsche, *Genealogy of Morals*, 218; Johnston, *The Ibsen Cycle*, 131. On the mergings of identity in mythological thinking, see Cassirer, *The Philosophy of Symbolic Forms*, II, 110–11.

90. Brandes, *Henrik Ibsen*, 116.

value and perversion of the spiritual, moral, and biological world, and this rich tension resides in every scene of Ibsen:

> That wind works on me like the breath of life. It comes to me like a greeting from captive spirits. I can sense them, the buried millions. I feel the veins of metal, reaching their curving, branching, beckoning arms out to me. I saw them before me like living shadows—the night I stood in the bank vault with a lantern in my hand. You wanted your freedom then—and I tried to set you free.
> But I lacked the strength for it. Your treasures sank back into the depths. (His hands outstretched) But I'll whisper to you here in the silence of the night. I love you, lying there unconscious in the depths and the darkness! I love you, you riches straining to be born—with all your shining aura of power and glory! I love you, love you, love you.
> (I, JGB, IV, 1021)

Like so many other speeches in Ibsen, this one powerfully traps in dialectical contention the lower ethic of duty and the higher one of self-realization, responsiblity to human love, and the rage for power. The mythic imagination seducing nature into metaphor and courting irresponsible power both widens the scene and refuses to justify the missionary ambition.

Nor can the mythic gestures of climbing, mining, calling out; the guiltless rhythms of death and rebirth; the fall of kings and gods; seasonal pathetic fallacies; topography—that fitful archetypal scaffolding of the plays—save the potential nobility of tortured power and passion from the indignity of biological and psychic grounding. Ibsen certainly imagines for myth the de-Christianizing task of subverting the moral world to which Nietzsche sets his mind: "We few or many who again dare to live in a dismoralized world, we pagans in faith: we are probably also the first to grasp what a pagan faith is:—to have to imagine higher creatures than man, but beyond good and evil, to have to consider all being higher as also being immoral. We believe in Olympus—and not in the 'Crucified'." But he could not imagine for his characters a life free of sexual and ethical guilt, nor for the creative will a pagan escape from their lingering power. Like mythology and psychology, nature was not free to offer a place above or below our pains, without becoming, itself, caught in a dialectical infection. Once, myth safeguarded the morality of community in the service of life and could comfortably inhabit the moral world. But when morality turned against life, it abandoned myth and perverted our spiritual and sexual instincts.

That is why it is so tempting to use myth and nature as chastening instruments of social and psychological deformation. Strindberg had claimed: "The naturalist has erased guilt along with God," though he cannot convert the society that punishes us.[91]

The relentless presence of guilt on Ibsen's stage is a sign that he could not leave the orphaned will pathetically stranded—as Zola, Hardy, Conrad, and Kafka had done—in a world narratively abandoned to impotent longing. His parody protested that abdication, as it refused the merely pathetic shadow of community of sentimental and necessary delusion left behind by Turgenev, Hardy, and Conrad. Naturalism could be tempted to evolutionary romance, but did not imagine a world to come where all that is "is alive, where there are no things, only beings participating in the same life-current—men, animals, plants or stones."[92] This is the binding of myth and nature evoked by its absence in the parlors of Ibsen and by the presence, on the stage, of the Great World. In a universe that is not only of man, both spiritual and sexual hunger find a worthy pasture.

Plekhanov, like other readers impatient with those writers who, passionately endorsing individual liberation, had no trust in political progress, scolds Ibsen for Brand's "purely negative revolution."[93] We would have difficulty imagining Ibsen as a hero of the proletarian cause, even if there were such a class in bourgeois Norway. And Terry Eagleton sees "impotent idealism" and the recourse to myth and naturalism as a response to the crisis of a ghosted middle-class society and community.[94] The mythical seduction of spirit in

91. Jung, "The Psychology of the Child Archetype," in Jung and Kerenyi, *Essays on a Science of Mythology*, 106; Johnston, *The Ibsen Cycle*, 148ff., 261ff.; Sandra E. Saari, "Of Madness or Fame: Ibsen's *Bygmester Solness*," *Scandinavian Studies*, L (1978), 2–3; Nietzsche, *Will to Power*, 533; Strindberg, preface to *Lady Julie*, in *Pre-Inferno Plays*, 78. See also Valency, *The Flower and the Castle*, 112: "In naturalist drama the worm never turns; the wicked do not repent and are not punished; and Providence never intervenes to save the situation."

92. Eric Dardel, "The Mythic," in Dundes (ed.), *Sacred Narrative*, 234. See also Bronislaw Malinowski, "The Role of Myth in Life," in *Sacred Narrative*, 199; Eliade, *Le Sacré et le Profane*, 81–82.

93. George V. Plekhanov, "Ibsen, Petty Bourgeois Revolutionist," in Angel Flores (ed.), *Ibsen: Four Essays* (New York, 1937), 37.

94. Speaking of the novelist facing the crisis of the middle class and a crumbling community, Terry Eagleton, *Exiles and Emigrés: Studies in Modern Literature* (New York, 1970), 222, writes:

> On the one hand, the intensifying problems of value, relationship and identity, raised by a society in prolonged crisis, broke beyond the traditional forms of literary realism within which they had been previously confined. From this movement emerged a kind of novel

the plays might well seem to the politically engaged critic a characteristic amateur escape from genuine moral and historical responsibility. But Ibsen used it because he saw so clearly that political
promises could be as double-edged as the recourse to mythology and
nature.

Sensitive to the common indictment of the purely negative her-
meneutic function of Marxist criticism itself, Frederic Jameson is
also responsive to "the ambivalent value" of Conrad's impres-
sionism which opens up "a life space" in which the opposite of "the
capitalist rationalizations" is "at least imaginatively experienced."[95]
The relationship between critical exposure and that space in Conrad's fiction might be cast as a pathetic version of Ibsen's fierce
opening of the Great World by an aggressive mythology. And every
texture in Ibsen carries a burden of criticism that prevents it from
escaping dialectical responsibility and impurity. We can hardly
imagine Ibsen speaking this line of Ulfheim: "Then we'll stand
there, free and easy—exactly as nature made us" (*I, WWDA*, III,
1086). But, like all calls to the happiness of the flesh in the plays, it
neatly humbles the spiritual ascent of Rubek and Irene, and takes
its place as a positive dialectical force. Weigand neglects the incessant energy of the mutual contention when he gives us another version of Brandes's complaint: "The recognition that the basis of life
is biological instead of ideally ethical deprived him of any tangible
objectives for his indignation." The objective for his indignation is
never single, for no origin or end is, finally, determinant of human
life. When, on the model of Claude Bernard, Zola converted the
Romantic writer's divine interest in *pourquoi* to the naturalist's
charting of *comment*, he willingly abdicated control and creation of
a single cause, despite his adoption of the determinism of heredity.

---

forced back on to crucial questions of private consciousness and individual value in a
society whose actual character came to seem increasingly elusive and remote. A form of
novel embodying many of the ideal values, definitions, and aspirations of a traditional
middle class . . . is driven increasingly to confront, and to withdraw from, the harsh ac-
tualities of the society which that same class has largely created.

A recourse to myth and naturalism and "characteristic feelings of guilt, cynicism, nostalgia,
impotent idealism and fantasy," are symptomatic of this problem. Eagleton's analysis concerns itself with England, but it certainly describes the dilemma of Ibsen's situation as well.

95. Frederic Jameson, *The Political Unconscious: Narrative as a Socially Symbolic Act*
(Ithaca, N.Y., 1981), 236.

And Ibsen shares in this rich demotion. But his own responsibility, rage, and desire assured him of the dialectical relationship to his society that Georg Lukács grants to Balzac, while lamenting its absence in Zola and his naturalism, forced into compensatory picturesque Romanticism. If Ibsen has the same problem as Kierkegaard binding the individual and collective revolutions, it derives from the fear that politics would abort the drama of creation and fail to leave the future to the Great World alone.[96]

Stockmann wants to put naturalism in the service of social conversion, to target the "spiritually common men" (*I, EP, IV,* 360) for indignation by preferring to them the mongrel boys whose natural instincts and spontaneity have not been repressed. An unlikely reformed society might seem a missing middle but that does not make Ibsen's revolution negative. He is after a life energetic and humble enough to tolerate both the rich collision of spheres and motives and an indefinite future, and he always needs to feed his purpose with the lower food of social liberation. Rousseau's recourse to the animal world is ever motivated by his interest in reforming the social structure of human society, and Strindberg clearly uses it for this polemical purpose. One target in the preface and short stories of Strindberg's *Getting Married,* we remember, is Ibsen's Nora, who, by walking out on the family, opposes nature when she flouts cultural inequality. Why does the peasant woman not suffer as much as the cultured woman of the nineteenth century from motherhood? Because she cooperates with the practical arrangements of nature's economy, in which the children help out in the struggle for survival. Nora, on the other hand, is a "romantic monstrosity" who throws out nature with culture, an "egoistical individualist." Ibsen's anger at his culture's deformation of the will and at the will's impotence to fight back—an anger he shared with other writers, Nietzsche, Butler, Shaw, William James, all worried that Darwinism left no room for the energies of creative desire—is turned not toward the recovery for the race of the social bonds of nature's herds, but towards the transformation of the guilt that plagues creative expression and building. Even Dr. Rank's Nietzschian antihumanitarian words, eliminated from the final version of *A Doll*

96. Weigand, *The Modern Ibsen,* 132; Emile Zola, *Le Roman expérimental;* Georg Lukács, *Studies in European Realism,* trans. Edith Bone (New York, 1964), 92–93.

House, are really aimed at saving not the species but the single spirit: "The unfit individuals in a herd have to make way for the better ones. And that is how nature progresses. It is only we human beings who forcibly *retard progress* by taking care of the unfit individual." His interest is not primarily in putting together, in a more practical arrangement, the family he scatters, but in the imperative call towards being to be answered by the strong individual.[97]

Even as Stockmann uses his animal imagery to chastise his culture's psychic murder of spiritual nobility, Ibsen's concern is to keep the individual from being tamed by social institutions intent upon leveling the higher types. The distinction between breeding and taming that Nietzsche makes in *The Will to Power* is, essentially, a diatribe against the morality that had sponsored the weak over the strong, frustrating the bird of prey in us. Morality is, in Nietzsche's phrase, "an illusion of the species" that impels the spiritually strong man to stand alone.[98] When Gregers asks old Ekdal how it is he can tolerate "the stuffy city" after his days in the forests, he is met by the resigned consent to acclimatization. Gregers's protest, in the name of the natural world (as we would expect in Ibsen), immediately takes on the cast of Romantic rhetoric because it grows out of a self-protective idealism: "But all those other things, the very roots of your soul—that cool, sweeping breeze, that free life of the moors and forests, among the animals and birds?" (*I*, WD, II, 432). Rubek's satiric submerging of the faces of domestic animals that "human beings have distorted in their own image, and that have distorted human beings in return" (*I*, WWDA, I, 1036) is vitiated by his own creative cowardice that had divorced art from life. It is only just that he should be mocked, in turn, by the bestial sexual energies of Ulfheim and Maja. No claim, short of the Great World's, is spared the irony of its exposed pretense. Ellida's regression to animal conversations with her sailor half does not capture a serviceable pattern for marriage. Rather, they widen the living space for the individual will driving to fullness, despite marriage. The alliance between nature and spirit against the established

---

97. Rousseau, *Emile*, 429–30; Strindberg, introduction to *Getting Married*, 42; *Ibsen's Workshop*, 112; Sverre Arestad, "Ibsen's Conception of Tragedy," *PMLA*, LXXIV (1959), 285–309.
98. Nietzsche, *Will to Power*, 214–15, 218.

moral world cannot settle a new social colony in the small world, or even in the world of exile.

Primarily, nature is John the Baptist to spirit, working like myth and childhood to demystify morality. When Ibsen pokes his pet scorpion into ejecting the poison that made him sluggish, he notes: "The laws of nature seem to apply to the spiritual life, too."[99] The morality of bourgeois Christian humanism is the poison that parody expels. The return to the wild animal, to our undomesticated feelings, is on the way to spiritual nobility. Ulfheim compares his fully aggressive struggle to master the wild animalism of life to Rubek's wrestling with marble. Even the stone, he says, "has something to fight for," and it "resists with all its strength being hammered into life" (I, WWDA, III, 1044). What struggles against the will, strengthens Ulfheim. But if we shorten the will's work, choose easy material, *we* are like the stone that will not be shaped into spirit. Not for Ibsen the guiltless will of Ulfheim's passionate struggle against eagles, wolves, women, elks; the dramatist must make creation out of the human obstacles to his will, the first and second family, and the pillars of society, who all *inhibit* the passions of body and soul in the name of protection.

In one of his most interesting genealogies, Nietzsche calculates the great advantages of polytheism. The disequilibrium and immoderation associated with the individual's positing of his own ideal from which he would derive "his own laws, joys, and rights" are avoided by projecting onto Olympus a "plurality of norms," making over to the "distant overworld" the "luxury of individuals":

> The invention of gods, heroes, and overmen of all kinds, as well as near-men and undermen, dwarfs, fairies, centaurs, satyrs, demons and devils was the inestimable preliminary exercise for the justification of the egoism and sovereignty of the individual: the freedom that one conceded to a god in his relation to other gods—one eventually also granted to oneself in relation to laws, customs, and neighbors.

The importation of animated metaphors from the mythological and natural worlds is certainly, in Ibsen, a way of combatting the monotheistic "doctrine of one normal human type" that results in a stagnating mono-morality. The repression of our animal nature has

---

99. Henrik Ibsen to Peter Hansen, October 28, 1870, in *Correspondence*, 200.

forced us into the "sublimated cruelty" of self-torture, the bad conscience. The human will desires to find itself guilty: "What a mad, unhappy animal is man! What strange notions occur to him; what perversities of idea burst from him, the moment he is prevented ever so little from being a beast of action."[100] In a universe systematically denuded of belief in mythic places and forces that could receive and soothe the sick conscience of creative missionaries, releasing it to action and expression, we look to the artist to banish the ghosts of Christianity's shrinking provinces in order to return us to our individuality and ready us for the Great World.

100. Nietzsche, *The Gay Science*, 191–92; Nietzsche, *Genealogy of Morals*, 225–26.

FOUR

The Great Divide

Unhousing bad marriages in the small world, Ibsen prevents the premature conformity that subdues the singular and uncommon spirit. He might have imagined the possibility of being the joyful leader Nietzsche demands, but his mission, rooted in guilt as much as in passion, in a terrible twist of irony, entered his plays as much an enemy of life as bourgeois morality (*I, R, III,* 555–56). Ibsen viewed Kierkegaard's bold disguise—to think like an uncommonly spiritual man and to live like a bourgeois philistine—as his own cowardice.[1] His passion for psychological honesty would not allow his fantasy of freely leading a new community to go unpunished, or his fantasy of the communion that Mrs. Wilton finds so natural, the union of two people who do not fear consequences (*I, JGB, III,* 1006). Borkman's reproach to Foldal that "there *are* no precedents for exceptional men" (*I, JGB, II,* 979) who dream life forward attracts the public demand for full restitution and full repression. And Foldal's doubts about his poetic projections of life anticipate the more arrogant remorse of Rubek: "The dreadful doubt—that I've botched my whole life up for the sake of a fantasy" (*I, JGB, II,* 980). Because Irene's sexual reality is

1. See Haakonsen, *Henrik Ibsen,* 257; and Binswanger, *Henrik Ibsen,* 37, who contends that the artist's self in his plays had to be sacrificed so that he could live. He might have been Hedda if he had not had the courage of his talent.

refused by a Rubek who is "an artist, only an artist. Not a man" (*I*, JGB, II, 1070), she becomes a ghost of life. Rubek confesses:

> It was the fact that all the talk about the artist's high calling and the artist's mission, and so on, began to strike me as basically empty and hollow and meaningless.
> *Maja.* What would you put in its place?
> *Rubek:* Life, Maja.
> (*I*, JGB, II, 1063)

Readers and viewers are quick to seize upon this confession as Ibsen's remorse over a life drained by service to art. They recognize it as a common one in the literature of the last half of the nineteenth century and first decades of the twentieth, though in artists like James and Mann, the mutual exclusivity takes on a pathetic or morbid cast, rather than that shed by the heartless parody of Ibsen's scene.[2] Ibsen could never be content with such a crude antithesis. For his art to have a power that could expand the life it so brutally exposed, it had to undergo all the temptations, special pleading, perversion, punishment that self-parody could conceive. The rudeness of art to life was paid back in kind by the constant reproaches of wounded wives, rejected mistresses, and those capable of unself-conscious *livsglede*, but both terms were submerged ceaselessly in dialectical contexts.

Ibsen saw the gap between public action and creative projection closed by both Bjørnson and Brandes. Brandes himself spotted the affinity between Ibsen's sponsorship of internal revolution and an inability to act. In a letter to Nietzsche, he admits, while recommending Ibsen to his correspondent, that the playwright does "not have the same stature as a human being that he has as a poet." For all Ibsen's hatred for theological reduction of life's fullness, he seemed to Brandes always to carry Brand in his blood. In addition, Ibsen himself contrasted Bjørnson's marriage of art with life to his own compensatory design. For this reason, he had to be one of those who was "cruel against his own inclination." Rosmer, like Ibsen's Bjørnson, might want to make his finest work of art his life, but Kroll confines him to his fictions: "That's how bad his judgment is when it comes to situations and people in real life" (*I*, R, III,

2. See Jirí Munzar, "Henrik Ibsen und die Tradition der Bürger-Künstler—Problematik in der deutschen Literatur," in Haakonsen (ed.), *Fifth International Ibsen Seminar*, 183–93.

557). Brendel's hopes point him, at last, towards the void: "Could you spare me an ideal or two? . . . A couple of cast-off ideals. You'd do me a good deed, then. For I'm wiped out, dear boy" (*I*, R, IV, 578). The noble missionary in the modern world is met by an indifferent or hostile community, a bad conscience, tenaciously held back from power by the torment of sexual conflict and marital guilt. Because his ambitious art has inevitably committed the double murder of which Ella speaks—"the love in another human being" and "of your own soul" (*I*, JGB, II, 985–86)—it meets, as well, the worst of his enemies, the self-mocking intolerance of his author.[3]

Ibsen could gain power for his art by transposing, as Rank puts it, "the will affirmation creatively"—that is, "express his will spiritually," converting the "unavoidable guilt feeling into ethical ideal formation, which spurs him on and qualifies him for ever higher performance in terms of self-development." But he knew that the dream of German idealism, of making the personality itself into a work of art, a dream still alive in Otto Rank, was almost bankrupt in the modern world where heroes like the Underground Man and the Country Doctor are always unequal to themselves. Nietzsche had persistently identified the modern Romantic thinker as one still full of desire to believe, but impotent to invest it in life and creation. Napoleon, the bird of prey, whose wings and sword commanded the pens of so many nineteenth-century writers, is, in Ibsen, a caged eagle:

> *Borkman.* I feel like a Napoleon, maimed in his first battle . . . And now I have to sit here like a wounded eagle and watch the others pass me by. (*I*, JGB, II, 974)

The mighty titans that challenged God, Job, Lucifer, Faust, stand behind the Master Builder's climb to high individualism, furnish a history of the rights of rebellion against providential and moral orders, but the bad conscience that surfaced in Karl Moor and paralyzed Ivan Karamazov is positively mortified by Ibsen's antiromantic

3. Georg Brandes to Friedrich Nietzsche, quoted in Nietzsche, *Will to Power*, 53n; Brandes, *Creative Spirits of the Nineteenth Century*, trans. Rasmus B. Anderson (New York, 1923), 375; Valency, *The Flower and the Castle*, 135; Henrik Ibsen to Bjørnstjerne Bjørnson, August 8, 1882, in *Correspondence*, 359; Ibsen to Bjørnson, September 12, 1865, in *Correspondence*, 86; Nietzsche, *Beyond Good and Evil*, 159; Henrik Ibsen to Bjørnstjerne Bjørnson, August 8, 1882, in *Correspondence*, 359.

detachment from utopian public possibilities and from the romance of self-sacrifice.[4]

The Napoleon and the Schlegel circle Brandes praised had wives who expanded the creative power and claim of the husbands. To the Danish critic, George Sand, Schleiermacher, and Shelley could be heroes and heroines of liberated marriage. Nietzsche exploits an older notion, that the artistic and sexual energies compete with each other: "The force that one expends in artistic conception is the same as that expended in the sexual act: there is only one kind of force. An artist betrays himself if he succumbs *here* if he squanders himself *there*."[5] Rubek could have used him as an ally in the self-defense he pleads before Irene. But Ibsen would never give the philosopher's authority to Rubek's special pleading. In fact, his protest in the name of purity seems entirely suspect as one of the causes of his ruined art. It spreads out into patterns of remorse and satire because it insisted on a pure origin, free from guilt and conflict, and not because it is an inevitable fate of the great artist in a bad world.[6] The worm of guilt gnaws at his claim: "And the conviction filled me that, if I touched you, or desired you in sensual terms, then my spirit would be profaned so that I couldn't have created what I was striving for. And I still think there's some truth in that" (*I*, WWDA, I, 1052). It is important to note, too, that the model herself is viewed as "a sacred creature" to be worshiped. The art, then, that would work to purify life of its conflicts is the source of Rubek's troubles, not Ibsen's own sense that he had wasted his life as an artist. This is the puritanism that must be punished so that we can know that some good can come out of an art that acknowledges the disturbed beginnings of the will's way in the world. How was Ibsen to punish Rubek's perversion of the creative task? To force it into marriage, where it longs for a lost innocent communion of spirit and desire never really had, and only possible in death. Not for Ibsen the celibate art of Proust triumphing over life's exhaustion.

4. Rank, *Truth and Reality*, 242; Gerald N. Izenberg, *The Existentialist Critique of Freud: The Crisis of Autonomy* (Princeton, 1976), 279; Bakhtin, *Problems of Dostoyevsky's Poetics*, 59. For discussions of the modern coupling of belief and impotence, see Nietzsche, *Twilight of the Idols*, 74; Nietzsche, *Will to Power*, 129, 184, 197; Nietzsche, *The Anti-Christ*, 166. See Rolf Fjelde's comments in *Ibsen: The Complete Major Prose Plays*, 939; Michaelsen, *Ibsens "Bygmester Solness" som tidsdiagnose*, 60.

5. Nietzsche, *Will to Power*, 432.

6. In *Contradictory Characters*, 272, Albert Bermel notes that when Rubek satirizes the human face, he is "showing mankind not only *its* predicaments but also his own."

Using Brand as a model, Unamuno claims that Ibsen's climbers are proud and promethean and, therefore, chaste like all heroes.[7] But we must remember that their chastity made for unhappy marriages. The bad marriages of the plays have often been read as reflective of Ibsen's disappointments in marriage, but it is more likely that they reflected the old guilt of the creative will blasting its way through the family's sexuality and shame. Why does Solness have to imagine himself the sole destroyer of Aline's creative life?

> Because Aline—she had her lifework too—just as I had mine. (*His voice trembles.*) But *her* lifework had to be cut down, crushed, broken to bits, so that mine could win through to—to some kind of great victory. Aline, you know—she had a talent for building too.
>
> (*I, MB, II, 826*)

He insists on adopting his society's identification of "good" with "dutiful" precisely in order to suffer the punishment he deserves for another crime, that of wanting to be the only builder. Solness's ready agreement with Hilda, that nobody but him should have a right to build, is behind his guilt over the death of the children, as it is behind Hedda's burning and killing of the future, behind Irene's furious sense of eviction from the act of creation and Maja's from life itself. By establishing a bleak morality as his legitimate prosecutor, Solness can accept Hilda's Nietzschian blasphemy as an ally of life:

> *Solness.* Because underneath, she's so kind—so good—such a fine person—
>
> *Hilda (impatiently).* But if she *is* all that—why does she run on so about duty.

If the ethic of duty and sacrifice is, as Nietzsche puts it, "an idealism inimical of life," is not the mission of self-realization trapped by marriage also made into a killer of life? If marriage is the protector of the mediocre type who dreads "exceptional needs," it also is a place that treacherously crosses common rights with the ideal missions of the higher type.[8]

The woman's question entered Ibsen's plays not only as a problem of inequality between partners in marriage, but also as the problem of the subservience of the artist to marriage. Hedda might

7. Unamuno, "Ibsen y Kierkegaard," in *Mi religión*, 56.
8. Nietzsche, *Will to Power*, 175.

struggle to rise to that realm of beauty, exiled by the institution of marriage, "in which she can achieve power over opposites without violence," and Rosmer might dream of overcoming the suffering that afflicts a bad conscience, by sheer nobility.[9] But they are plagued by a marriage they dishonestly chose. Camilla Collett and other feminists were just as attentive to the renunciations of self-realization enforced after marriage as those demanded of women before marriage.[10] But in many cases, Ibsen exposes a premarital sexual conflict and guilt as the impure source of the missionary desire after marriage. The state of marriage, which Strindberg and Lawrence insist should be the difficult but rich scene of self-realization, is for Ibsen's missionaries a place of protection *from* the demands of self-realization, though it appears to be an agent of torture. As a cultural absolute, it waved the flag of form ideal enough to suppress ambivalence. When Nora's art becomes serious enough to let life conduct it, it makes Torvald enormously uneasy because it threatens the domesticated game of marriage, but it is for Nora, too, a register of anxiety. Torvald's sexual demands, at a moment of great spiritual crisis, are not only reminders of male insensitivity to woman's autonomy, but a tyrannical defense against a competing absolute ideal, supported for years by Nora. One of Kierkegaard's most emphatic justifications for celibacy was the terrible temptation in marriage to direct absolute passion to a relative term, whereas in faith, that passion would find an absolute end. The betrayal of Nora's false use of marriage leads her to a Kierkegaardian exile from the false prophets of morality. It is the Great World that reverses the circuit so perversely connected by the overly moral world, making rich play of the tension between relative and absolute, properly married.

This is the place of true marriage, in which both members of the partnership come into their own before coming together, and it is in the name of this order that Ellida counterexcludes herself from the family she prematurely entered. The imagined purity of marriage to an ideal makes it difficult to face the conflicts of marriage as it is. It leads, in Ibsen, to a confusion between the first and second family, a displacement of sexual conflict to an ideal public mission

9. *Ibid.*, 422.
10. In *The Oxford Ibsen*, VII, 470, James W. McFarlane translates a letter of Camilla Collett to Ibsen, February 24, 1889, in which she speaks of renunciation *before* marriage.

(a parody of the art that overcomes opposites), and the search for an ideal communion. Marriage in Ibsen is not a place in which the terrible guilts of personal and public history can be soothed. Because it is sought as a refuge from self-development, it serves as its resentful enemy. Stockmann never needs to use his public mission as an escape from marriage, and that is why his wife can firmly ask: "Does a man with a wife and children have no right to proclaim the truth?" (I, EP, III, 340). A telling contrast to this balance is the attempt of Allmers to make his son's life into a noble mission in order to escape uxorial demands. No lines are more searingly ironic than those in which he claims to have been able to shift his noblest purpose from self to son in the mountains: "Here at home I never could have managed it. Never could have forced myself to that renunciation. Never here, at home" (I, LE, I, 883). The unwritten book on responsibility, renounced for a life of paternal responsibility, is a farcical exchange and will only aggravate the contest between marriage and mission. When Rita vents her frustration by naming the son a greater rival than the book, she accuses Allmers of mutilating "the holiest thing between us" (I, LE, I, 888). The characteristic yoking of unstable allusions to sex, child, marriage is a powerful demonstration of the fullness of the competition between the mission and marriage that so ardently torture each other.

Only Kafka allowed the family to torment art as much as art tormented it, and he scrupulously refused to *his* artist types the possibilities of both self-idealization and responsible exile. Art could not elope because it was bound up with guilt—this side of marriage, the father's realm—and because it served as a way of rebelling against the father without leaving his home. In some sense, that is what Kierkegaard's literature was to him, as well, for the father's marriage, its origins shadowed by convenience and incontinence, was a place of guilt that had to be overcome by a higher marriage to faith. Brand takes over Kierkegaard's question, stirred by a religious father who was sexually guilty. He seeks a

> place on the Earth where one can be
> Wholly oneself,
> That is Man's right.
> To be wholly oneself! But *how*
> With the weight of one's inheritance of sin?
> (M, B, II, 46)

The inheritance, spurring the compensation of absolute idealism, kills a wife and child. We see the connection between mission and sexual guilt in Gregers, who cures his inheritance by plaguing a relative marriage, already forced into an ideal fiction, with absolute demands. It is directly after he blames his father for his mother's misery and dalliance with Gina that he clearly sees his mission (*I*, *WD*, I, 409). [11] His interest in exposing the background of Hjalmar's marriage is anything but disinterested. We can only partially credit the claim of Werle Sr. that his son's "conscience has been sickly from childhood . . . an inheritance from" the mother (*I*, *WD*, III, 450), because we see the direct connection between the son's sense of having been sacrificed in the marriage of his parents and his deadly pleas to Hedvig to sacrifice a life. No wonder Werle senses the danger of his son's departure from the house.

Lyngstrand's fantasy of wife as Muse is one Bolette views with immense suspicion:

> *Bolette.* All the same, I think he'd do best simply to live for his art alone.
> *Lyngstrand.* Well, naturally he will. But he can do that just as well if he's also married.
> *Bolette.* Yes, but what about her?
> *Lyngstrand.* Her? Who?
> *Bolette.* The one that he marries. What's she going to live for?
> *Lyngstrand.* She'll live for his art, also. I think that a woman must feel a profound happiness in that.
> (*I*, *LS*, IV, 651)

G. B. Shaw had convinced Dickens's daughter that her mother had a case against her father, too; it had been well noted that "the sentimental sympathy of the nineteenth century with the man of genius tied to a commonplace wife had been rudely upset by a writer named Ibsen." [12] Otto Rank exposes, like Bolette, the egoism of Lyngstrand's claim. The artist might make his wife or lover into a muse "transforming a hindrance into a helper," but this absorption, notes the psychoanalyst, "renders no service to life." Marriage insists

11. Valency, *The Flower and the Castle*, 187, notes that "Ibsen invariably gives his reformers the worthiest rationalizations, but he usually suggests the erotic impulse that underlies their zeal."

12. This comment of Shaw in *Time and Tide*, July 27, 1935, addressed to Dickens's daughter, in response to her prejudice against her mother, appears in Madeline House and Graham Storey (eds.), *The Letters of Charles Dickens* (5 vols.; Oxford, 1965), I, xxii, n. 2.

upon aggravating the first family wounds and dooms idealists to self-doubt and destruction.[13]

Plagued by an idealizing dream of guiltless love and power, the Ibsen missionary calls out a suffering in marriage that cannot be excused by a justifiable recourse to cultural cause, Relling's "national disease" of "moralistic fever" (*I, WD,* IV, 451). Too much familial guilt and rage hide behind Gregers's desire to make of his society's families ideal Christian trinitarian paradigms of mutual subjection: "Oh, there's so very much to think about. You three have got to stay together if you're ever going to win through to a self-sacrificial, forgiving spirit" (*I, WD,* IV, 469). That this is Gregers's mission prevents it from being that selfless love Rosmer calls "the most magnificent thing in life, if it really exists" (*I, R,* IV, 576). Mortensgaard has, with difficulty, overcome the sexual indiscretion he claims had cured his freedom to act, but only by giving up ideals (*I, R,* II, 536). Perhaps that is why he is, despite his political nature, assigned a crucial question when he asks Rosmer if he really is as innocent as he claims to be. Whoever would shift responsibility from inner to outer ennobling motive will be unable to overcome or transform a marriage into a creative place that tolerates doubt and renounces the possibility of innocence (*I, R,* II, 544).

The moralism of nobility is a symptom of suppressed sexual conflict. As a stand-in for art, it manifests its dangerous and potential misuse as an enemy of life. When Rebecca moves into a position of marriage, she renounces her "uncontrollable drive" for the sake of Rosmer's nobility (*I, R,* IV, 575), but since this means a future of no crying children and no laughing adults, marriage can be consummated only in death, which can stop, but not cure, the mixed motive behind all communions. The highest marriage, which can hold together art and morality, passion and responsibility, belongs to the Great World and cannot, in this one, hide behind "wider and wider circles" of noble happiness (*I, R,* II, 543). Even the marriages of Asta and Borghejm, Ellida and Wangel, Rita and Allmers will not close the wound opened by erotic guilt in the child's will,

---

13. Otto Rank, *The Myth of the Birth of the Hero and Other Writings,* trans. Charles F. Atkinson, ed. Philip Freund (New York, 1964), 160. See comment of Kerans, "Kindermord and Will in *Little Eyolf,*" 205: "Ibsen's heroes are almost invariably sexually estranged from their wives, who inherit typically, the 'providing' characteristics of the primary mother, and yet they cannot . . . execute their 'act of will' with the secondary mother."

and the demand of that will can never be granted here: "I want you whole and undivided" (I, LE, III, 923). There is clearly a sense in Ibsen, as in Freud, of a tendency in modern man, generated by cultural, personal, and ontological conflicts, to split affections between the tender and the passionate sentiments.[14]

What is certain is that an inner hierarchy of repression will cooperate with an outer one. The idealizing hero might pretend to a morality higher than his culture, but he only confirms its infectious influence. Rosmer's delusion that his relation with Rebecca was spiritual is supported by his confession of a guilt that his noble friendship was misread as lust by his wife (I, R, III, 555). Rosmer and Rebecca, by using renunciation only for death, fail to drive on the deep inward development in life that creatively produces beauty and power out of guilt and frustration. They are still possessed by purity. More patently, the celibate Gregers, like his culture, needs to ennoble marriage from without. This allows Ibsen to raise in a draft of his play an interesting question concerning the relationship between marriage and art that is everywhere played out, more subtly, in its final form:

> Gregers. Do you think any great problem *can* ever be solved by an imperfect individuality?
> Relling. Do you mean that photography cannot be raised to the level of an art so long as the photographer's relation to his wife is not a true marriage?[15]

Caught by a mission that serves self-preservation in the name of the family ideal, both Gregers and Hjalmar are purveyors of low art, unable either to redeem honor or to change the world. In his assessment of Hjalmar's character and Gregers's disease, Relling helps us to see the inner nobility of Hedvig and her wild duck as the inevitable sacrifice to the need to ennoble and be ennobled from the outside. Ironically, Relling, because he is not a self-overcomer, is also parasitic on other relationships for his negative hierarchy of value. The dependence of family unity on a fiction of appearance, even if it is fostered by a consenting inner circle, is precisely what makes it so vulnerable to Gregers's attack. The incestuous dream of true

14. Downs, *Ibsen: The Intellectual Background*, 75, contends that, as an anti-Romantic, Ibsen was not an "apostle of sexual passion." See also Peter Gay, *The Bourgeois Experience: Victoria to Freud*, Vol. II, *The Tender Passion*, 123ff.

15. *Ibsen's Workshop*, 241. This is a question that fascinated James as well.

marriage is vitiated by suppression and cooperates with the society it seems to flout by denying ugliness, conflict, and suffering. We are not as surprised at the use of a retreat to incestuous marriage by All-mers and Asta, to avoid the conflicts of marriage, as we are by the use of marriage itself to avoid the ambivalence of all affective reality.

The contest between personal creative demands and social duty is inevitably painful, but more so than necessary, and uselessly, when the artistic mission leaps over its origins in guilt and double-ness. Even if, like Ibsen's wife, the marital partner is, as John Fowles puts it, "the strongest ally of his consciousness, his outward self," she might very well be, at the same time, "the greatest threat to his inward, unconscious one." The Ibsen hero feels impelled to seek communion *out* of marriage that promises to elide both the equal claim to creativity and the moral censorhip that supports the in-stitutional ideal. Given our distance from the Great World, it seems difficult to believe that Nora's hope for marriage as a place of mutual self-realization can come about both sexually and spiritually intact. Mrs. Stockmann's question concerning the rights of a married man to tell public truths is only one issue. The higher question is, where can we find the man who, in marriage, has not dishonestly pur-veyed public service as a rationalization rather than a reality? No character in Ibsen, not even Stockmann, who is too direct for his age, has the prophetic power, psychological subtlety, and moral courage, to endorse Nietzsche's manifesto: "He shall be greatest who can be loneliest, the most concealed, the most deviant, the human being beyond good and evil, the master of his virtues, he that is overrich in will. Precisely this shall be called *greatness*; being capable of being as manifold as whole, as ample as full."[16]

The destruction of children, in Ibsen, represents, among other things, a protest against the difficulty of reckoning original guilts and losses as necessary roots of creation. The guilt in all creation involves competition with God the father, and the fear of very young rebellion is clearly registered by the Master Builder.

The novelist, Fowles, makes a helpful analogy:

For the simple truth is that creating another world, however imper-fectly, is a *haunting* experience, very similar indeed to the creating of a

16. John Fowles, "Hardy and the Hag," in Lance St. John Butler (ed.), *Hardy After Fifty Years* (London, 1977), 33; Haaland, *Seks Studier i Ibsen*, 62; Nietzsche, *Beyond Good and Evil*, 139.

"real" perspective on the actual world that every child must undertake. As with the child, this experience is heavy with loss—of all the discarded illusions and counter-myths as well as of the desires and sensibilities that inexorable adulthood (or artistic good form) has no time for.[17]

It is that loss that Kierkegaard repeats up to faith. But Ibsen, refusing the leap of high repetition, while honoring the spiraling struggle with his parody of transcendental hope, grants us instead the cool waiting presence of the Great World which might someday be lived in when art is no longer burdened with reproach and retribution. Our task is to turn the necessary haunting into a willing acknowledgment of the compromised connections among first and second loves, creative ambition, and the moral world, and between cursing and competing with God, the young, the wife. Meanwhile, the great visible scene of guilt is strewn with the bodies of those sacrificed, behind which the author's secret self is played out in the struggle demanded by its realization as a personal goal and an agent for a new world.[18]

If, on the one hand, Ibsen's mission requires the ruination of his missionaries, their missions also require the mutilation of others, and in this somewhat sadistic pattern of justice, a major burden of drama in the age of individualism is raised. Here is Lukács:

> The new drama that emerges is the drama of individualism. For one of individualism's greatest antinomies becomes its foremost theme: the fact that realization of personality will be achieved only at the price of suppressing the personalities of others (which, in turn, require for their realization the ruin of the personalities of others).[19]

Unjoyful leaders and fathers of sick conscience might try to head off this recognition by taking on the outrageous mission of developing the individuality of another. Allmers, Hilda, Gregers, Hjalmar, Rosmer, and Hedda have this in common, but the displacement is a cheat, an act of cowardice since they are not sufficiently ennobled from the inside to assume the necessary cost of a useful mission. Ibsen's art insists on the knowledge that "the champion of truth,"

17. Fowles, "Hardy and the Hag," in Butler (ed.), *Hardy After Fifty Years,* 29.

18. *Ibid.* Fowles notes that "in a highly territorial species like man, such repeated loss of secret self must in the end have a quasi-traumatic effect." See also Binswanger, *Henrik Ibsen,* 37; and a discussion of the idea by Georg Lukács in de Man, *Blindness and Insight,* 42.

19. Georg Lukács, "The Sociology of Modern Drama," in Herzfeld-Saunders (ed.), *Essays on German Theater,* 153; Haaland, *Seks Studier i Ibsen,* 113.

as Brandes puts it, is "himself involved in injustice and guilt."[20] These sterile artists of a dishonest life were the necessary reminders by which Ibsen continually kept faith with his woundings and losses. Solness's rehearsal of losses is sentimental and rhetorical, albeit a clear source of suffering, because he has not separated his creative urge from ethical responsibility, checkmating, instead, his art by resentment disguised as sympathy for a wronged wife. While Solness complains about the pain his building has caused his wife, himself, and others, he still holds onto the dream of innocent power. If we listen closely to the relation between his art and his past, we hear the deceit that makes of determinism a server of pure origins, and since the autobiographical element is large, we feel it to be a strong authorial temptation.

Perhaps even the possibility of innocence could be domesticated into the marriage, that place of guilt, and bless the displaced determination to "follow human responsibility through—in [one's] own life" (I, LE, I, 883). Rita pounces on Allmers's cheat, "Then you *can* divide yourself," as he divides all that is dialectically held together in the superior beauty of the Great World. In a draft of the play, Allmers reads an early Ibsen poem that tells of a couple whose marriage has burned down, like their nice and cozy house, through all ideal expectations to a resigned acceptance of demotion from joy to happiness to livability.[21] But Rita claims the poem refers really to the lost relationship with Asta, and we have to credit her bias, at least partly, because one of Ibsen's ways of sabotaging the escape into childhood is by exposing the dream of innocent communion to the same scorching as marriage. The calling out of the semimythical communion is motivated by the exhaustion of belief, a by-product of untrue marriages. Kierkegaard and Dostoyevsky insist on resting both reality and miracle on the foundation of belief, but this religious transvaluation was not available to Ibsen. The terrible courage of standing alone is rare enough in the age of individualism, but it is a trap as well as a supreme value. Marriage, if blamed for rendering power guilty, can no longer serve it, as it does in the anachronistic Stockmann family. It might justifiably be replaced by communion which, in the past, suffered the sacrifice of its sexual content in order to bind innocent power and love. Death claims this preten-

20. Brandes, *Henrik Ibsen*, 4.
21. *Ibsen's Workshop*, 507–508.

sion, and reproaches against the severing of spiritual and sexual love mar the dialogue.[22]

In his lust for power, Borkman claims that "any woman can be replaced by another" (I, JGB, II, 986), and the motto has a searingly ironic truth. But the great paralyzed man of action turns to the poor paralyzed poet, Foldal, for the communion of belief he killed in both his wife and her sister. In *Fear and Trembling*, the dramatic dialectical relationship between the poet and the man of action testifies to the possibility, however difficult, of an inner dialogue between faith and action in the world. The doubling of two old men in self-justifying conversation is a scene that predicts the death sentence for the communions of action and poetry in Ibsen's plays.[23] Kierkegaard's Johannes de Silentio is a vital dialectical poet who comments disparagingly on his own capacities for faith, and Abraham is a man of such wholeness that his faith and action are indistinguishable. But almost all ideal action in Ibsen leads to death and destruction because it seeks, by belief in another, the sanction for avoiding the difficult dialectical relation between and within life and art. If only, as in a draft of *Little Eyolf*, the wife would herself invite the sister into the marriage. Infantilizing her competition, she pleads with Allmers to let Asta stay in the family:

> Rita. You must! What you need is a tranquil, warm, passionless feeling. A child or a sister.[24]

But even that dreamed-of consent must be rejected when the sister is sexually available. When marriage is used as an escape from conflict, excuse for paralysis, or a host for missionary plans, it cannot gain credence as a legitimate enemy of art.

All art this side of the Great World represents, in some way, the perennial dream of recovery of wholeness lost on the conflicted journey to adulthood, a dream particularly strong in the creative

22. Lyons, *Henrik Ibsen: The Divided Consciousness*, 120, comments on the ambiguities of the erotic temptation offered to the hero in the last plays by a woman. It is disguised as a spiritual one in order to cover up an earlier disability in the face of an earlier sexual attraction.

23. Arne Røed, "The Utter Necessity," in Haakonsen (ed.), *Fourth International Ibsen Seminar*, 159, comments on Foldal's lament at the loss of Borkman's belief in him: "As long as the man of action believes in the ideals the poet stands for, so long the poet has the power to inspire. . . . If the man of action destroys the artist in himself, he also destroys himself as a man of action."

24. *Ibsen's Workshop*, 504.

will that resists resignation and adjustment most tenaciously and vividly. That is what Irene thinks is behind her choice to act as muse to Rubek's talent:

> Irene. It was the rebirth of my childhood, to go with you.
> (*I*, WWDA, I, 1052)[25]

But the sacrifice of her own creativity to Rubek's artistic mission is destructive of the communion of love and power, for it feeds the resentment born in the slave unable to obligate mission to marriage, spirit to sex. When Rubek asks Irene if it was jealousy of his appreciated creation that killed her, Irene calls it, rather, hate, the terrible price of communions of sacrifice, as of the Christianity of sacrificed strength. Irene makes the claim for herself that Solness makes for Aline: "I should have brought children into this world. Many children. Real ones, not the kind buried away in mausoleums. That should have been my vocation" (*I*, WWDA, II, 1074). Her sacrifice is only an aesthetic beauty of the past to Rubek, a life of murderous resentment to Irene. They are both unwilling to admit that all art in this world must overcome an impure source, not hang onto a myth of its pure origin. Darkness and light have been radically and fatally separated in an angelic creation that features spiritually antithetical patterns as bourgeois Christianity parades morally antithetical ones. In the end, the couple joins the darkness and light, mythically healing, albeit in death, psychology and morality, for they realize too late that "one does not," in the words of Jung, "become enlightened by imagining figures of light, but by making the darkness conscious."[26]

The transformation of Emilie Bardach into Hedda Gabler wickedly trying to break up a communion that is a muse to art doubtless owes its power to Ibsen's renunciation of adultery. His own dream of guiltless mission, or faultless masterpiece, is continually corrected by a parody directed as much against communion as marriage. It is doubtful that Ibsen's prudent and silly dalliance opened up, as Else Høst contends, the possibility of earthly fullness and happiness in a man who had faced down the impurity of his origins and the origins of his art. Tony Tanner suggests that the urge of fiction's adultery to

25. See Durbach, *Ibsen the Romantic*, 144.
26. Jung, *Psychological Reflections*, 219–20.

"leap into limitlessness" serves, in a profane world, as a leap of faith. Flaubert attacks this dream by brutally forcing Madame Bovary to admit that adultery has all the monotony of marriage. Especially in his last play, Ibsen saves the sacred dream of art's power to survive disillusion by killing the sacred dream of art's purity. Maja's resurrected sexuality successfully humiliates the art that takes as its model the "purest, most ideal of women" (*I*, WWDA, I, 1051), who burns with the rage of frustrated spirit and sensuality. The enormous gap between the two couples exposes the fantastic nature of the final communion, a hyperbolic marriage provoked by the spiritual death of community, sexual conflicts of marriage, and nostalgia for the first ego's doubling, whole and undivided.[27]

The great divide between spiritual ascent and sexual descent, both isolated from any middle ground that could receive passionate aspirations, vividly signals the "crisis of the knowable community" that Raymond Williams, among others, has charted, particularly in the novel of the nineteenth and twentieth centuries.[28] Rosmer could hope that liberal reform would bring more independence of thinking and its sponsoring individualism a stonger sense of self. The old power of a Viking culture that invades the plays as metaphor, a legacy of the long tradition of the Norwegian fisherman's self-reliance, and the new romanticism that honored an individualism scornful of a previous altruism, would seem to have been an adequate protection against the leveling of the majority, the crowd's untruth, feared by both spiritual aristocrats and liberal reformers. A *Doll House* clearly adumbrated the major recognition of Stockmann that truth is the greatest enemy of a society bureaucratically ordered by fearful and fantastic men plying the letter of dead ideals. The question Rousseau raised, of what kind of community we must recover if we would save both the self and civilization, could no longer be answered by social contracts. The religious reality of active love, with which Dostoyevsky closed the gulf between father and son, brother and brother, answered the obsessive Russian inquiry of what is to be done, which had been too readily solved by socialist utopian engineers of a new society, free of pain and conflict. But

27. Else Høst, *Hedda Gabler: En Monograf* (Oslo, 1958), 107–108; comment of Haaland on Høst's theory in *Seks Studier i Ibsen*, 84; Tanner, *Adultery in the Novel*, 376.

28. Raymond Williams, *The English Novel from Dickens to Lawrence* (New York, 1970), 16.

this solution could be only tentatively touched at the end of a play like *Little Eyolf*. The last exchange has no energy so transcendentally and socially hopeful as in that cry of Alyosha's crew: "Hurrah for Karamazov!" More expressive of Ibsen's deferment of full society to the Great World is the cry of Hilda: "My Master Builder!"

D. H. Lawrence faulted Hardy and Tolstoy for not drawing out of transgression a new colony of morality, but already in *Bleak House* and *Little Dorrit* the new couple is dwarfed by a badly parented and bureaucratic world of circumlocuted responsibility. More and more, as the century progressed, did the chosen alternative of Romantic communion become the impelled compensation for a lost community. Hegel had not allowed this substitution to remain unopposed by a healthy dialectical backlash, and his great antagonist, Kierkegaard, reconnected Christianity with the Platonic pattern of nonpreferential love as a requirement for the self that would make relationships real by having, first, a dedicated, individual misunderstanding with God. Ibsen would hit head on communion as a *substitute* for the difficult state of marriage. The Hegelian paradox of individuality's persistent evasion of the self, of its personal and historical fear of standing alone, bereft of the "feeling of kinship with others, finally with the *All*," is one that Ibsen parried by keeping an ironic distance from liberalism, while he drove his characters into paroxysms of false individuality and impotent communion.[29] Lawrence's later complaints about the "absolute frustration of his primeval societal instinct" derived from the recognition that the individualism of bourgeois democracy was a rhetorical rather than a spiritual attribute:

> *Be Thyself!* does not mean Assert thy Ego! It means, be true to your own integrity as man, as woman; let your heart stay open to receive the mysterious inflow of power from the unknown. . . . *Be Thyself!* is the grand cry of individualism. But individualism makes the mistake of considering an individual as a fixed entity: a little windmill that spins without shifting ground or changing its own nature. And this is nonsense. When power enters us, it does not just move us mechanically. It changes us.[30]

29. Kierkegaard, *Works of Love*, 69; Rank, *Will Therapy*, 155; Egil Törnqvist: "Individualism in *The Master Builder*," in Haakonsen (ed.), *Third International Ibsen Seminar*, 135.

30. D. H. Lawrence to Dr. Trigant Burrow, July 13, 1927, in *Selected Letters*, 264; Lawrence, *Phoenix II*, 456.

False individualism is what drives the spiritually starved in life, in the novels of Flaubert, Tolstoy, and Hardy, and in the plays of Ibsen, to isolated and failed transcendental communions and death instead of new colonies of morality. Lawrence's definition of healthy individualism claims the necessity, for both life and literature, of struggling, exhilarating marriages between sexes, with brothers and sisters, with the will-less natural world—marriages surrendering the projections and guilts that have closed off a universal community of gods, beasts, and constellated couples.[31] The "old stable ego," ossified by a morality of self-preservation and an aesthetic of type, will give way, in and out of the novel, to allotropic alternations, responsive and vulnerable to their teeming universe. We have some sense of this kind of relief from the hysterical responses of false individualism in the last, tentative movements of *Little Eyolf*. If, for all his desire and energy, Lawrence could not bridge the gap between marriage and community, how much less could Ibsen, who willfully *refused* the possibility, both aesthetically and ethically, in his art. Like Kierkegaard, he feared the temptation to settle for lesser freedoms than the Freedom beckoning from the Great World.

That is why we must be so cautious of ascriptions of political allegory, so painfully reductive of the richest response to the plays. It is not very satisfying to say that Borkman's will is lodged in a capitalistic titan because, for all his talk of subjection of social and natural resources, his ethical and legal abuses can no more be judged primarily as the calculated moves of a giant of liberal individualism moving up the chain of command in his new society than they can as a late Romantic rebellion of inspired lawlessness, in the name of a new community of justice, the legacy of heroes of Schiller and Kleist. It would be just as disturbing to link Rosmer's passion to uplift the country and the self in joyful leadership, with the German tradition of conservative individualism that wanted to close the gap between individual and state by raising history to a creative and organic drama that could accommodate the single striving soul.[32] If Brandes, who, even as a fellow radical aristocrat, was identified

31. See Georg Lukács, "The Sociology of Modern Drama," in Herzfeld-Sanders (ed.), *Essays on German Theater*, 143: "Destiny is what comes to the hero from without. If we are to continue composing dramas, we must hold to this definition regardless of whether it is true in life."

32. Steven Lukes, *Individualism* (Oxford, 1973), 19, 45.

with the liberal cause, could confess confusion over Ibsen's anarchism, it was because he failed to sense, since everything in the middle plays seemed to ask for social reform, that neither State nor Society could possibly answer the needs of the will rooted in the erotic and spiritual yearnings of childhood:

> I understand how men like Lorenz Von Stein and Gneint see in modern history one constant feud between state and society, and how they, with a new invigorating conception of the state idea, turn against society. I can also understand how a new conception of society may lead to abhorrence of the State; but I cannot quite understand the ambiguity of Ibsen's attitude and do not even know whether Ibsen himself is conscious of any ambiguity in it. [33]

In his protest against false individualism and its identity with liberalism, Ibsen seemed to have affinities with political thinkers of both the right and the left. Much to the irritation of liberal social thinkers, he was, after all, intent on separating individualism from liberalism, but to *prevent* it from finding a home in this world, or from settling for the political freedoms promised by European republics and parliaments. The tendency in bourgeois marriages and politics to seek the consummation rather than the struggle for rights made them treacherous traps for the will. Ibsen could make the mischievous statement that he could put up with the ambitions of socialists and nihilists because at least, consistent and passionate, they patently dissolved the conflict between self, state, society instead of pretending to befriend the individual's interest in self-realization through social laws and contracts. [34] The flirtation with anarchy in so many writers of Ibsen's era is certainly a protest against legal and moral repression of a wild and rich mythopoeic world. The humiliating of hyperindividuality in writers like Flaubert and Brecht, the neutralizing of its tragedy by parody in Ibsen, risk an anarchy of values to foster, by negative persuasion, the memory and hope of a living culture in or past our history.

Ibsen's radical individualism, which could survive state and society only by punishing them for the sake of the Great World, might have smiled appreciatively at Shaw's reversal of the usual liberal

33. Brandes, *Henrik Ibsen*, 60.
34. Kristofer Janson quotes Ibsen's statement in his diary of 1880: "The only people I have any real sympathy with are the socialists and nihilists. They want something wholeheartedly and are consistent" (Meyer, *Ibsen*, 520).

order in the claim that Rita can come to socialism because she is a brave individualist. At least the two levels of rights and freedoms are not confused, though there is always the danger of misunderstanding that the reeducation of Nora, Stockmann, Rita means a radical shift of emphasis from fact to feeling. In a letter to Bjørnson, around the time of A Doll House, Ibsen claims a purpose for art that he was never to vary: "I do not think it is our task to take charge of the state's liberty and independence, but certainly to awaken into liberty and independence the individual, and as many as possible." The liberal prejudice against the aristocracy of spirit and intellect threatens to reduce Norway to a "mob-community," he writes after Ghosts. And Stockmann makes a clear distinction between his brother, the mayor, who is plebeian, and himself, who seeks spiritual kinship instead of a state in which freedom is rhetorically invoked but never lived for. A diaspora of spiritual kinship is the place for the individual in restless transition to the Great World, and it is a place opened by the false individualists of Ibsen's plays whose ethical failures, redeemed by parody, prevent us from honoring Mortensgaard's acclimatization to the political arena that could never positively prepare us for the larger medium. In an opinion that has, after the fact, become ironically familiar, Ibsen contended that had the Jews remained in Palestine, they would long ago have lost their individuality in the process of constructing a state, like other nations. The state, however liberal, screens out the task of inward revolution, while exile continually reminds us of our struggle.[35]

We can sell out this freedom to the State, or we can sell out individuality to communion, elicited from mysterious needs and justified by the delusion of a sacred past:

> Rubek (hesitantly). What I now feel so powerfully—even painfully— that I need, is to have someone around me who can reach my innermost self.
> (I, WWDA, II, 1062)

Of course, we hear this wish in every play, but it is not to be had under these conditions, not in this life. Løvborg's body must be separated from the progressive society based on the creative compan-

---

35. Shaw, The Quintessence of Ibsenism, 157; Henrik Ibsen to Bjørnstjerne Bjørnson, July 12, 1879, in Speeches and New Letters, 86; Meyer, Ibsen, 521; Ibsen to Georg Brandes, February 17, 1871, in Correspondence, 208.

ionship of men and women that, in Ibsen's notes to *Hedda Gabler*, is projected as the subject of his book. Otto Rank, speaking of the therapist's relation to the patient, admits that "the making good of our will through the other" momentarily seems to free the will from its terrible ethical conflict, and in the guilty act of individuation, "transforms our difference, at least temporarily into likeness and mutual striving," easing the extreme anxiety and loneliness of self-realization. But when the communion spiritualizes away sexual conflict and the will's celibate ambitions by dissolving them in death, it serves as no compensation for a lost community. It escapes the struggle of true marriage by courting death. Thomas Whitaker's remarks do not seem outrageous in the case of these couples: "Their talk of marriage and expiation hides a will-to-end all mutuality, all living together with guilt, confession, forgiveness, freedom."[36]

A moment of insight does not exhaust the truth. Rosmer realizes he cannot be made innocent from without by a selfless love that exists only as a cover for desire (*I*, R, IV, 576). And he cannot press communion, in this life, into public service, without degrading it and without recognizing the impurity of its origin. He calls Rebecca on the mixed motive: "You believed you could make something great out of your own life. And that you could use me along the way. That I could serve your purpose. *That's* what you believed" (*I*, R, IV, 572). Earlier, in a more optimistic moment, it was the nefarious Kroll who had to remind Rosmer of the ominous doubling of his faith:

Kroll. You're not a man who can stand alone.
Rosmer. There are two of us to bear the solitude.
Kroll. Ah!—That too, and Beata's words.
(*I*, R, II, 520)

As in *Hedda Gabler*, the epithets of companionship are plagiarized and passed around, making the phrase, "vi to" vulnerable, in its ironic debasement, to Kroll's political uses. Borkman, who cynically claimed that one woman is as good as another for his needs, wants to be understood by one human being only to free himself from the old recriminations of a wife and society that have forgotten his power. He did not need it when power seemed within reach

36. *Ibsen's Workshop*, 459; Rank, *Will Therapy*, 56; Whitaker, "Killing Ourselves," in *Fields of Play*, 48.

of his great passion. And the dying Ella's projected appropriation of his son as host for her influence and immortality makes a retrospective mockery of the purity of a lost communion.

The secret companionship of Hedda and Løvborg bypasses an idea of society and is not a mere flouting of its conventions. It borrows Rousseau's sword, in a severely qualified version of his crusade, to divide sweet confessions of sin from the compelled confession of weakness, the sweet society of two from the imperative society of Bracks. Løvborg can call the old communion "a companionship in a thirst for life" (*I*, HG, II, 739), but it must destroy life to serve its ceaseless hunger for expansion. The plays abound in obsessive and magnetic pairings, sometimes those that settle for the lower and more realistic marriages of two who need someone to work for, and sometimes those treacherously artificial spiritual kinships, of Hedvig and Gregers, Helmer and Nora. The deepest and most moving recognition of a companionship that renounces the magic of innocent communion, *liebestod*, utopian high purpose, is that of Rita who comes to sense how useless a consolation it is to imagine a community of sympathy and feeling:

> Rita (*staring straight ahead*). Nothing, in fact, *has* happened. Not to the others. Only to the two of us.
> (*I*, LE, III, 927)

On the ashes of their mutual inquisition and resignation, Rita, with Allmers, gropes towards the transformation of personal loss into public benefit. But it is not missionary zeal, the sentimentality of social idealism, that impels her. That motive has been thoroughly exposed as a protection against the creative and responsible uses of guilt. Allmers is now honest enough to sense that it is not love that is behind Rita's dedication, and Rita herself will call it only "something in the shape of love" ("noe, som kunne ligne en slags kjaerlighet"), a phrase that catches up an earlier one, "a kind of birth" ("en slags fødsel") (*I*, LE, III, 933; III, 928)—a modest beginning for a new parent. And the schooling starts with her own reeducation for, like Nora, she has been badly trained by state, society, and marriage for the challenge of freedom. Ibsen's art refuses to see beyond this painful, humble, binding of self-judgment and responsibility, even as it evokes the continual presence of the Great World.

EPILOGUE

Robert Brustein, with other perceptive critics of drama, remains dissatisfied by the many Ibsen endings, starting with *Brand,* which seem at times a cheat rather than a challenge.[1] And Brand himself laments, in the last act:

> I am weary of this game which no one wins
> And no one loses.
> (M, B, 92)

True Freedom's fear of consummation and climax makes a friend of irony and parody in Ibsen's art, dedicated to *not* finishing off the struggle to reach the Great World. To stay honest, it needs as continuous a story as does the Romantic return to original innocence, to keep us from dying of disappointment: "If the writer's secret and deepest joy is to search for an irrecoverable experience, the ending that announces that the attempt was once again failed may seem more satisfying."[2] Ibsen's failures and tenuous, fragile successes never point us backward to a state of merged maternal peace, but always, by way of exile, deeper on the way to our natural, renounced medium of rich mystery and glad fullness of being. The endings of all his major plays, not just the last one, help us to understand what he means by the truth of the self. Jung names the shadow that haunts Ibsen's scene a moral problem that challenges the whole character, for no one can be spiritually and morally rich without acknowledg-

1. Brustein, *The Theatre of Revolt,* 58.
2. John Fowles, "Hardy and the Hag," in Butler (ed.), *Hardy After Fifty Years,* 35.

ing the "dark aspects of the personality as ever present and real."
Even if Rubek is not up to Ibsen's fierce irony, he at least helps the
necessary blurring of scene when he says of the mountain place of
"marriage": "All the powers of light will look kindly on us. And
those of darkness, too" (I, WWDA, III, 1091). Like the therapist,
Ibsen confronts us "with our own shadows," and like the patient, he
stands as his own judge between his darkness and his light.[3] This is
the depth from which we can sense, from time to time, even if we
are not quite ready for a real homeland, that we might become citizens of the Great World that has been for so long feared, so long
desired.

3. Jung, *Psychological Reflections,* 219–20.

BIBLIOGRAPHY

Abrams, M. H. *Natural Supernaturalism: Tradition and Revolution in Romantic Literature.* New York, 1973.

Adams, Robert M. "Ibsen on the Contrary." In *Modern Drama,* edited by Anthony Caputi. New York, 1966.

Adorno, Theodor. *Minima Moralia: Reflections from a Damaged Life.* Translated by E. F. Jephcott. London, 1974.

―――. "Reconciliation Under Duress." Translated by Rodney Livingstone. In *Aesthetics and Politics: Ernst Bloch, Georg Lukács, Bertolt Brecht, Walter Benjamin, Theodor Adorno,* translation editor Ronald Taylor. London, 1977.

Althusser, Louis. *For Marx.* Translated by Ben Brewster. London, 1979.

Andreas-Salomé, Lou. *Henrik Ibsens Frauengestalten nach seinen sechs Familien-Dramen.* Berlin, 1892.

Archer, William. *William Archer on Ibsen: The Major Essays, 1889–1919.* Edited by Thomas Postlewait. Westport, Conn., 1984.

Arestad, Sverre. "Ibsen's Concept of Tragedy." *PMLA,* LXXIV (1959), 285–309.

Arnheim, Rudolf. *Art and Visual Perception: A Psychology of the Creative Eye.* Berkeley, 1966.

Arup, Jens. "On *Hedda Gabler.*" *Orbis litterarum,* XII (1957), 3–37.

Bachelard, Gaston. *The Poetics of Space.* Translated by Maria Jolas. Boston, 1969.

Bager, Poul. "Uendelighedens tilbageslag." *Kritik,* II (1969), 46–68.

Bakhtin, Mikhail. *The Dialogic Imagination: Four Essays.* Translated by Caryl Emerson and Michael Holquist. Edited by Michael Holquist. Austin, Tex., 1981.

―――. *Problems of Dostoyevsky's Poetics.* Translated and edited by Caryl Emerson. Minneapolis, 1984.

Bang, Herman. *"Hedda Gabler."* Tilskueren, IX (1892), 827–38.

Barranger, M. S. "Ibsen's Endgame: A Reconsideration of *When We Dead Awaken.*" Modern Drama, XVII (1974), 289–99.

———. "Ibsen's 'Strange Story' in *The Master Builder:* A Variation in Technique." Modern Drama, XV (1972), 175–84.

———. *"The Lady from the Sea:* Ibsen in Transition." Modern Drama, XXI (1978), 393–403.

Barthes, Roland. *Mythologies.* Translated and edited by Annette Lavers. New York, 1972.

Bayley, John O. "The Order of Battle at Trafalgar." *Salmagundi,* LXVIII– IX (Fall, 1985–Winter, 1986), 19–29. Reprinted in John Bayley, *The Order of Battle at Trafalgar and Other Essays.* London, 1987.

Becker, Ernest. *The Denial of Death.* New York, 1973.

Beer, Gillian. *Darwin's Plots: Evolutionary Narrative in Darwin, George Eliot, and Nineteenth Century Fiction.* London, 1985.

Bermel, Albert. *Contradictory Characters: An Interpretation of the Modern Theatre.* New York, 1973.

Bentley, Eric. *The Life of the Drama.* New York, 1965.

———, ed. *Theory of the Modern Stage: An Introduction to Modern Theatre and Drama.* Harmondsworth, Middlesex, 1968. Selections from the commentary of Emile Zola, W. B. Yeats, Georg Brandes, Georg Lukács, Arnold Hauser, *et al.*

Beyer, Harald. *A History of Norwegian Literature.* Translated by Einar Haugen. New York, 1956.

———. *Nietzsche og Norden.* 2 vols. Bergen, 1959.

Bien, Horst. *Henrik Ibsens Realismus: Zur Genesis und Methode des klassischen kritische-realistischen Dramas.* Berlin, 1970.

Binswanger, Ludwig. *Being-in-the-World: Selected Papers of Ludwig Binswanger.* Translated and edited by Jacob Needleman. New York, 1963.

———. *Henrik Ibsen und das Problem der Selbstrealisation in der Kunst.* Heidelberg, 1949.

Bouchard, Donald F., ed. *Language, Counter-Memory, Practice: Selected Essays and Interviews by Michel Foucault.* Translated by Donald F. Bouchard and Sherry Simon. Ithaca, N.Y., 1977.

Bradbrook, M. C. *Ibsen the Norwegian: A Revaluation.* London, 1966.

Brandes, Georg. *Creative Spirits of the Nineteenth Century.* Translated by Rasmus B. Anderson. New York, 1923.

———. *Friedrich Nietzsche.* Translated by A. G. Chater. New York, 1909.

———. *Henrik Ibsen: Bjørnstjerne Bjørnson: Critical Studies.* Translated by Jessie Muir. Revised by William Archer. London, 1899.

———. *Main Currents in Nineteenth Century Literature.* Translated by Diane White and Mary Morison. Vols. I, II, V, VI of 6 vols. London, 1901.

Brecht, Bertolt. *Understanding Brecht*. Translated by Anna Bostock. Edited by Hannah Arendt. London, 1973.

Bredsdorff, Elias. *Den store Nordisk Krig om seksualmoralen: En documentarisk fremstilling af saedelighedsdebatten i nordisk litteratur i 1880'erne*. Oslo, 1973.

Brooks, Peter. *The Melodramatic Imagination: Balzac, Henry James, Melodrama, and the Mode of Excess*. New Haven, Conn., 1976.

Brustein, Robert. *The Theatre of Revolt: An Approach to Modern Drama*. Boston, 1964.

Butler, Lance St. John, ed. *Hardy After Fifty Years*. London, 1977.

Calderwood, James L. "*The Master Builder*: Failure of Symbolic Success." *Modern Drama*, XXVII (1984), 616–36.

Campbell, Joseph. *The Flight of the Wild Gander: Explorations in the Mythological Dimension*. New York, 1969.

Camus, Albert. *The Myth of Sisyphus*. Translated by Justin O'Brien. New York, 1955.

Carlson, Marvin. "Ibsen, Strindberg, and Telegony." *PMLA*, C (1985), 774–82.

———. *Theories of the Theatre: A Historical and Critical Survey, from the Greeks to the Present*. Ithaca, N.Y., 1984.

Carr, Joan. "'The Forest's Revenge': Subconscious Motivation in *The Wild Duck*." *Modern Language Review*, LXXII (1977), 845–56.

Carstens, Erik. *Fra en Psykoanalytikers arbejdsvaerelse: Korte afhandlinger og artikler*. Copenhagen, 1970.

Cassirer, Ernst. *An Essay on Man: An Introduction to a Philosophy of Human Culture*. New Haven, Conn., 1966.

———. *The Philosophy of Symbolic Forms*. Translated by Ralph Manheim. Vol. II of 2 vols. New Haven, 1965.

Chamberlain, John S. *Ibsen: The Open Vision*. London, 1982.

———. "Tragic Heroism in *Rosmersholm*." *Modern Drama*, XVII (1974), 277–88.

Chase, Richard. *The American Novel and Its Tradition*. Garden City, N.Y., 1957.

Cima, Gay Gibson. "Discovering Signs: The Emergence of the Critical Actor in Ibsen." *Theatre Journal*, XXXV (March, 1983), 5–22.

Cole, Toby, ed. *Playwrights on Playwriting: The Meaning and Making of Modern Drama from Ibsen to Ionesco*. New York, 1960. Selections from the commentary of Emile Zola, Anton Chekhov, Maurice Maeterlinck, W. B. Yeats, et al.

Cortinez, Carlos, ed. *Borges the Poet*. Fayetteville, Ark., 1987.

Culler, Jonathan. *Flaubert: The Uses of Uncertainty*. Ithaca, N.Y., 1985.

Davis, D. Russell. "The Death of the Artist's Father." *British Journal of Medical Psychology*, XLVI (1973), 135–41.

Davis, Rick. "The Histrionic Hedda." *AIT: The Repertory Reader*, I (Spring, 1984), 2–3.

De Man, Paul. *Blindness and Insight: Essays in the Rhetoric of Contemporary Criticism*. New York, 1971.

D'Heurle, Adma, and Joel N. Feimer. "Lost Children: The Role of the Child in the Psychological Plays of Henrik Ibsen." *The Psychoanalytic Review*, LXIII, 1 (1976), 27–47.

Dickens, Charles. *Bleak House*. Edited by George Ford and Sylvere Monod. New York, 1977.

———. *Dombey and Son*. Harmondsworth, Middlesex, 1970.

———. *Martin Chuzzlewit*. Edited by P. N. Furbank. Harmondsworth, Middlesex, 1968.

———. *The Selected Letters of Charles Dickens*. Edited by F. W. Dupee. New York, 1960.

Dostoyevsky, Feodor. *The Brothers Karamazov*. Translated by David Magarshack. 2 vols. Harmondsworth, Middlesex, 1958.

———. *The Double*. Translated by George Bird. Bloomington, Ind., 1958.

———. *Notes from Underground and The Grand Inquisitor*. Translated by Ralph E. Matlaw. New York, 1960.

Downs, Brian W. *Ibsen: The Intellectual Background*. New York, 1969.

———. *Modern Norwegian Literature, 1860–1918*. Cambridge, 1966.

———. *A Study of Six Plays*. New York, 1950.

Dumas, Alexandre. Preface to *Le fils naturel*. In *Théâtre complet d'Alexandre Dumas fils*. Vol. III of 8 vols. Paris, 1890–98.

Dundes, Alan, ed. *Sacred Narrative: Readings in the Theory of Myth*. Berkeley, 1984.

Durbach, Errol. "The Apotheosis of Hedda Gabler." *Scandinavian Studies*, XLIII (1971), 143–59.

———. "The Denouement of *Rosmersholm*." *Educational Theatre Journal*, XXIX (1977), 477–85.

———, ed. *Ibsen and the Theatre: Essays in Celebration of the 150th Anniversary of Henrik Ibsen's Birth*. London, 1980. Contributions by Inga-Stina Ewbank, Janet Suzman, John Northam, Evert Sprinchorn, James McFarlane, et. al.

———. *Ibsen the Romantic: Analogues of Paradise in the Later Plays*. Athens, Ga., 1982.

———. "On the Centenary of *Vilanden*: The 'Life-Lie' in Modern Drama." *Scandinavian Studies*, LVI (1984), 326–32.

Durkheim, Emile. *Le Suicide*. Paris, 1897.

Duve, Arne. *Henrik Ibsens hemmeligheter?* Oslo, 1977.

———. *The Real Drama of Henrik Ibsen*. Oslo, 1977.

———. *Symbolikken i Henrik Ibsens skuespill*. Oslo, 1945.

Dyrenforth, Harold O. "Georg Brandes: 1842–1927." *Educational Theatre Journal*, XV (1963), 143–50.

Eagleton, Terry. *Exiles and Emigres: Studies in Modern Literature.* New York, 1970.

———. *Walter Benjamin: Or Towards a Revolutionary Criticism.* London, 1981.

Eliade, Mircea. *Le Sacré et le Profane.* Paris, 1965.

Ellis, Havelock. *The New Spirit.* New York, 1930.

Engels, Friedrich. *The Origin of the Family: Private Property and the State: In the Light of the Researches of Lewis H. Morgan.* New York, 1972.

Fjelde, Rolf, ed. *Ibsen: A Collection of Critical Essays.* Englewood Cliffs, N.J., 1965. Essays by Eric Bentley, F. W. Kaufmann, P. F. D. Tennant, Halvdan Koht, John Northam, Robert Raphael, Richard Schechner, et al.

———. "*The Lady from the Sea:* Ibsen's Positive World-View in a Topographic Figure." *Modern Drama*, XXI (1978), 379–92.

Flaubert, Gustave. *Madame Bovary.* Translated by Alan Russell. Harmondsworth, Middlesex, 1970.

———. *The Selected Letters of Gustave Flaubert.* Translated and edited by Francis Steegmuller. New York, 1953.

Flores, Angel, ed. *Ibsen: Four Essays.* New York, 1937. Essays by Friedrich Engels, Franz Mehring, George V. Plekhanov, Anatol Lunacharsky.

Forster, E. M. *Abinger Harvest.* London, 1946.

Foucault, Michel. *Language, Counter-Memory, Practice: Selected Essays and Interviews by Michel Foucault.* Translated by Donald F. Bouchard and Sherry Simon. Edited by Donald F. Bouchard. Ithaca, N.Y., 1977.

Fowles, John. "Hardy and the Hag." In *Hardy After Fifty Years*, edited by Lance St. John Butler. London, 1977.

Freud, Sigmund. *Civilization and Its Discontents.* Translated by James Strachey. New York, 1961.

———. "Some Character Types Met with in Psycho-Analytic Work"; "One of the Difficulties of Psychoanalysis"; "The 'Uncanny'." In *Collected Papers*, translated under supervision of Joan Riviere, edited by Ernest Jones. Vol. IV of 4 vols. London, 1950.

Frye, Northrop. *Fables of Identity: Studies in Poetic Mythology.* New York, 1963.

———. *A Study of English Romanticism.* New York, 1968.

Gabrieli, Iselin Maria. *Rilettura di Ibsen.* Naples, 1977.

Gaskell, Ronald. *Drama and Reality: The European Theatre Since Ibsen.* London, 1972.

Gay, Peter. *Education of the Senses.* New York, 1984. Vol. I of *The Bourgeois Experience: Victoria to Freud.*

———. *The Enlightenment: The Rise of Modern Paganism.* New York, 1977.

————. *The Tender Passion.* New York, 1986. Vol. II of *The Bourgeois Experience: Victoria to Freud.*

Gide, André. "L'Evolution du théâtre." In *Oeuvres complètes,* edited by L. Martin-Chauffier. Vol. IV of 14 vols. Paris, 1932–39.

Gravier, Maurice. *Le Féminisme et l'amour dans la littérature norvégienne d'Ibsen à Sigrid Undset.* Paris, 1968.

Gray, Ronald. *Ibsen: A Dissenting View.* Cambridge, England, 1977.

Grene, David. *Reality and the Heroic Pattern: Last Plays of Ibsen, Shakespeare, and Sophocles.* Chicago, 1967.

Haakonsen, Daniel. *Henrik Ibsens Realisme.* Oslo, 1957.

————. *Henrik Ibsen: Mennesket og kunstneren.* Oslo, 1981.

————, ed. *Contemporary Approaches to Ibsen: Proceedings of the First International Ibsen Seminar, 1965.* Oslo, 1966. Essays by Alex Bolckmans, Inga-Stina Ewbank, Brian Johnston, James W. McFarlane, John Northam, *et al.*

————, ed. *Contemporary Approaches to Ibsen: Proceedings of the Second International Ibsen Seminar, 1970.* Oslo, 1971. Essays by Edvard Beyer, M. C. Bradbrook, Inga-Stina Ewbank, Rolf Fjelde, Maurice Gravier, Daniel Haakonsen, Jens Kruuse, *et al.*

————, ed. *Contemporary Approaches to Ibsen: Proceedings of the Third International Ibsen Seminar, 1975.* Oslo, 1977. Essays by Atle Kittang, Helge Rønning, Gerd Enno Rieger, Egil Törnqvist, Alex Bolckmans, John Northam, *et al.*

————, ed. *Contemporary Approaches to Ibsen: Proceedings of the Fourth International Ibsen Seminar, 1978.* Oslo, 1979. Essays by Edvard Beyer, Daniel Haakonsen, Andrew K. Kennedy, John S. Chamberlain, Derek Russell Davis and Daniel Thomas, Sandra E. Saari, Maurice Gravier, Arne Røed, *et al.*

————, ed. *Contemporary Approaches to Ibsen: Proceedings of the Fifth International Ibsen Seminar, 1983.* Oslo, 1985. Essays by Errol Durbach, Sandra E. Saari, Jírí Munzar, Philip E. Larson, *et al.*

Haaland, Arild. *Seks Studier i Ibsen.* Oslo, 1965.

Heidegger, Martin. *Being and Time.* Translated by John Macquarrie and Edward Robinson. New York, 1962.

————. *An Introduction to Metaphysics.* Translated by Ralph Manheim. New Haven, Conn., 1959.

Henriksen, Aage. "Henrik Ibsen som moralist." *Kritik,* II (1969), 69–84.

Herzfeld-Sander, Margaret, ed. *Essays on German Theater.* New York, 1985. Selections from commentary by Friedrich Schiller, G. W. F. Hegel, Friedrich Hebbel, Gerhart Hauptmann, Georg Lukács, Carl Sternheim, Arnold Hauser, *et al.*

Hettner, Hermann. *Das moderne Drama.* Berlin, 1924.

Hinden, Michael. "A Reading of The Master Builder." Modern Drama, XV (March, 1973), 403–10.

Holtan, Orley I. Mythic Patterns in Ibsen's Last Plays. Minneapolis, 1970.

Hornby, Richard. Patterns in Ibsen's Middle Plays. Lewisburg, Pa., 1981.

———. Script into Performance: A Structuralist View of Play Production. Austin, Tex., 1977.

Høst, Else. Hedda Gabler: En Monograf. Oslo, 1958.

———. Vilanden av Henrik Ibsen. Oslo, 1967.

Hovde, B. J. The Scandinavian Countries, 1720–1865: The Rise of the Middle Classes. Vol. II of 2 vols. Ithaca, NY, 1948.

Howells, William Dean. "Henrik Ibsen." North American Review, CLXXXIII (July, 1906), 1–14.

Hurrell, John D. "Rosmersholm, the Existentialist Drama, and the Dilemma of Modern Tragedy." Educational Theatre Journal, XV (1963), 118–24.

Hurt, James. Catiline's Dream: An Essay on Ibsen's Plays. Urbana, Ill., 1972.

Ibsen, Bergliot. The Three Ibsens: Memoirs of Henrik, Suzannah, and Sigurd Ibsen. Translated by Geri K. Schjelderup. London, 1951.

Ibsen, Henrik. The Correspondence of Henrik Ibsen. Translated by John N. Laurvik and Mary Morison. London, 1905.

———. From Ibsen's Workshop: Notes, Scenarios, and Drafts of the Modern Plays. Translated by A. G. Chater. Edited by William Archer. New York, 1978.

———. Speeches and New Letters. Translated by Arne Kildal. Boston, 1910.

Izenberg, Gerald N. The Existentialist Critique of Freud: The Crisis of Autonomy. Princeton, N.J., 1976.

Jacobsen, J. P. Niels Lyhne. Translated by Hanna Astrup Larsen. New York, 1967.

James, Henry. "The Altar of the Dead." In The Cage and Other Tales, edited by Morton Dauwen Zabel. New York, 1958.

———. Literary Criticism: French Writers; Other European Writers; the Prefaces to the New York Edition. Edited by Leon Edel, assisted by Mark Wilson. New York, 1984.

———. The Portrait of a Lady. Edited by Leon Edel. Boston, 1963.

———. The Scenic Art: Notes on Acting and the Drama 1872–1901. Edited by Allan Wade. New Brunswick, N.J., 1948.

Jameson, Frederic. The Political Unconscious: Narrative as a Socially Symbolic Act. Ithaca, N.Y., 1981.

Johnston, Brian. The Ibsen Cycle: The Design of the Plays from Pillars of Society to When We Dead Awaken. Boston, 1975.

Jorgenson, Theodore. Henrik Ibsen: A Study in Art and Personality. Northfield, Minn., 1945.

Jung, Carl G. *The Basic Writings of C. G. Jung.* Translated by R. F. C. Hull. Edited by Violet S. de Laszlo. New York, 1959.

―――. *Psychological Reflections: A New Anthology of His Writings, 1905–1961.* Translated by R. F. C. Hull. Edited by Jolande Jacobi and R. F. C. Hull. Princeton, N.J., 1978.

Jung, Carl G., and C. Kerenyi. *Essays on a Science of Mythology.* Translated by R. F. C. Hull. New York, 1949.

Kafka, Franz. *The Basic Kafka.* Translated by Martin Greenberg, with Hannah Arendt, Tania Stern, James Stern, Elizabeth Duckworth, Richard Winston, and Clara Winston. Edited by Erich Heller. New York, 1979.

―――. *The Diaries of Franz Kafka: 1914–1923.* Translated by Martin Greenberg with Hannah Arendt. Edited by Max Brod. Vol. II of 2 vols. New York, 1968.

―――. *Letters to Milena.* Translated by Tania Stern and James Stern. Edited by Willi Haas. New York, 1953.

Kaufman, Michael W. "Nietzsche, Georg Brandes, and Ibsen's *Master Builder.*" *Comparative Drama,* VI (1972), 169–86.

Kerans, James E. "Kindermord and Will in *Little Eyolf.*" In *Modern Drama: Essays in Criticism,* edited by Travis Bogard and William I. Oliver. New York, 1965.

Kermode, Frank. *Continuities.* New York, 1968.

Kierkegaard, Søren. *Concluding Unscientific Postscript to the Philosophical Fragments.* Translated by David F. Swenson and Walter Lowrie. Edited by Walter Lowrie. Princeton, N.J., 1941.

―――. *Either/Or: A Fragment of Life.* Translated by David F. Swenson, Lillian Marvin Swenson, and Walter Lowrie, with revisions by Howard A. Johnson. 2 vols. Garden City, N.Y., 1959.

―――. *Fear and Trembling* and *The Sickness unto Death.* Translated by Walter Lowrie. Revised by Howard A. Johnson. Edited by Walter Lowrie. Garden City, N.Y., 1954.

―――. *Letters and Documents.* Translated and edited by Henrik Rosenmeier. Princeton, N.J., 1978.

―――. *On Authority and Revelation: The Book on Adler.* Translated and edited by Walter Lowrie. New York, 1966.

―――. *Søren Kierkegaard's Journals and Papers.* Translated and edited by Howard V. Hong and Edna H. Hong, assisted by Gregor Malantschuk. Vols. I, II, III, VI of 6 vols. Bloomington, Ind., 1967–78.

―――. *Works of Love: Some Christian Reflections in the Form of Discourses.* Translated and edited by Howard Hong and Edna Hong. New York, 1962.

Knight, G. Wilson. *Henrik Ibsen.* New York, 1962.

Knox, John. *Myth and Truth: An Essay on the Language of Faith*. Charlottesville, Va., 1964.

Knudsen, Trygve. "Phases of Style and Language in the Works of Henrik Ibsen." *Scandinavica*, II (May, 1963), 1–20.

Lagerkvist, Pär. "Modern Theatre: Points of View and Attack." Translated by Thomas R. Buckman. *Tulane Drama Review*, VI (November, 1961), 3–31.

Laurence, Dan H., ed. *Platform and Pulpit: Bernard Shaw*. New York, 1961.

Lavrin, Janko. *Ibsen and His Creation*. New York, 1972.

Lawrence, D. H. *Aaron's Rod*. New York, 1961.

———. *Apocalypse*. New York, 1960.

———. *Phoenix: The Posthumous Papers, 1936*. Edited by Edward D. McDonald. Harmondsworth, Middlesex, 1978.

———. *Phoenix II: Uncollected, Unpublished, and Other Prose Works*. Edited by Warren Roberts and Harry T. Moore. Harmondsworth, Middlesex, 1978.

———. *The Rainbow*. New York, 1967.

———. *The Selected Letters of D. H. Lawrence*. Edited by Diana Trilling. New York, 1958.

———. *Studies in Classic American Literature*. New York, 1972.

Lukács, Georg. *Studies in European Realism*. Translated by Edith Bone. New York, 1964.

———. *The Theory of the Novel*. Translated by Anna Bostock. Cambridge, Mass., 1971.

Lucas, F. L. *The Drama of Ibsen and Strindberg*. New York, 1972.

Luke, F. D. "Nietzsche and the Imagery of Height." *Publications of the English Goethe Society*, XXVIII (1958–59), 83–108.

Lukes, Steven. *Individualism*. Oxford, 1973.

Lyons, Charles R. *Henrik Ibsen: The Divided Consciousness*. Carbondale, Ill., 1972.

McFarlane, James Walter. *Ibsen and the Temper of Norwegian Literature*. London, 1960.

———, ed. *Discussions of Henrik Ibsen*. Boston, 1962. Selections from the commentary of G. B. Shaw, Eric Bentley, James W. McFarlane, James Joyce, *et al.*

———, ed. *Ibsen: A Critical Anthology*. Harmondsworth, Middlesex, 1970. Selections from the commentary of Knut Hamsun, Rainer Maria Rilke, James Stephens, Mary McCarthy, *et al.*

Mason, Herbert. "Myth as an 'Ambush of Reality.'" In *Myth, Symbol, and Reality*, edited by Alan M. Olson. Notre Dame, Ind., 1980.

May, Keith M. *Ibsen and Shaw*. New York, 1985.

Merton, Thomas. *New Seeds of Contemplation.* New York, 1961.
Meyer, Hans Georg. *Henrik Ibsen.* Translated by Helen Sebba. New York, 1972.
Meyer, Michael. *Ibsen.* Harmondsworth, Middlesex, 1971.
Michaelsen, Aslaug Groven. *Ibsens Bygmester Solness som tidsdiagnose.* Tangen, 1982.
———. "Individualisme og personlighetslaere, plassert i forhold til dem modernistiska isolasjon." In *Festskrift til Tollak B. Sirnes.* Bergen, Norway, 1982.
Mill, John Stuart. *The Subjection of Women* (with Mary Wollstonecraft, *The Rights of Women*). London, 1970.
Mueller, Janel. "Ibsen's *Wild Duck.*" *Modern Drama,* XI (1969), 347–55.
Nietzsche, Friedrich. *Beyond Good and Evil.* Translated by Walter Kaufmann. New York, 1966.
———. *The Birth of Tragedy and The Genealogy of Morals.* Translated by Francis Golffing. Garden City, N.Y., 1956.
———. *Briefwechsel: Kritische Gesamtausgabe.* Edited by Giorgio Colli and Mazzino Montinari. Vol. II' of 3 vols. Berlin, 1977.
———. *Daybreak: Thoughts on the Prejudices of Morality.* Translated by R. J. Hollingdale. Cambridge, England, 1985.
———. *Ecce Homo.* Translated by R. J. Hollingdale, Harmondsworth, Middlesex, 1979.
———. *The Gay Science.* Translated by Walter Kaufmann. New York, 1974.
———. *Human, All Too Human: A Book for Free Spirits.* Translated by R. J. Hollingdale. Cambridge, England, 1986.
———. *Thus Spoke Zarathustra: A Book for Everyone and No One.* Translated by R. J. Hollingdale. Harmondsworth, Middlesex, 1969.
———. *Twilight of the Idols and The Anti-Christ.* Translated by R. J. Hollingdale. Harmondsworth, Middlesex, 1968.
———. *Untimely Meditations.* Translated by R. J. Hollingdale. Cambridge, England, 1983.
———. *The Will to Power.* Translated by Walter Kaufmann and R. J. Hollingdale. Harmondsworth, Middlesex, 1968.
Noreng, Harald, ed. *En ny Ibsen: ni Ibsen-artikler.* Oslo, 1979. Essays by Harald Noreng, Atle Kittang, *et al.*
Norris, Margot. *Beasts of the Modern Imagination: Darwin, Nietzsche, Kafka, Ernst, and Lawrence.* Baltimore, 1985.
Northam, John. *Ibsen: A Critical Inquiry.* Cambridge, England, 1973.
———. *Ibsen's Dramatic Method.* London, 1953.
Nussbaum, Martha C. *The Fragility of Goodness: Luck and Ethics in Greek Tragedy and Philosophy.* New York, 1986.

Ortega y Gasset, Jose. *The Dehumanization of Art and Notes on the Novel.* Princeton, N.J., 1948.

———. *The Modern Theme.* Translated by James Cleugh. New York, 1961.

Paul, Fritz. *Symbol und Mythos: Studien zum Spätwerk Henrik Ibsens.* Munich, 1969.

Pendleton, Austin. Interview in *Ibsen News and Comment*, II (1981), 7.

Pettazzoni, Raffaele. "The Truth of Myth." In *Myth, Symbol, and Reality*, edited by Alan M. Olson. Notre Dame, Ind., 1980.

Quigley, Austin E. *The Modern Stage and Other Worlds.* New York, 1985.

Rank, Otto. *The Myth of the Birth of the Hero and Other Writings.* Translated by F. Robbins and Smith Ely Jelliffe, Charles Francis Atkinson, Mabel E. Moxon, and Jessie Taft. Edited by Philip Freund. New York, 1964.

———. *Will Therapy* and *Truth and Reality.* Translated by Jessie Taft. New York, 1950.

Raphael, Robert. "From *Hedda Gabler* to *When We Dead Awaken*: The Quest for Self-Realization." *Scandinavian Studies*, XXXVI (1964), 34–47.

———. "Illusion and the Self in *The Wild Duck, Rosmersholm*, and *The Lady from the Sea.*" *Scandinavian Studies*, XXXV (1963), 37–50.

Ricoeur, Paul. *The Conflict of Interpretations: Essays in Hermeneutics.* Translated by various people. Edited by Don Ihde. Evanston, Ill., 1974.

Rilke, Rainer Maria. *The Notebooks of Malte Laurids Brigge.* Translated by M. D. Herter Norton. New York, 1949.

Roach, Joseph R. "Ibsen and the Moral Occult." In *Telling Right from Wrong: Morality and Literature.* University College Occasional Papers, No. 5, Washington University. St. Louis, 1987.

Robbe-Grillet, Alain. *For a New Novel.* Translated by Richard Howard. New York, 1965.

Robins, Elizabeth. *Ibsen and the Actress.* New York, 1973.

Rose, Phyllis. *Parallel Lives: Five Victorian Marriages.* New York, 1983.

Rosengarten, David. "*The Lady from the Sea*: Ibsen's Submerged Allegory." *Educational Theatre Journal*, XXIX (1977), 463–76.

Rousseau, Jean-Jacques. *The Confessions.* Translated by J. M. Cohen. Harmondsworth, Middlesex, 1954.

Saari, Sandra E. "*Hedda Gabler*: The Past Recaptured." *Modern Drama*, XX (1977), 299–316.

———. "Of Madness or Fame: Ibsen's *Bygmester Solness.*" *Scandinavian Studies*, L (1978), 1–18.

Sennett, Richard. *The Fall of Public Man: On the Social Psychology of Capitalism.* New York, 1978.

Shafer, Yvonne, ed. *Approaches to Teaching Ibsen's A Doll House*. New York, 1985. Contributions by Cary M. Mazer, Barry Witham and John Lutterbie, Irving Deer, *et al.*

Shaw, George Bernard. *Major Critical Essays*. In *Collected Works*. Ayot St. Lawrence Edition. Vol. XXIX of 30 vols. New York, 1932.

————. *The Quintessence of Ibsenism*. New York, 1957.

Silk, M. S., and J. P. Stern. *Nietzsche on Tragedy*. Cambridge, England, 1981.

Sprinchorn, Evert. "Science and Poetry in Ibsen's *Ghosts*: A Study in Ibsen's Craftsmanship." *Scandinavian Studies*, LI (1979), 354–67.

Steegmuller, Francis. *Flaubert and Madame Bovary: A Double Portrait*. Boston, 1970.

Steiner, George. *The Death of Tragedy*. New York, 1961.

Strindberg, August. *A Dream Play and Four Chamber Plays*. Translated and edited by Walter Johnson. New York, 1975.

————. *Getting Married*. Translated by Mary Sandbach. London, 1972.

————. *Inferno, Alone and Other Writings*. Translated and edited by Evert Sprinchorn. Garden City, N.Y., 1968.

————. *Plays of Confession and Therapy: To Damascus I, II, III*. Translated by Walter Johnson. Seattle, 1979.

————. *Pre-Inferno Plays: The Father, Lady Julie, Creditors, The Stronger, The Bond*. Translated by Walter Johnson. New York, 1970.

————. *Queen Christina; Charles XII; Gustav III*. Translated by Walter Johnson. Seattle, 1955.

————. *The Son of a Servant: The Story of the Evolution of a Human Being, 1849–1867*. Translated and edited by Evert Sprinchorn. Garden City, N.Y., 1966.

Sulloway, Frank J. *Freud, Biologist of the Mind: Beyond the Psychoanalytic Legend*. New York, 1979.

Szondi, Peter. *Theory of the Modern Drama*. Translated by Michael Hays. Minneapolis, 1987.

Tanner, Tony. *Adultery in the Novel: Contract and Transgression*. Baltimore, 1979.

Taylor, Richard, ed. *The Will to Live: Selected Writings of Arthur Schopenhauer*. Translated by R. B. Haldane and J. Kemp. New York, 1967.

Templeton, Joan. "Of This Time, of *This* Place: Mrs. Alving's *Ghosts* and the Shape of the Tragedy." *PMLA*, CI (January, 1986), 57–68.

Thompson, Alan R. *The Dry Mock: A Study of Irony in Drama*. Berkeley, 1948.

Tufts, Carol Strongin. "Recasting *A Doll House*: Narcissism as Character Motivation in Ibsen's Play." *Comparative Drama*, XX (1986), 140–59.

Unamuno, Miguel de. "Ibsen y Kierkegaard." In *Mi Religión y otras ensayos breves*. Buenos Aires, 1942.

Valency, Maurice. *The Flower and the Castle: An Introduction of the Modern Drama: Ibsen and Strindberg.* New York, 1963.

Van Laan, Thomas F. "Generic Complexity in Ibsen's *An Enemy of the People.*" *Comparative Drama,* XX (1986), 95–111.

Webb, Eugene. *The Dark Dove: The Sacred and the Secular in Modern Literature.* Seattle, 1975.

Weigand, Hermann. *The Modern Ibsen: A Reconsideration.* New York, 1960.

Weiskel, Thomas. *The Romantic Sublime: Studies in the Structure and Psychology of Transcendence.* Baltimore, 1986.

Welsh, Alexander. *George Eliot and Blackmail.* Cambridge, Mass., 1985.

Whitaker, Thomas R. "Killing Ourselves." In *Fields of Play in Modern Drama.* Princeton, N.J., 1977.

White, Hayden. *Metahistory: The Historical Imagination in Nineteenth Century Europe.* Baltimore, 1973.

Williams, Raymond. *Drama from Ibsen to Eliot.* London, 1961.

———. *The English Novel from Dickens to Lawrence.* New York, 1970.

Zwicker, Steven N. "Lines of Authority: Politics and Literary Culture in the Restoration." In *Politics of Discourse: The Literature and History of Seventeenth Century England,* edited by Kevin Sharpe and Steven N. Zwicker. Berkeley, 1987.

INDEX

Absolutes: parodied, 128; tension between relative context and, 128,
150, 216; in *The Master Builder*, 195
Aestheticism: in *Hedda Gabler*, 20,
115–17; in *Madame Bovary*, 25;
Ibsen's native, 106; as disguise,
106n61; Ibsen vs., 111–12, 119,
121, 124, 128, 132, 135; temptation of, 112n73; as evasion,
113–16, 120–21, 146; Nietzsche
and, 129; symbolism as, 131; parodied, 139
Aesthetics: morality and, 20–21, 27,
28n44, 31, 57–58, 185
Altruism. *See* Self-sacrifice
Ambiguity: of Ibsen's endings, 52,
233–34; and truth, 189
Anarchism: Ibsen's, 85–86, 170, 201,
228; his contemporaries' flirtation
with, 229
Art: nature and function of, 2, 7,
83–84, 112–13, 139, 186, 200,
224–25, 230; vs. purity, 79, 142,
226; and sexuality, 79, 214–15,
226; ambitions toward, 82–83; suspect, 100; relationship to life,
103–105, 106n61, 111, 122,
224n23; and distance, 105, 112,
151; of the small world, 112–13,
221; Ibsen's attitude toward and
treatment of, 142–43, 144, 214;

and evolution, 145–47; and childhood, 185n60, 224; and guilt, 186,
222; universalized by exile, 192; and
marriage/family, 217–18, 219–21,
224–26. *See also* Creativity
Artists: isolation of, 95; mission of,
96–98, 100; maimed, 148, 149;
compared to children, 185n60,
221–22, 225; compared to women,
187; Ibsen's portrayal of, 211n1
Austen, Jane: correspondence between
language and morality in, 152;
and social convention, 171; mentioned, 53
Authority: Kafka and, 93; decay of
civic and spiritual, 95, 102, 155,
158–59, 160

Balzac, Honore de: and melodrama,
123; dialectical relationship to society, 207; mentioned, 158
Beauty. *See* Aestheticism; Aesthetics
Bible: Ibsen and the, 44n74, 114,
121, 129n105
Bjørnson, Bjornstjerne: Ibsen impressed by, 120; mentioned, 181
Bourgeoisie: Lawrence and Joyce vs.,
133; art's changing treatment of,
141n125
Brandes, Georg: vs. aestheticism,
119–20; author of liberal break-

249